CW00621545

Looking Through Bubbles

TO ANNE

HOPE YOU ENJOY THE BOOK
AND FIND IT USEFUL

Matthew

Looking Through Bubbles

Patricia Greenwood

© Patricia Greenwood 2011

Published by Reeth House

All rights reserved. Reproduction of this book by photocopying or electronic means for non-commercial purposes is permitted. Otherwise, no part of this book may be reproduced, adapted, stored in a retrieval system or transmitted by any means, electronic, mechanical, photocopying, or otherwise without the prior written permission of the author.

A CIP catalogue record for this book is available from the British Library.

ISBN 978-0-9569044-0-9

Cover design by Clare Brayshaw

Prepared and printed by:

York Publishing Services Ltd
64 Hallfield Road
Layerthorpe
York YO31 7ZQ
Tel: 01904 431213
Website: www.yps-publishing.co.uk

Dedicated to Karl.
Our gentle giant.
We love you. We miss you.
Everyday we think of you.

CONTENTS

Chapter 1

FALLING IN LOVE

It was a cold, sunny Sunday morning as I curled up on the soft cushioned chair and gazed out of the window at the early mist rolling across the hillside. My emotions were being stretched further than at any time in my life and in more ways than I could ever have imagined. I was deliriously happy because I had fallen in love and it felt wonderful. My attention moved to the bed behind me, which I had left ten minutes earlier, and to the beautiful man who was sleeping peacefully. He also looked happy and contented.

Despite this idyllic state, tears were forming in my eyes. The tears began to run down my cheeks and were soon so intense that damp patches formed on the cushion that I was cuddling tightly to my breast. I knew it couldn't last. I knew that sooner or later, I was going to have to say goodbye to Keith and never see him again. I looked back at the view from the window. Through my tears, I could just make out the stark mountainous terrain that surrounded the quaint village of Reeth.

Suddenly I felt his hands on my shoulders, and as he started to kiss my neck, I felt a warm glow developing inside. Miraculously, it dried my tears and ensured that he was unaware I had been crying. Without speaking, he gently lifted me from the chair and while kissing my lips, carried me back to the warm bed. The painful thoughts of what was to come were still there, deep inside me, but on this, our last Sunday morning together, I was determined to enjoy every second.

My first meeting with Keith had been a low-key event, ten years earlier, in the autumn of 1970. He and his wife Maureen lived in a house identical to the one that my husband Dennis and I owned, on a small housing development in the village of Wyke on the southern outskirts of the City of Bradford. Very similar couples populated the houses – twenty-something, newlyweds, without children. We were all out working during the day, but at weekends and during holiday periods we got to know one another. Chitchats over the garden fence developed into strolls to the local pub and eventually to group get-togethers. Any anniversary or birthday or new job or whatever, was an excuse for a party. We did the rounds, taking it in turns to be the host and hostess. As the host, you had the chance to invite friends and relatives from outside Wyke, which meant there were nearly always new people to meet.

On one particular occasion, Dennis and I accepted an invitation to a neighbour's birthday party celebration. The beginning of the evening was very pleasant and I enjoyed catching up with the news of several friends who were there. As it started to get quite late, most of the people who had to travel any distance headed home. This left about a dozen people still enjoying the party. Some of the young men in the group began to organise tricks and others joined in and tried to come up with more interesting variations and challenges. As usual on these occasions, serious competition brought with it serious drinking. I had enjoyed the party and was ready to leave but to my husband the night was still young; he had no intention of leaving. To me there is nothing worse than hanging on at a party when it's time to go, but I had no choice, and so, reluctantly, I found myself a place to sit in a corner on the sofa, away from the increasingly rowdy activities and settled to wait until it was time to go home. After a short space of time a young man came and sat next to me. At the time, it never crossed my mind to ask why he wasn't joining in with all the other men. It just seemed quite natural for him to be there. Our conversation flowed easily from one subject to another. We chatted about our connection with the people at the party and we talked about where we had both grown up, where we had gone to school and about our families. It was strange to find out that he was exactly six months older than me and that our childhoods had developed with only five miles between us. It was a very pleasant hour or so. I do remember that he didn't smile a lot but when he did he had such a lovely smile – his whole face was animated. That was my first meeting with Keith and when I mentioned this to him, many years later, sadly he had no recollection. Some impact I must have made!

Gradually many of the couples had babies. Most of the mums did not go back to work after having their babies and lots of strong friendships were forged. As the babies grew into toddlers, a playgroup was formed in the village church hall. The activities for the children were well planned and the group grew in numbers. A fundraising committee was formed and the money raised was used to buy much-needed equipment for the children. Summer concerts and Christmas fairs were planned and adult dances were held twice a year. Keith and I were probably in each other's company at many of the various events over the years but I cannot remember speaking to him again until several years later at a children's party that they were having for his son Richard. Our youngest son Jonathan was invited. We all had a good time and played all the children's games you would expect and sang lots of songs. This seemed like a good party to me, not too stressful, and with the work shared by both parents. Keith organised all the games with the enthusiasm of a child. He was obviously having fun. Keith's wife Maureen and I had become good friends by this time and regularly met at each other's houses with the children.

I spoke to Keith and once again I enjoyed his company. When he was in the presence of children he was animated, happy and sunny, with endless patience. When he was with several adults he became nervous and reclusive. To most of the men in the group, Keith was seen as an oddball. He seemed much more comfortable with the women, not flirting, in no way a threat, but simply chatting about everyday things.

The men, meanwhile, would be in a huddle talking about football and work. I had now spent two long sessions with him, several years apart, just talking. And although I had to agree that he seemed to behave differently to other men, there was something about him that I found endearing.

The following year, 1978, a small group of ten couples set up a circle with the intention of having, in turn, a dinner party at each other's houses, to be held about every two months. We all had similar lifestyles, not a lot of money and difficulties with babysitting and so we had a babysitting rota running in tandem with the events. These activities eventually ran their course and then a much smaller circle came out of it. This consisted of three couples, one of which was Maureen and Keith. It very quickly became apparent to the third couple that there was a very good reason why the other two couples wanted these occasions to take place more and more often. It became obvious to them that a strong chemistry was developing between my husband and Keith's wife. This was quite acceptable to both Keith and myself as we also had very strong feelings for each other. It wasn't long before the third couple dropped out of the circle entirely. Inevitably, the regular get-togethers developed into something deeper for each "new" couple.

Arrangements were made, usually by Maureen and myself, which created situations for one couple to be together while the other partners looked after their respective children. The next seven months were very exciting and romantic. Not only did we have numerous dates that involved the cinema, theatre, restaurants and pubs, but we also developed a very adventurous sexual liaison. We didn't need to search out seedy hotels for this purpose. Our arrangement meant that one of the houses would be made available for us on a rota basis with the other couple. However, we did sometimes make love in the back of Keith's car, which added to the excitement.

Although the house availability sounds like a perfect arrangement, it wasn't without its difficulties. Not only did we have to creep about to avoid nosy neighbours and wide-awake children, we also had to find suitable clothing to negotiate the route between the houses. Keith would dress up in an old overcoat and wellingtons to climb over a fence and through the gardens to avoid detection. This was too much of a tortuous route for me, so I would use the footpath, wearing a coat that was very similar to one Maureen would wear. As we were a similar height, with the hood pulled up, people were unlikely to recognise the wearer. We are sure that none of the neighbours suspected anything because of these carefully arranged plans. However, Keith nearly blew it one morning as he walked past my house on his way to the shops. He spotted me upstairs at the open window and shouted to me in a loud voice, *"Did I leave my watch there last night?"*

Yes he had, but fortunately no-one was around to hear him or to see my embarrassed mimed reply.

The more that Keith and I were together, the more we seemed to connect. Here we were, both in our early thirties and yet acting like teenagers. It was a wonderful, happy, time. We were having lots of fun without hurting our families. We were so natural with each other, like best friends, able to share our innermost thoughts and feelings, our hopes and disappointments. Although I had seen that Keith was ill at ease in a large group, on a one to one with me, he became confident and able to talk in a relaxed manner. Sadly we knew that, even though we were falling in love with each other, sooner or later this exciting period of our lives would come to an end and our meetings would be just a memory. For the sake of our children and their future, we would have to walk away from this perfect arrangement. For now though, we were determined to enjoy every minute while we could. We decided that if we had to end our relationship, we needed to do it in style. We needed quality time together away from normal routine, everyday pressures and our local environment. I discussed our idea with Maureen and it was agreed that each couple would have a weekend away. They decided to go to the Lake District. Our choice of destination was the Yorkshire Dales.

After finishing work on Friday evening, the two of us headed up the A1. We chatted, non-stop, all the way, as the evening sun danced across the windscreen. By the time we reached our destination, the picturesque village of Reeth in Swaledale, the sun had long since dropped below the horizon. Although the village was small, it was the first visit for both of us and it took us some time to locate the hotel. Eventually we pulled into the car park. We didn't go inside immediately. We just sat in the car kissing and cuddling, taking in the atmosphere, enjoying the moment. Keith clasped my hand and gave me a gentle squeeze as we walked towards the front door. We entered reception and a smartly dressed young lady in a dark blue suit asked if we had a booking. Keith gave all the information that was needed. While he did so, I took the opportunity to look around. Firstly my eyes landed on a beautiful pink antique chaise-longue, and above this hung a very large delicate chandelier. Over to the right was an extensive library of antique books and to the left a roaring log fire surrounded by a marvellous display of polished horse brasses. Immediately I felt at ease and I knew that I would enjoy relaxing here with Keith. After checking in as husband and wife, he picked up our two cases and we ran up the stairs. In true romantic style he carried me over the threshold into the bedroom, gently laid me on the bed and produced a huge box of chocolates. At last we were alone, away from the world, wanting no more than to give pleasure to each other. After a few lingering kisses he asked, *"Where do you want to eat? What kind of food would you like?"*

I thought about this and was about to answer his questions when he kissed me again, this time much more passionately and then more urgently. The box of chocolates, still unopened, fell to the floor. I knew then that our meal would have to wait.

The following morning we were awake early and the sun was streaming through the window. We had not closed the curtains the evening before as our nearest neighbours were the sheep halfway up a hillside in the far distance. The birds were singing happily and we were both at peace. Once again we kissed, held each other tightly and were instantly engulfed in passion. After making love, we talked and laughed and joked together that we could happily stay in this room all weekend, just making love and occasionally eating and drinking. We took a long, leisurely bath together and talked about where we would go that day. Keith's plan was that after having breakfast we should explore the countryside and then maybe the following day, spend our time walking around Reeth before we needed to leave for home. I agreed and we had breakfast together in the old oak furnished dining room. I felt so relaxed it was as if this had been our normal pattern forever. We enjoyed simply talking to each other about everyday things and even talking about something as ordinary as food seemed exciting. In this area also we were very similar; we both had very few dislikes.

We talked happily throughout our short journey to High Force. We walked along the riverbank and skimmed stones in the River Tees. I have never been any good at this. I think it must be a man thing, so after a few feeble attempts, I stood back and watched Keith enjoy himself for at least ten minutes. As I was watching him, a sad thought crept into my mind. My boys would love to be enjoying the adventure of being here skimming stones. As he walked across to me and gave me a hug, I quietly told him of my thoughts. *"Yes,"* he said. *"I was thinking exactly the same."* He hugged and kissed me for a full five minutes and then gently whispered, *"Remember, this is our time, we will be back in normal time soon enough. For now let's enjoy every minute to the full."*

This we did. We walked and talked and hugged throughout the rest of the day. We had thought about going to the theatre in Richmond that evening but planning this and fitting in a time to eat started being difficult to organise. We both felt that we would much rather enjoy a leisurely romantic meal together before going to bed early. So that's exactly what we did. All weekend we were never out of each other's sight, never more than a few yards away from each other, never out of touching distance. It felt natural and it felt perfect. We both agreed that we felt the same, at ease, as one.

Sunday was our last day in Reeth and, as discussed, we did explore the village, every nook and cranny, hand in hand. We did not talk as freely as we had on the previous days as a sad feeling was hanging over both of us. We knew that we were enjoying the last few hours that we would ever spend together. Even though I was excited about going away with Keith, I had secretly half wished that we would not be compatible. It would have been a period of fun and excitement but once it had passed I would not give it another thought. Why is life never straightforward? That was not how I felt at all. I felt sad and emotional as I walked in the fields, hand in hand with him. I looked up at him, neither of us spoke but I could see tears well up in the corner of his eyes. He was obviously feeling sad that this friendship that had turned into a love affair was about to come to an end. We did not eat lunch as neither of us was hungry. In fact I don't think we wanted to share our last short hours with anyone.

All too soon Sunday evening arrived. It was a painful and silent drive back to Bradford. Keith pulled into a lay-by on the outskirts of the city. He stroked my hair and, gently touching my cheeks, leaned across and kissed me for several minutes. Tears slowly filled my eyes and started to run down my face. No words were spoken between us. I looked deep into Keith's eyes and I could see that he too had tears welling up. We held each other, without movement, for what seemed like eternity. Then, without talking, he broke away, started the car and drove in the direction of home. We met our partners at a pre-arranged spot. Pleasantries were exchanged but I couldn't look at Keith. I avoided his eyes and walked to the other car. This was the most emotional period that I had experienced in my life. I felt numb and empty.

When we arrived at my parents' home I was so pleased to see my children. We had planned to collect them and take them home, but as it was the Easter holidays and because they had really enjoyed the weekend, they persuaded us to let them stay a few more days. Dennis and I organised bath time for all three boys. We had supper together and talked about the fun they had had with their grandparents. My dad always made visits fun for them. He would organise games and always include his grandsons in tasks around the garden where possible as this helped them to be independent and add to their confidence. My mum was a superb cook and always made them treats. She would also encourage them to make cakes or biscuits, with her support and this was great fun. Gran would allow her grandsons to choose how to ice the cakes they had made and also help to choose the trimmings. Once the children were settled in bed and bedtime stories read, Dennis and I headed home.

On arrival we settled in the lounge together. Normally we would probably have watched television for an hour before going to bed but on this occasion, I said I needed to talk. I explained that Keith and I had felt it was time for the arrangement that we had been enjoying for the past seven months to come to an end. For all our sakes, especially for our children, it was time to end the "affairs". We had been lucky so far, in that no-one had been hurt, and that our children and the rest of our families were unaware of what was happening. But it would not stay this way forever if we carried on. I said that now my thoughts were about us working together as a family.

Our two families had planned to go on holiday together in the summer and for this purpose we had booked a villa in Spain. I firmly stated that this would have to be cancelled. Dennis had listened carefully to what I had said and then replied with, *"Yes I agree, we should probably stop seeing each other – but surely we could leave the holiday booked as something to look forward to?"*

Once again I stated firmly that the affairs had to stop and that the holiday should be cancelled as soon as possible.

At some point he obviously relayed this to Maureen as the following day she came round to our house to talk to me. The children were still at their grandparents and our husbands were at work so we were able to talk without interruption. She was very unhappy that I had said that we were cancelling the holiday and shocked when I told her that we would probably move house shortly afterwards. I felt overwhelmingly that I could not continue to live there and see Keith regularly either driving or walking past our house. A clean break was the best thing for all of us. Those were my thoughts and the only way I could move forward positively. Twenty-four hours went by and Maureen contacted me again. What she told me came right out of the blue and I was quite shocked. She explained that she could not see a future without Dennis being in it and that after a great deal of thought she said she wanted to be with Dennis in the future.

The children were happy and safe with their grandparents and so it was an easy act for the two men to simply swap houses and join their new partners. It seems quite glib and indeed comical, looking back, but it was, of course, a very emotional and traumatic end to a pair of twelve-year marriages.

It was, however, the start of a new exciting journey for both couples. I was waiting in the house eagerly anticipating Keith's arrival. It seemed like forever but suddenly there he was, standing in front of me. We did something we thought we would never be able to do ever again. We fell into each other's arms and simply held each other for what seemed like hours. In reality it was only a few minutes. We knew this was it. We knew this was the first day of our life together. We knew it wouldn't be easy, but we knew it was right. We didn't need to say anything, we just knew. Neither of us slept that night, talking and agonising over the future of our four children. How we would explain to them what had happened and how we would reassure them that we loved them. I had three boys, Karl aged nine, Darren aged seven, and Jonathan aged three, and Keith's son Richard was almost five. We knew that if our relationship was to survive, then our relationships with our sons had to continue and be nurtured. We made an unwritten pact that they came first. The hardest decision had already been taken. We had discussed the future with Dennis and Maureen and we had agreed what we felt was the best solution for the boys.

We all felt that is was important that they spent as much time as possible with both sets of parents. However, they each had to have a base, which would be the least disruptive to them, as individuals, in their developing lives.

So the scene was set. Our youngest son, Jonathan, would have his base with Keith and me, and our older boys would be with us on a regular basis. I knew it was not going to be easy but we were very much in love and I was confident that we would make it work, even though the date was All Fools Day, 1st April 1980.

I had no idea, however, what was waiting for me just around the corner. I had no idea that my life was about to be turned completely upside down.

Chapter 2

STRANGE BEHAVIOUR

The following day Keith went to work as though nothing had changed and that really was my first clue. This was the first full day of our new life together and yet he seemed to have slipped back into a routine that he was familiar with. Over the past few months I had seen an adventurous, spontaneous, challenging man, and today, he seemed somehow more formal, and much more serious. He seemed to take on another character from the moment he got out of bed. There was a kind of military precision to his preparation. I can't really pick out any one thing that illustrates this. It was just an uncanny, unnerving sensation that I felt. I thought no more about it as I carried out my jobs around the house.

When Keith returned from work he came in with a big beaming smile as usual. Ah, I thought, this is the Keith I know. But the hurried kiss and cuddle were an indication that I was wrong. At that point, he was not ready to relax. After a few words, he took his briefcase, scooped up the letters that had arrived in the post that morning, and went upstairs without venturing into the lounge, where Jonathan was watching television. I was confused, but carried on preparing an evening meal. Ten minutes later, I heard noises on the stairs and the sound of a door closing. I went to investigate and found him in the lounge. He was no longer wearing his suit; he had changed into something more casual and was laid on the floor playing games with Jonathan. He looked up at me and smiled, and from across the room I could instantly sense the difference in his manner, it was very strange! Whatever had happened to him during the day had gone. That magical spark that existed between us was there again. It had returned.

That night, our first official night living together, I was dealt another clue, and what a surprise it was. Before getting into bed, he lifted the pillow and there underneath was a very old homemade burgundy coloured plastic pyjama case. He opened the case and there inside was a pair of neatly folded pyjamas. He took them out carefully, put them on and buttoned them up to the neck in a very formal fashion. I was shocked and intrigued. They had not played any part in our relationship until that point. In fact if I had been questioned on bedtime routines I would have said, "*No, Keith never wears pyjamas.*" And where had they come from? How had the pyjama case got under the pillow? I had made the bed during the day and it wasn't there then. When I challenged him with regard to the pyjamas and their case he took on a manner I had not seen before. He became indignant at the fact I was challenging his routine and quite upset at my burst of laughter. His mind seemed to be closed to any suggestion of change. So I decided to drop the subject. After all, it was really unimportant and it didn't detract from our lovemaking, which was as passionate and exciting as always. And yet after only one day I was seeing a different person to the lover I had known. It was as though that period was for him something completely different. Now we were together, he was able to re-immerse himself in his own version of reality.

Early next morning my sleep was broken by the sound of Keith pacing forwards and backwards in front of the wardrobe. "*What are you doing?*", I said.

"*Not sure what to wear,*" he replied.

"*Well just keep looking,*" I said with a yawn, snuggling back under the duvet. "*You're bound to find something.*" I soon realised that he was still pondering so I suggested that he wear something similar to what he wore the day before. He didn't say anything to me. He just pulled some clothes from the wardrobe and marched out of the bedroom. A few minutes later he returned, fully dressed, telling me that he was going to work. He gave me a kiss but it bore no resemblance to the passionate kisses we had shared the previous evening.

When he came home in the evening, it was virtually a repeat of the first evening's performance. A big smile, a hurried kiss, collect the post, disappear and then transformation once the formal clothes had been replaced by casuals. It was really weird and then the following morning it was the same procedure as before with the pacing in front of the wardrobe and the indecision.

What I didn't realise at the time was that he had never been in the habit of choosing his own clothes. He had gone from living with his parents and his mother choosing his clothes to a first marriage where his wife then continued to chose his clothes. This was both in the purchase of the clothes and the ongoing decisions about what to wear on which occasion. It was obvious that he needed daily help in being told what to wear. I did not do this for him and he was obviously struggling. He was trying to cope without any regular signals from me. For my part we had young children who I had encouraged and taught to choose their own clothes daily. When they were very young I dressed them and then at a later stage I put out their clothes the night before in neat piles so that they were in no doubt as to what they should wear. Then with each son the time came when they challenged my decision. This was healthy, so for some time I would continue to guide them until eventually they were confident and I was confident that they were able to make their own choices. I suppose it came to my knowledge early on in our relationship that Keith hadn't gone through this process but I handled it badly and probably did more to confuse him.

The first significant acknowledgement of a problem was when he was going away for a week to an exhibition being held in Birmingham at the National Exhibition Centre. He asked me if I could help him pack his case. This was not a problem for me, as I always liked to pack if the family were travelling anywhere. I was responsible for my children when we arrived somewhere, and I had to know that all the necessary clothes and equipment were with us – I could not leave packing to chance. So I just saw this as Keith being cautious, which I understood. He stayed with me while I was about to pack his suitcase but he gave no instructions as to which suits or shirts to pack for the week. First I checked which suits he would be wearing. This was new to me, as I did not know what the week involved. After we had sorted out three suits my next task was to fold shirts.

"*Which shirts would you like me to fold?*" I asked.

"*Which do you suggest?*" was his reply.

I was surprised at his reply as my father and my ex-husband had a clear dress sense of their own. Although they had not ignored my support in this area, on a day-to-day basis they went about it without asking my opinion. At this time I was confused. I thought he was being tactful and asking for my input but it quickly became obvious that he did not have a sense of what he was supposed to wear and that it was all very confusing for him. He told me that at his request, his previous wife had always put a list in his suitcase stating which shirt, tie and socks he was to wear with each suit and which suit to wear on what day. Reluctantly I agreed to carry on the practice but I made it plain to him that I thought that at his age he should be able to work it out for himself. This was quite a trivial matter to me, and a cause of frustration from time to time, but it was a very serious problem for Keith. It was a long time before I realised I should be seriously helping him instead of trying to make light of it and dismissing it as if it were unimportant.

I had another strange experience with him during our first weekend together. We were sitting in the car listening to the radio. It was Grand National day and the race was being broadcast live. Every year the staff at the bank where I worked would organise a sweepstake on this race. It was a bit of fun and our total stake 'flutter' was only 50p each. I turned the volume up a little so that I could hear more clearly. Keith was horrified and switched the radio off immediately. I found it quite funny but was also a little shocked at his extreme reaction. He said that it was ridiculous that ordinary people who knew absolutely nothing about the sport of horse racing could spend money and get excited about this one race. I thought it a strong reaction but said nothing. I don't think we ever discussed it again until years later when we decided to put a £1 each week on the National Lottery.

Our second week together followed much the same pattern as the first although during the times when he was relaxing he seemed to be even more relaxed; this was highlighted by more and more frequent bouts of giggling and the uttering of very strange phrases. And then one evening his parents came to visit. As soon she entered the house and saw Keith, his mother said, "*Keith. You need a haircut!*" I found it odd that at thirty- four- years of age and having left home more than twelve years ago his mother would make such a comment. Even though I had thought myself that it needed cutting, I never dreamt about voicing my thoughts. It was his hair and his decision.

But following this incident, I took more notice and realised it was not something he had ever worked out for himself. When we talked about it, he told me how he found the whole process difficult. Working out when to have it cut was only part of the problem. When he went to the barber's shop, he said he felt like a fish out of water.

"How would you like it cutting sir?" Firstly he just didn't know how to answer. All the other customers seemed to understand the right terminology to use. But more particularly, as he kept to the same barber for years and always had the same style throughout, he couldn't understand why he always insisted on asking that question at all. In his mind it was obvious. He just wanted it cutting shorter. How hard can it be? He did not appreciate that men often changed their styles and that the barber had to make sure that he was creating the effect the customer wanted.

Each day I saw something else, something different that at the time I labelled as strange behaviour. I had not had any experience of this before. My love for Keith was growing and yet I couldn't put my finger on what it was that I was seeing and feeling. He seemed to switch from a very serious, formal man when he was going out to work, to a very immature child when he was at home. He would regularly let out strange noises and screams and his silly walks could easily compete with anything that John Cleese portrayed. When he came in from work he would walk in with his big beaming smile, give me a big kiss and assess the situation. Often the room would be untidy with toys all over. His first task would be to tidy up all the toys. He always did this and it always upset me. Why couldn't he just play with the children and let me get on with the meal and then we could all sit and chat? He thought he was helping me and I felt ungrateful saying we could tidy up later. After he had put all the toys away he would go upstairs and open his mail, finish off paperwork and unwind until the meal was ready. This was his way of saying, 'There, I've said hello, and I've helped you, now I need space.' I tried on several occasions to challenge this behaviour and get him to help me but after several frosty replies, I decided to accept it.

If he was working at his desk in the study and he took a personal phone call I would see him tidying papers and generally fidgeting and fiddling with things. If he took a call in the lounge where the telephone was on a low table in the corner, he would lie on the floor and spread out. All the time he was on the phone he would roll about, often on his back with his legs up in the air. When I mentioned this to him he denied it happened. He was a very serious person and found social phone calls very difficult to handle. Sometimes we would relax together by watching a film. If he became engrossed in a film I would see him relax, although his body language said the opposite. He would sit with his legs wound round each other and his arms would be close to his chest and entwined and twisted like the branches of a tree. He often looked like Houdini trussed up in his chains all ready to start his escape act. If the events in the movie were emotional, Keith would get very emotional. Watching a sad film, would leave us both in tears.

Like many people of our generation, during the 1970s both Keith and I wore flared trousers. Our children referred to them as Flarey Marys. The short-lived fashion had virtually disappeared by the early 1980s but not in our household. Keith did not insist on continuing to buy new flares but he did continue to wear his old ones for many years. Getting him to buy any new clothes was always a nightmare. We would discuss his need for a new item, and then go to the shop, but in the shop and always at the last moment he would insist he did not really need the item. He had another one at home so it was an extravagance to buy it. We always had this embarrassing exchange just before we parted with the money. Once the money was handed over, the subject was closed. We would go home happily together.

One of the nice things about Keith is that after any exchange of words on whatever subject, he was always the same even-tempered person, no sulking.

As he would say, *"We don't **do** sulking."*

Our two older boys, Karl and Darren, were taking a healthy interest in fashion at this time and were often at a loss to understand why Dad was all dressed up to go out for the day in clothes which looked as if they were even too out of date for a jumble sale. This caused many headaches and quite a bit of friction. One day I had just had enough and said, "*We are not ashamed of you but there are times when everyone, even tramps, have to part with things which are worn out.*"

Unknowingly I had hit on the answer and a solution.

"*Yes,*" he said, "*but these trousers are not worn out, they are just out of date and I don't mind that.*"

He was right: they didn't contain any holes and someone, somewhere, might get some wear out of them. We just wished it was not Keith. So against my better judgment I set up my sewing machine and made straight jeans out of flared jeans – not an easy task but I got there. This I did with three pairs of jeans. Our sons found this hilarious but it did ease the situation and it also pleased Keith, as he was always reluctant to spend money on new clothes. Over a period of time he relegated the jeans to wear when doing household jobs, painting or gardening and he catalogued them into these three areas by labelling the boxes in which they were kept.

One particular occasion that stands out in my memory is when I made an arrangement to collect a friend on a Sunday and go to a mill shop to buy a tapestry kit. I got in the car and found that the petrol level was very low. I went back into the house and as Keith was still in bed I apologised but asked if he would mind getting up and taking the car to the garage to get some petrol before I set off. I felt guilty, as he did not get the chance to stay in bed and catch up on his sleep very often. However this trip had been arranged with his blessing and unfortunately his Visa card was only in his name and therefore I could not use it to put petrol in the car myself. Our budget was very tight as always at this time and if I had used my only cash to put some petrol in the car I would have had no money to go to the factory. Keith insisted that I take his card to the garage and sign on his behalf. He said that if the bank realised it was my signature and not his, it would be all right as they would simply send for his signature and everything would be just fine. Having worked in a bank I knew this to be illegal and could cause a lot of problems. And if nothing else, it would certainly cause embarrassment. It was not my Visa card and even though it was my husband's and not a stranger's it would still be classed as fraud. After trying to argue the point with him for at least five minutes he got very cross and said I was just being very silly. With this I went to ring my friend and apologise and give an excuse for not going. The second I picked up the phone it was as if by magic he was out of bed and at my side. Very calmly he took the phone from me and put it down before I was able to make the call. Then he went out to the car, drove to the garage and filled it up with petrol. I set off with very mixed emotions. It was not imperative that I make this trip. I knew he had no objections to me seeing our friend for an hour or two and he had never criticised or made comment on any money I had ever spent. He trusted me on both counts. I could not understand why he had refused to put the petrol in the car in the first place. If he had said, "*I need my rest and you can go later,*" I could have understood it. But the issue seemed to be that I was making a mountain out of a molehill at the very idea of using his Visa card.

In the afternoon when I got back he had made lunch for the children. I had left the food out and written instructions. Everyone was busy and quite happy. After I got in he literally took my coat off made me a drink and sat me down and then proceeded to apologise for his behaviour. He said how selfish he had been and was so sorry and it would never happen again. To say I was shocked was an understatement, as he usually stuck to his guns with unwavering resolve if he thought he was in the right. The issue to me was not who was right or who was wrong – we had moved on from the problem. The thing that worried me, however, was that he had not grasped that what he had very casually asked me to do was in fact illegal. He explained to me that after I had gone he had understood this and that he was sorry he had been so stubborn. He handed me an envelope. I pulled out a handwritten letter from him. Receiving a letter from Keith was not unusual. We had often communicated this way before and we found it a good way of expressing our love for each other.

But this letter was different. It was a full apology for getting things so wrong. He said he was trying really hard to get things right and was determined to learn from today's episode and from my example. The last line had just three words written in large capitals: I LOVE YOU! I felt quite sorry for him at this point but I soon found reason to smile because he had drawn the outline of a man at the bottom of the letter. The man was shown with unkempt hair, needing a shave, wearing old flared trousers, and cowboy boots. A heading underneath asked the question 'Guess Who?' but this was immediately answered with the inscription 'KTG going for petrol on a Sunday morning'. This showed me that he was aware of his two halves. He was aware of the fact that he just went to an extreme when he was not at work. I would regularly point out that he could go for days without shaving and showering and would wear clothes that even tramps would discard, if he was not going out to work. He had made a joke about it, but really it was concerning. He didn't seem to recognise that it was an important issue and something he should be tackling.

We formalised our liaison in October by getting married. Shortly afterwards we moved away from Bradford. We chose to live in a newly built bungalow in Snaith, East Yorkshire, which is about forty miles away. It had taken several months of house hunting to arrive at that decision; endless days of trailing around different towns and villages, looking at a large variety of properties. I remember one particular Saturday when we were both feeling quite low after a full day of looking at houses with nothing suitable being found. It was early evening by now as we said our goodbyes to the young couple in the final property of the day and walked a short distance to our car, parked in a deserted lane. We both exhaled in unison and gave each other a kiss and a cuddle as a means of comforting one another. Before long we had converted the car into a bedroom, but not, of course for sleeping. I remember being concerned about where we were parked, but I was having too much fun to worry unduly. Keith showed absolutely no concern for our whereabouts. It was about three years later when we were driving along a busy bus route that he asked me if I could remember making love here when we were house hunting. I could recall the occasion very clearly. But I told him he was mixed up about the location. He smiled, and drove a short distance down a narrow lane, which led to the last house that we had visited on that day. It was just as I had remembered it and made all the more poignant by the fact that it was up for sale again. Perhaps it had been on the market for all this time? I had no idea that we had been so close to a main road and would have been devastated if I had known at that time. That wasn't our first time in the open, of course, and we were to repeat the experience on several occasions in the future. These activities were never planned by both of us. It was always just one of us that decided it was going to happen on a particular day, and engineered our movements to ensure that we ended up in a suitable location.

Keith planned our house-moving with military precision. Once a deposit had been taken on the house, we acquired several packing cases and all none essential items were packed. He hired a van and organised a gang of family helpers and timings were checked and double-checked. He wouldn't let me help, insisting that I should ensure that the children had their normal routine during this traumatic transition. Then the lady who was moving into our house asked if we could move out a day earlier so that they could have more time to move in on the Saturday. After several objections Keith very reluctantly agreed and revised his plans. On the Friday evening, after they had finished work, my dad, my brother John and his fiancée Janet all helped Keith to load the van. After loading, Keith went from room to room carefully checking that each one was left neat and tidy for the new owners. He was meticulous in his endeavour. He made sure that all light bulbs were left in place, holes which had been uncovered by the removal of furniture and appliances were filled, that he had plastered behind the cooker and left all bathroom accessories so as not to leave any unnecessary unsightly holes in the tiles. Finally he ensured that all floors were swept and washed. The whole team was shattered by the end of the night as they had already put in a full day's work before coming along to fill the removal van.

That night we slept at my parent's house. When we woke up next morning there were several inches of snow on the ground. How were we to get the van on its way in all this snow? It was only years afterwards that we talked about this and realised that if there had been an accident we would have lost all our worldly possessions as we had not taken out any extra insurance cover. With a great deal of strength and pushing from our super band of helpers, the van finally moved. Keith's parents also joined the team that morning which made unloading to be a little faster than loading. Everything went smoothly and we have always been eternally grateful to our helpers.

Keith, the children and I were living with my parents for a week while Keith was travelling daily to decorate as much of the bungalow as possible before we moved in. He was up early each day and came back early evening. On the first evening he returned home I had his tea waiting. I was excited to hear about his progress and any reports on our new neighbours. I was finishing off his meal when I heard my dad open the door for him. I waited for him to come into the dining room and give me a kiss and say hello to the children as they had been in bed when he left that morning.

Five minutes went by, then ten minutes, and still no Keith. I went to investigate. There he was sitting in front of the television glued to his favourite programme of the time, *Star Trek*. I should have known. He had obviously calculated the timing perfectly. He had painted for the maximum amount of time possible, allowed for his journey time, and arrived on the dot to watch his programme. What he had forgotten to do was leave enough time to say hello to his wife and children. I took his meal to him to eat on a tray. He grunted at me but his gaze never left the screen. He had worked so hard that day, how could I be so ungrateful? But ungrateful I was as it seemed like the return of a stranger who I was not allowed to communicate with until he was ready. I was very appreciative of how hard he was working and yet I was unable to understand why I could not have two minutes of his time for a kiss and hello and then we could have watched the programme together.

Something that I had found very frustrating about him was dramatically highlighted when we started to consider furnishings for our new home. Shopping with him was always a nightmare. He could never make a decision. Not just his personal wardrobe but also anything for the house such as furniture, curtains, carpets. Eventually I realised that I had to do the choosing myself and then simply gain his approval for my choice. So it was a major surprise to me when, out of the blue, he came home with a piece of furniture which he had chosen himself. We had discussed buying a coffee table for our new lounge with some money that my mother and father had given to us as a wedding present. Whenever I mentioned it, he would put me off and say that we would do it later. After persistent attempts to get him to act he stormed in this particular day and put a package in front of me.

"There!" he said very sharply. *"That's what you wanted."* But then almost immediately he sat back and watched with excitement as I tore off the brown paper. Inside was a nest of tables that were identical to those which had been among the lounge furniture of his previous home with his previous wife. They had been purchased some eleven years earlier. By now they were out of fashion and did not blend with our other pieces of furniture. But his expression was just like that of

a child who had made his first birthday card for you at school. How can you knock that sort of enthusiasm? It was years later when I found that the financial gift from my parents had disappeared into a black hole and that our newest household addition had arrived by courtesy of Barclaycard.

Soon after we moved into our bungalow I took the children over to Bradford for a day out with my parents. Keith was decorating the bedroom. When we got back he had finished and tidied up. He took me to show me his handiwork and how spacious the room was. It certainly was more spacious and I soon realised that something was missing. *"Where is the dressing table?"* I said. It was an antique, which I loved and was very attached to. It had been given to me by my previous mother-in-law.

"Oh, I thought it would give us more room in here if I put it in the loft," he said, with an air of authority and confidence.

"But I didn't think it would go in the loft," I replied.

"Oh it went in easily after I chopped the legs off," he stated, very matter-of-factly.

I gulped in astonishment. I could have cried but something inside me was telling me not to react. I knew that he had worked all day, probably non-stop. If he has a project and he is busy he can soon forget to eat. Keith had obviously wanted the room to be ready for when we got home. I was very pleased with the result. It looked very fashionable. I just could not bring myself to tell him how upset I was at losing my favourite dressing table. Weeks afterwards I did tell him and he just said, *"Well it was old, I thought it was better in the loft."*

He looked thoughtful for a while. *"I was just thinking that I could glue the legs back on and bring it back down again."*

Nice idea, I thought to myself, but I really hope he doesn't. I needn't have worried, because his next statement enabled me to relax: *"But then I remembered that I had thrown them out."*

A lot of Keith's idiosyncrasies were financially based and he did seem to have a total lack of appreciation about prioritising where money was concerned. He would come home regularly on a Friday without any cash, which meant we couldn't buy any food. As with hairdressers, he also had a hang up about banks and avoided them like the plague. He wouldn't use the 'hole in the wall' on principle, and spent lots of energy complaining about the hours that banks opened, or more precisely didn't open. After several attempts to get him to understand, I found it was easier to open an account of my own, so that I could manage to buy food for the household without aggravation.

One of the most challenging periods during our first year together was the run up to Christmas. I had been used to a long period of celebration with family groups, meals, games, friends, relaxation and generous gifts exchanged. Keith had been used to a quiet family get-together. We ended up planning something in the middle and even that made him very uncomfortable. But the strangest thing for me was his attitude to buying presents. He appeared to have no concept about the cost of Christmas and threw a wobbly every time I discussed presents. He also had no idea about making choices. He just found the whole thing too much and was unable to cope with it. I soon realised I had to get on with the arrangements myself. This was fine but each time I asked him for more money his face took on an incredulous and disapproving appearance, which made me feel very uncomfortable. I bought all the presents on my own. I wrapped all the presents on my own, and I even bought and wrapped the present which Keith would give to me on Christmas Day. Despite all this aggravation, though, the festive period itself was enjoyable. However, Keith enjoyed it as a child would enjoy Christmas. He had magic in his eyes as he stuffed himself with food of all varieties, which eventually made him violently sick. And when it came to cooking and serving and clearing away? Well children don't do that, do they? It was certainly a strange Christmas and a great learning experience for me.

As we had agreed on our first night, the children would come first and indeed they did. Despite all his idiosyncrasies, Keith was a great dad to all our children. He did have one difficulty though. We each had joint custody with our previous partners for our children. At the beginning, Keith was finding it difficult to establish a new routine, a new relationship with our middle son, Richard, who was living with his mother. There was no refusal or aggression towards his requests to see his son at all. He just found the whole experience of contacting his ex-wife too frustrating. There was no conspiracy to stop him seeing Richard – it was all in his mind and probably part of his strange behaviour at that time in his life. I can remember so clearly him not being able to get to sleep one night. He was sobbing away and saying, *"It's no good. I will have to stop seeing Richard, even though I don't want to."*

I questioned him as to why he thought this was best. He said he couldn't take all the aggravation and thought it was no good for Richard. I just let him talk and talk and get lots of things off his chest. Then I said, *"If you do take this action, just imagine Richard in the future when he is a man living on his own making his own decisions. He will never understand that you did it for him. He will just think that his Dad did not love him enough to be around for him. It might not be easy but you have to make the effort for his sake."*

He accepted my advice but still found it hard to communicate in order to fix up meetings and so I took this over. He never mentioned this difficulty again until many years later.

Keith had many 'hang ups' from his youth. He told me about his feeling of loneliness. It was, he said, an inner loneliness that he had been unable to share with anyone until now. He told me how as a child, he had developed an obsession for pictures of women. He felt it was not the normal titillating schoolboy interest in females. It was an obsession. His mother had caught him masturbating and she had castigated him for being so 'dirty minded'. This had left a very strong impression in his mind that made him greatly confused about himself. It was during one of our long talking sessions following an enjoyable period of sexual pleasure, while we were away on honeymoon, that he admitted to me that he had continuously purchased men's magazines from the age of thirteen and, indeed, right up until that present day. He said he felt ashamed. I asked about his magazines and where he kept them. He said he had stored them in his garage but when we moved in together he had burned them all in case I found them and thought he was a freak. It was obvious he was confused about the situation. The magazines had been a big part of his life but now he felt it was wrong to buy them. I explained that I did not feel they were part of a grown up relationship, but I knew that there were probably a lot of men who regularly relied on them. I also explained that as a teenager I had had a male work colleague who had a weekly order at a local newsagent for a men's magazine and on occasions I would collect it for him. I never made any judgement of this and often looked at the book myself or together we often discussed the models in the books. It always seemed no more than everyday conversation to me at the time. I asked Keith what he liked about the books and his reply was that, apart from the obvious sexual stimulation that he got from the erotic pictures and lurid stories, it was somewhere for him to escape and relax. The very next day we called at a newsagent and together we looked at the books on the top shelf. We studied the covers, thumbed through the pages, and finally made a purchase. I have to admit I had always been curious to know what all the different books were about and now I was finding out. It was a further two days before we settled down together in the hotel and shared the contents of the book. We looked at the pictures together and read the stories and readers' letters to each other. We found out a lot more about each other, such as our likes, dislikes and prejudices. Over a period of the next eighteen months, Keith would occasionally come home with a new magazine and we would enthusiastically pour over the contents together. Then eventually no more books arrived. He didn't need them anymore. Rightly or wrongly I had made a decision to share with him something that had been part of his life but had troubled him. I think that if I had been judgemental at the time and called him dirty or disgusting and simply refused to talk to him about it, he would have carried on using this avenue as a means of escape from reality.

He also had a major hang up about 'bath nights' and intercourse and the relationship between them. In his former life 'bath nights' were Friday and Sunday and sex usually followed the same pattern. At least he knew when he was going to get it, but Monday to Thursday must have been quite frustrating at times. I was used to a daily bath and couldn't understand why everyone didn't do the same.

"Does this mean we should have sex every night?" I asked him. We had a laugh and went on to develop our own pattern of when we needed each other, irrespective of the day of the week.

Despite his odd behaviour, that first year was a very happy time for me. From the first time we slept together, we seemed to know what each other wanted. We would regularly set the alarm clock to wake us very early, so that we could have some private time together before having to make breakfast for the family. We found early morning love making much more enjoyable than late at night, but of course, we were often able to take advantage of both sessions. After the evening sessions we would talk, sometimes for hours, into the early morning.

But Keith wouldn't just talk; he would often sing songs or recite poetry. I always found this endearing, even if a little frustrating at first. The songs were usually ones that had a repeated chorus after each verse or a poem he had learnt at school. This included a repertoire of playground chants, which contained lines such as, 'Holy Moses had a cow he called it Fatty Horrocks'. Although very childish it was new to me and far from being annoying it displayed his continuing need to communicate with me after we made love. Both the sex itself and the aftermath were tremendous fun and very fulfilling. If ever I was upset or made it clear I had a problem, when we went to bed at night Keith would act like a clown. I would think 'for goodness sake, leave me alone. I have enough problems, stop clowning about.' But while his activities were usually very corny, without exception it always worked. Just as I was telling him to go to sleep and stop being so silly, something in his actions or his voice would make me crack up and laugh with him. I have to admit it must have been hard for him to keep up the stamina to make me laugh when I had no intention of laughing. He always felt he had to cheer me up and this was the only way he knew. He could not offer me solutions, as very often he was the reason for me being down, but he could always relieve the tension and frustration that I had developed.

Keith was never jealous of my relationship with my children, and, in his own way, he did show me that he loved me. However there were so many times when I felt I did not have enough hands to hold everyone or enough strength to support us all. Unbeknown to me, Keith was becoming my extra child. He needed constant reassurance of my love. Like a child, he used to perform for attention, for hugs and laughs. All these things grew naturally between us. I did not realise it as it was happening, but not only was the strong bond of love between us growing, but also developing was Keith's dependence on me socially and often practically. This would continue for another eighteen years until he finally started to grow up. The signs were all there from the beginning but at this stage in our relationship I did not know how to read them. Life with Keith was like being a lover, a mother and a teacher. Fortunately, I didn't have to be more than one at a time. These were the signs but I was unable to interpret them at the time. Sometimes he was a very serious man who frowned a lot and sometimes he was a very adventurous cheeky young boy. I found it very difficult living with the different characters he seemed to project. Probably the most difficult year of my life so far was just coming to an end. I didn't know it yet, but there were many more challenging years ahead.

Chapter 3

ALONG COMES MATTHEW

Matthew was born at lunchtime on Wednesday 14th January 1981. The waiting was over. Owing to the challenges of the previous year, my pregnancy had seemed endless and yet there are some very special memories for me – particularly when I look at the photographs of the heavily pregnant bride at our wedding. But it was the fact that our four sons were so happy about the forthcoming addition to our family that gave me the most pleasure. We had broken the news to them while enjoying a picnic in Pickering, North Yorkshire, on one of our very many days out. Both of us had been very nervous about making the announcement not really knowing how they would react to yet another major change to their young lives so soon after the trauma of their parents' separation. But they were all instantly thrilled with the news although a little disappointed that they were going to have to wait several months before they could see 'our baby'.

Keith and I arrived at the hospital at 5.30 in the morning and Matthew was born at two minutes before twelve, lunchtime. Keith, who was with me throughout the labour, was fascinated with the monitor that had been set up to induce me. This was a new experience for me as my other three babies had come into the world naturally without much help – although I had needed help in breaking my waters. This time was different. My baby had suddenly gone to sleep after several hours of advanced labour. Keith scanned the monitor constantly, telling me when a contraction was approaching but, of course, as I was feeling each pain, the last thing I needed was a running commentary. He was very impressed that, thanks to technology, he could follow the progress of the impending birth, but I really wished that the monitor was anywhere but at my bedside. We were both delighted when our new son came into the world. He was beautiful and we could not wait to show him to his four brothers. Keith went home to tell everyone the news and to get some much-needed sleep. When he visited me that evening I was very surprised to learn that he was still planning to attend the monthly sales review meeting in London the following day. He felt that as a manager, it was his responsibility to be as up-to-date with sales figures and information as possible. I pointed out that if we had been on holiday at the time of the meeting he would have missed it. This statement made no difference to him, because as far as Keith was concerned he had a responsibility to his company and that came first. The fact that he had a newborn son was irrelevant as we were in hospital and being well looked after by nurses and, therefore, he didn't need to be there. He couldn't understand what I was making all the fuss about. Yes, in an ideal world he would like to spend the time with us, but surely I could see that it was not possible, as he had things to do and expectations to fulfil. The next afternoon our two mums came to visit and brought with them their four grandsons, Karl, Darren, Richard and Jonathan, who were all eager to meet their new brother. They took it in turns to nurse Matthew, each one bonding with him immediately. I had a wonderful afternoon as I listened to our sons and all their news, while my mum and Keith's mum had lots to tell me themselves, in between holding their new grandson for the first time. I just sat back and listened, enjoying our sons' enthusiasm and excitement. I was so happy as it felt just like being at home. They were all over my bed telling me their stories. We talked about the immediate future and especially what gift we would buy for Matthew when we returned home from the hospital. One of the nursing staff was fascinated by the fact that we had a large family of boys. She remarked on the similarity in appearance between Karl and Richard, which made me smile to myself, as they are, in fact, stepbrothers. The visiting period that evening, however, was a very different story. All the other mums in the ward had a visitor, either a husband or a partner, but as Keith had chosen to go to London, I was alone with my thoughts and so I pretended to sleep. I tried reading but as I felt lonely I could not concentrate. My thoughts were drifting to Keith and the children. The following day, my best friend Christine came to visit us and we had a special afternoon together. She had crocheted some little jackets for Matthew and her mum had knitted one for him. Christine was six months pregnant with her third child, and so we swapped notes and chatted about her progress. The same evening I got a happy surprise as John, my brother, walked in to the ward clutching a bunch of beautiful flowers. John and Janet were to be Matthew's Godparents, along with my sister, Judith. His visit was all the more special, as I knew babies were not his thing at that time in his life, his mid-twenties. But he loved all his nephews and nieces and liked to be with them, so I wasn't surprised when he eagerly scooped Matthew from his crib and held him for a short while. His conversation helped me to relax and we had a good laugh together. The biggest laugh, though, came as the bell rang for the end of visiting and before John had a chance to leave, the man visiting his wife who was in the next bed to me approached him and said in a loud voice, *"Did you get what you wanted lad?"*

John just nodded and was let off the hook as the man, who was quite inebriated, went on to tell us how this was their fifth baby and had turned out to be the only boy among his family of four girls. He was floating on cloud nine.

At last, Saturday arrived and I was so excited to be going home. Keith had returned from London late the previous evening, too late to come and visit us. He arrived mid morning as planned and we were so pleased to see each other. It was obvious that he had missed us and that now that work was out of the way, his time was all ours, and he had even booked some holiday to look after us. Before he arrived at the hospital, I was very disappointed to be told that, because Matthew was slightly jaundiced, he would probably not be allowed home for the weekend. As I was explaining these developments to Keith, a nurse came to us to confirm that they would have to keep him in until Monday, when another blood sample would be taken. The nurse saw the disappointment we were both feeling, took pity on us and said she would take a blood sample at once and deliver it to the laboratory herself there and then. She said that she could not promise it would be tested as it was Saturday, but she would try her best. Well, it was tested and it was negative, so with relief and joy we all headed for home. It was late afternoon when we arrived there, very happy to be a family once again. Keith was now on holiday for a whole week but what a strange week it turned out to be.

Once we arrived home we took Matthew straight to our bedroom. Grandparents had arranged for all the children to be together and it was really special when they all sat on our bed and took it in turns to cuddle their new brother and welcome him into the family. Keith was very eager to be involved in the task of looking after Matthew's needs such as nappy changing and he didn't hesitate when it came to giving him his first bath. Even though he was my fourth baby I was, as I had been with the others, very nervous of his fragile state in the first few days, until I got into a routine. The weekend was a very happy time and it felt good. However when Monday arrived, so did the routine. I spent the morning feeding and bathing Matthew. About halfway through the morning, I was startled to see that the midwife was suddenly standing in front of me. Keith had obviously let her into the house and yet there was no sign of him. In fact, I had seen little of him since breakfast and by noon I was beginning to feel a distinct lack of Keith's presence. It was after the midwife had gone that he appeared and asked what I wanted for lunch. We had lunch together and when this was over he disappeared again until just before teatime, when he woke me up from an afternoon nap to ask what he should cook for the evening meal. Before going into hospital I had organised all our meals for two weeks at least. I had spent hours cooking a variety of dishes and stocking up the freezer and I had prepared a list of the various dishes and their cooking times. All he had to do was take something out each evening and reheat it. It was not until early evening that I asked him what he had been doing all day.

"*I have to get my paperwork up to date,*" was his indignant reply. The following day was exactly the same. He made sure I was fed, but he never came into the bedroom to talk or relax with us. In the morning I spent my time organising Matthew and washing nappies. During the afternoon I tried to get a short nap. Once again he woke me up to ask what he should cook for tea. He seemed to be unable to make a choice from my list, so I decided that on the following days I would do it myself. It was just as well because he had received a message from work that a meeting had been called on what should have been the third day of his holiday. He perceived it to be a very important meeting that he could not miss. Off he went at six in the morning and arrived home after I had fed, bathed and put the children to bed. Keith had asked his mother to give me some support in his absence and so she arrived after she finished work, in the early afternoon, as I was ironing. Great, I thought, as I looked at the pile of clothes, which had been growing taller, day-by-day. Although I hated ironing it was something I would normally keep on top of and not allow to accumulate. I was only part way through the pile when it was time to turn off the iron and feed Matthew. The signal went unnoticed, as Keith's mum decided that I seemed to be coping well and thought she would visit her ex daughter-in-law Maureen for an hour or so. With Jonathan's help I fed Matthew, changed him, and played with him for a little while. Then it was back to the pile of ironing. Before long it was time for me to sort out dinner and Matthew's next feed. I was serving our evening meal as Keith's mum arrived back just in time to sit down at the table with us. She was so full of excitement when she relayed what she had been discussing with Maureen that she failed to recognise my workload and how tired I was feeling. So the week continued. This was not the family week I had expected. Keith's work intervened every day for several hours. It was part of his annual leave so we should have been relaxing together with our family. Surely this was our time – why did we have to be fitted in around his job? Why did he allow his job to encroach on holiday time? It was not as if he **had** to fit us in around his job, but he did. It was not the idyllic period I had envisaged. During Keith's holiday I'd hoped that we would enjoy making our new routine together and sharing our time together with the children, until it was time for him to return to work the following week.

The days and weeks went by and although our life together was still new and I knew he was a good and loyal person, and most of all that I was in love with him, I was concerned that our family time seemed to get less and less. I was very aware that he always helped with good grace, was never offhand but never ever anticipated that I needed help. Whenever I needed assistance, I had to ask for it; not just with the little things, but with the glaringly obvious as well. He did not seem to notice that I needed support sometimes. My first job each day was to wash and dress and then I could feel smart and reasonably confident and I was then ready to face anything. Like most busy mums with very young babies, hair brushing and re-applying make-up were not a standard daily routine and once dressed that was usually the only time I had for myself until bedtime. Sometimes I must have looked a fright, but then who was going to see me. I would make more of an effort if Keith was coming home, but rarely did he seem to notice either way.

Matthew was an easy baby to look after: he ate well and he slept well and at just a few weeks old he was sleeping through the night. Little teeth popped through at the appropriate times without any problems. He would sit contentedly with his brothers around him and was often unaware of what they were doing. Lots of babies interfere with their sibling's games but Matthew did not and he only ever showed interest in his own bits and pieces. He rarely played with conventional toys, preferring instead to use pans, containers, sticks and pieces of paper. Although these actions were different from what I experienced with the other boys, I didn't pay serious attention to it at the time. My boys and I got lots of fresh air as I found the best place for me to relax was outside. We lived in a lovely area and with our baby in his pram and children alongside we could enjoy a long walk together, either down country lanes or into the park area. At home, however, I found life somewhat more stressful. Keith had made one of the bedrooms into a study. He insisted that he needed an office as he worked from home. We had the double bedroom and so four boisterous boys and one baby boy were all neatly packed into the other bedroom. Very frequently I had to answer business telephone calls during the day when Keith was out and I always tried to answer these in a professional manner. This was not always easy with a baby in one hand and a four-year-old pulling my arm or leg for attention, not to mention one or more of the older boys shouting questions at me from the other side of the house. When Keith came home from work, he maintained his well rehearsed routine. After a brief greeting, he tidied away all the toys and other items, and then disappeared to the study. Almost as soon as the study door had closed, I would rescue some of the toys for the children to play with and then I would go into the kitchen to cook the meal, working hard between cooker and baby for the best part of the next hour.

As time moved on I felt happy, confused by Keith's behaviour, but nevertheless happy. But I did feel very tired, often exhausted at the end of each day and increasingly at several points during the day. I had known moments like this before when our other children were babies, but eventually I caught up on my rest and felt stronger; it was a normal part of motherhood. But this time it felt different, somehow more permanent. Obviously I was older now and couldn't expect myself to cope with a baby at thirty-four as easily as I did at twenty-three when Karl was born, but it was concerning for me. The breastfeeding was very tiring, even though I enjoyed this contact with him and for a brief period I felt very relaxed. That was until an abscess appeared in my right breast, which made me feel as though someone was jabbing thousands of needles into me at every feed. This was a new experience for me, but the doctor assured me that it was common and prescribed some antibiotics, which eventually eradicated the problem. I was able to continue breast-feeding until Matthew was four months old.

But there was something more sinister that was causing my daily lethargy and I needed to find out what it was. For three years before Matthew's birth, I had been having monthly injections to help with my allergy to house dust mites. I had stopped these when I was pregnant, but now, after discussion with the doctor, I decided to begin again. After the first injection I came out of the surgery and felt very uncomfortable. After several minutes I found I could not push Matthew in his pushchair in a straight manner and yet it was only because of the pushchair that I was able to get home; it acted like a Zimmer frame for me. Without the pushchair I would have given the appearance of someone still suffering the after-effects of a very good night out. I spent a very difficult day looking after the family and was relieved Keith was coming home that evening. Once he was home I could relax and I soon fell asleep in the chair after which Keith carried me to bed and I slept until two o' clock the next afternoon. Fortunately he was working at home on that day on a special project, so he kept an eye on me and looked after Matthew between his work. When I explained what had happened to the doctor he said we would try one more injection and if I reacted this time we should stop the injections and think again about different treatment. Next time I reacted in exactly the same way and so there were no more injections. In fact, that was the last injection I ever had. I have boycotted all types of vaccination ever since and even refused to go on holiday when vaccination was deemed essential. In hindsight, I realised that the doctor should have started me on a lighter dose and gradually built up to the previous level rather than prescribing the previous level immediately. Both Keith and I are convinced that those dust mite injections started a chain of events of personal ill health that continue to this day. The first indications of this chain of events were my frequent fainting episodes. I passed out on several occasions – in church, in our garden, even in the street. I wasn't choosy and often ended up with a variety of multi-coloured bruises. Over the next two years I lost a stone and a half in weight and saw various specialists. At first, multiple sclerosis was suspected but fortunately all the tests and brain scans ruled this out. It was the early 80s and the illness Myalgic Encephalomyelitis (ME) was just coming to light. We both watched programmes and read articles about this and everything pointed to the fact I was suffering from ME. The medical profession did not agree, however, but nevertheless it gave us a route to follow. We spent a lot of money at this time trying to make me well. The NHS had no tests for ME so many doctors preferred to believe it did not exist. One very helpful specialist set me off on the very slow road to recovery. He did tests and it became obvious I was intolerant to wheat and dairy produce. I followed wheat free and non-dairy diet and this did have a positive effect on me but although improved, I never regained my full health. We both believe that it is because it was not detected early enough and acted upon at the time that I continue now to suffer from both ME, and Fibromyalgia, a very painful condition which attacks the fibrous tissue in tendons and ligaments.

It was a very difficult period in our lives, but I was surprised, amazed and delighted that Keith totally supported me in my search to get better. We were united in finding a cure for me. He would conscientiously check things out if he had heard that there was some new information about intolerances and chronic fatigue, and he spent a lot of time and energy following up leads. That said, however, and just as before, once he was into his work mode another set of rules applied. The worst time I can remember was during a week's school holiday period when I was in so much pain I could not get out of bed. The problem was my back and kidney area, which was later revealed to be a serious kidney infection. Despite the fact I had been in agony for most of the night and had told Keith how difficult it was for me, he insisted on leaving home at six o' clock that morning, as planned, for a day in Glasgow. I can remember praying that if only I could have another couple of hours' sleep, I would be able to get up as normal. Fortunately it was well after 9.00am when Matthew woke up and needed attention. Although the extra sleep had been good for me, the pain was no less severe. I could just about sit up but it caused agony for me when I attempted to get my legs to the floor. Eventually, Karl, who realised that something must be wrong, as I would normally be up and about long before this time, came to find me. He sprang into action sorting out breakfast for Matthew and his other brothers. I realised that I couldn't expect Karl to look after us all day, but I wasn't sure what I was going to do, as I just could not stand properly. Regardless of my health, my boys came first. I had to know they were all safe. As different solutions kept coming into my head and then disappearing as impractical, I suddenly thought of my good friend Ann. She worked in a school, but as it was the school holidays she should be at home. She did have two children of her own but as they were a little older than ours, I thought it was worth a try. Karl rang her and explained that I was ill. He didn't need to say anymore; she was wonderful, arriving very soon after the call, organising things in the house, attacking the washing basket, putting wet washing on the line and preparing lunch and tea for the five boys and myself. I know she went home very exhausted but she was a lifesaver that day and for this support I will be eternally grateful. When Keith arrived home late that evening from Scotland he was shocked to find me trying to cope with the boys while suffering tremendous pain. Because he was now 'off duty', he could recognise the problem and yet in the early hours of that morning he had either not seen the state I was in, or simply chose to ignore it, electing instead to stick to his original planned trip up the motorway. This was the strongest indication to me that, whenever I needed help from him in the future, I would need to demand it. It wasn't that he wouldn't give me the support; it was just that he could never see for himself when help was needed. I had expected to cope well with Matthew's arrival and expected him to fit into our family easily. After all, he was not my first child. Perhaps if Keith had been there to fully support me, I would have coped well. In some ways it might have been easier if he hadn't been there at all because in reality I had to be mum to him as well. Although I was frustrated, I was still very much in love with him. The best times were when we were all together, all seven of us.

One of the most memorable moments for me was on our first wedding anniversary when Karl and Darren organised a concert in celebration. They spent a whole day planning and organising the two younger boys, and then at around ten o'clock the following morning Keith and I were asked to take our seats in our lounge. Matthew, too young to participate, made us an audience of three. Firstly we were presented with anniversary cards that our sons had individually made for us. This led inevitably to lots of hugs and kisses, and then we were ready to settle down for the entertainment. Karl and Darren had found some suitable outfits for them all to dress up in and they were instructing Richard and Jonathan on what to wear. They had rehearsed magic tricks, jokes, sketches, poems and songs. We spent a very happy day together and felt very privileged that our little family wanted to help us celebrate our first anniversary. Over the years, the boys and I spent many anniversaries together but Keith was invariably working away. Work always came first even when it was an important family occasion. Keith's company sponsored Watford's football team for a number of years and they held a firework display and refreshments on Bonfire Night every year, which he always attended. Hence I was usually a grass widow on Bonfire Night and the children and I sometimes enjoyed a few fireworks at home. More often than not, though, we joined our neighbours at a locally organised fireworks display.

Despite these difficulties in Keith's behaviour regarding everyday matters, he was superb in supporting me in other areas. I have already mentioned his backing for me in finding a solution to my failing health and there are many examples of him helping me to improve and believe in myself. Learning to type is the one that sticks in my memory, as it opened up a career for me in years to come. When I said I wanted to go to a typing class he supported me, he helped me and whenever I felt like quitting because of my slow progress, he always talked me round to a positive attitude and persuaded me to get back in there. After gaining my RSA and Pittman certificates I didn't have long to wait in order to put my new skill to good use. Despite the additional workload that Matthew had given me, despite the challenges that Keith gave me, and despite my far from perfect health, I felt that I needed outside stimulation.

Keith had been heavily involved with church life in Bradford and when we came to Snaith, he was keen to re-establish himself. He was over the moon when I agreed to join him. In fact it was to become part of our family life for several years into the future. We became very friendly with our vicar, Gareth, and his wife Kathleen. I was talking with them one day and the subject of the church magazine came up. Gareth had visions of a vibrant publication, which would be a source of information and inspiration for the vast majority of people in Snaith and Cowick. The magazine that was around at that time was a far cry from Gareth's vision and he knew that he didn't have the expertise or time to pull it off on his own. I listened with increasing interest and that evening talked to Keith with enthusiasm. I persuaded him that the production and advertising of the magazine was something I could get involved in. With a little bit of extra help from him, I could easily fit it into my week. Imagine my surprise when he said, "*Yes.*" I had expected a bit of a fight – after all I was asking him to change his routine. But in hindsight, as long as I wasn't asking him to give the extra help 'during office hours', he was fine. In fact it wasn't a simple yes; it was a very supportive and positive response.

I joined a small group of people who met on a monthly basis to collate all the snippets of information from the area and decide on the content and page layout. I evolved as the typist, which was fantastic. One area that had been neglected was the financial structure of the magazine. Clearly, if it was to develop, it needed to be sorted, and I felt that this too was an area that I could manage. At the time there were six small advertisements covering part of an A5 page. Some of those advertising were paying a nominal annual amount, probably seeing it as a contribution to church funds, but the majority had not paid anything at all in recent times. I rushed home from one of the meetings, full of enthusiasm, pouring out my plans to Keith about how I was going to revolutionise the income. I asked for his help and this was where his organisational skills clicked in. He quickly drafted a size chart for the advertisements: Singles, Doubles, Quarter Page, Half Page and Full Page with a price list for the different sizes. He was putting together a sales pack for me. Hang on a minute, I thought, am I getting out of my depth? I had never sold anything in my life. My new voluntary occupation had suddenly grown into a monster and it was to get bigger, because he went on to say that the current hand-typed adverts had to be scrapped and replaced by professional looking ones. All this created a larger challenge than I had at first thought, but I was determined to continue. My first task was to sort out the quality issue. A local printer was most helpful and agreed to create the artwork for all future advertisements. Armed with my presentation folder, which Keith had put together, I set off one morning with the intention of visiting all six current advertisers. The first one I chose was The Downe Arms, one of the five pubs in the village of Snaith. Although a village, Snaith and its neighbouring village of Cowick together make up a township. Once a thriving market township, first established in medieval times, it has now settled back to enjoy its semi-retirement before it is once again awakened by the progress of time, probably in the form of tourism. I sheepishly knocked on the door of the pub. A well-dressed young lady answered almost instantly and listened intently to my story. Then she let me down gently by explaining that the landlord, Bob Wood, was out for the day. Not a problem, I thought, but she continued to explain to me that he had refused to pay for the current advertisement because the details were incorrect and had been so for the past year. When he took over the business and made a number of improvements no-one had contacted him regarding the advert and it was by now very out of date. No wonder he wouldn't pay for it – it was of no use to him. I came away dejected, what a start. When I returned home I related the experience to Keith who could see my disappointment. He explained that I needed to make an appointment to see Mr Wood. When I made the call, it wasn't Mr Wood who answered but the young lady that I had spoken to on my visit and despite the negative comments that she had made earlier, she checked his diary and we agreed an appointment. The due date arrived and I was very excited but also very nervous about this, my first official appointment. I approached the appointment with all the enthusiasm of starting a new job. The only difference was that there was no salary with this one, but I was to meet some great people over the next few years and make some lasting friendships because of it. There I was in the restaurant, very nervous, my head buzzing with figures, terrified I would be asked questions that I was unable to answer. I just went for it. I apologised for the fact that his advertisement had never been updated, explained our future plans and told him his advertisement would be going into over two thousand homes in the area. To my absolute amazement I came away with a year's contract for a new style advert, not just the single size that had been there before but a Full Page! I could not believe the success that I'd just experienced. I was on cloud nine as I rushed to the printer with the required layout details that I knew had to be correct. After my first success, it gave me the confidence to visit the other five customers. One had passed away, a second one totally refused to advertise, but although disappointed by these setbacks, I was determined to succeed in this role. Keith helped me put together a list of potential advertisers and I systematically visited them all. It was a case of 'Have pushchair, will travel' as I walked miles with Matthew securing new customers and collecting annual payments. The number of customers rapidly increased and so it was decided that additional pages were required, which meant there was more room for articles, features and information. Keith decided to get involved and to introduce a Profile section. Each month he would go and interview a local 'celebrity' and then he would write a profile for the magazine. It was incredible to see his ability to interview these people while knowing that if he had met them at a social gathering, he would be too nervous to communicate with them at all.

His organisational strength also enabled him to make a huge difference to the Church Council, of which he was a member. Frustrated at the time consuming way in which decisions were made and then no action was taken, he persuaded the council to let him draw up a 'by whom, by when' chart which he would use at each month's meeting. From this he gained the nickname 'Action Man'. This is exactly how the outside world saw him. I also often saw him this way: an organised, well balanced person who was teaching me to like myself and be myself for the first time in many, many years.

But I often saw him behaving in completely different ways.

Sometimes he was a very severe and serious man who had a set pattern to his life and couldn't change it. He was so busy working to provide for the family, that he was totally unaware of the everyday needs of that same family.

Sometimes he was a little boy who didn't have a clue about life; Everyday social things that most people seemed to take for granted would cause him such nightmares. When he was with our children, he acted as if he was just one of them.

It was a very difficult time in my life, reacting to these different behaviours. It often felt as though I was married to three totally different men: action man, serious man, child-like man.

Chapter 4

SOMETHING IS DIFFERENT

We spent many happy hours in parks all over Britain, enjoying swings and slides when our boys were young. As you can probably imagine, Keith enjoyed the play equipment often as much as the children did. Yet for all I used to enjoy these experiences, I always felt I could not relax and had to be very alert. Watching five children between the ages of one and eleven and an adult child as well took some doing. The boys were always on the look out for parks and play areas as we went on our journeys. *"There's one!"* One of them would shout. Because Keith had planned the day and it obviously didn't include deviating, he would come out with a scripted reply:

"Perhaps we could go there one day." He would never say that we didn't have time because it wasn't on his plan, but in essence his reply meant the same thing. One park visit that stands out in my memory happened as we were returning from a day at the coast. After a long journey, tempers were getting a bit frayed. With five children all seated in the back of the car there was no space to move about. We decided it would be good for us to get some fresh air, let off steam and stretch our legs and so we stopped at the next park we came across. Keith and the four older boys decided to play football. I strapped Matthew into his pushchair and we took up our positions on the touchline. After only a few minutes' play, Keith was stripping off his jumper which he deposited on the handle of the pushchair. After running round the field several more times, he took off his shirt, which he placed on top of his

sweater. So there he was, naked to the waist, chasing about the park, thoroughly enjoying himself, just like one of the boys. Jonathan broke away from the game and headed for the swings and I followed in order to push him. I parked Matthew in his pushchair beside the swings. One by one, the boys followed Keith's lead and discarded firstly their sweaters and then their T-shirts, throwing them over the pushchair handle. I could see what was going to occur, but I wasn't quick enough to react as the inevitable happened. The pushchair tipped up under the weight and there was our youngest looking up at the sky. The pile of clothes scattered all over his body resembled a table top at the local jumble sale. I am not sure if he was more upset by the fall itself or by the fact that he was missing some neat goal scoring, but I soon calmed him. I always needed eyes in the back of my head. Needless to say Keith was totally oblivious to the incident.

The first indications that something was different with Matthew became apparent quite early when he would regularly bang his head against the side of the cot for no apparent reason. His brothers jokingly called him 'head banger'. It was when he was around fifteen months old that I became really concerned, because he was not yet attempting to walk. We began to visit the GP more regularly as well as the health visitor at the baby clinic. At this time Matthew could speak very clearly and had in fact started talking at one year old. By the time he was eighteen months, his words were very precise and very clearly understood, and he would question everything, but he was still not walking. The health professionals could offer no reason for his inability to walk. We just had to be patient and keep encouraging him. He was almost two years old when he finally took his first unaided steps. Once he had cracked it, however, he became a noisy whirlwind. Everything was done at speed. We noticed he had poor co-ordination and had many accidents – his legs were always full of bruises. He was clumsy and he often fell off his bike or tripped over things. On several occasions we were quizzed about how he came to have so many bruises on his body, because most of them were on his legs and very visible. Although it was never said, we often thought we were suspected of physically abusing him. Something else that came with his walking were tantrums, and we had not experienced this with our other children. For no apparent reason, he would stop whatever he was doing, stand still, and his whole body would shake. His face would turn red and take on a very pained expression and he would shout and scream at a very high pitch. The session could last anything from ten minutes to an hour and it made me feel very upset and quite inadequate. The first time it happened I was worried that there was something seriously wrong. I picked him up and cuddled him but this had no effect as he struggled to break out of my arms. His arms and legs were hitting out all over the place. I had to carefully lower him into a chair for fear of dropping him. He carried on screaming and kicking for a further fifteen minutes and no amount of sympathy from me seemed to make any difference. Eventually the screaming subsided and I was able to speak more rationally to him. He just sat there quietly, looking very confused. It was another thirty minutes before he spoke to me, but not about the incident – what he said was totally un-related. I sat beside him and after a while he put his head on my arm and we continued in this manner for a while longer. Normally he did not like to be touched, but now he was welcoming my hand as I gently stroked his hair. As I couldn't see any obvious cause for his outburst, I decided to put it to the back of my mind and treat it as a one-off incident. Within a few days, however, the episode was repeated and this time I was very worried as, once again, I could not pinpoint the reason. This second attack lasted for over an hour. I tried the sympathetic approach without success, so I now tried a firmer approach, and this was equally ineffective. The following day I took him to the doctor, but he dismissed my concerns saying that Matthew was just badly behaved and needed firmer control. I came away feeling lost and dejected. The doctor had not helped at all, in fact, quite the opposite. When the third tantrum occurred a few days later my reaction was to ignore him. As long as I knew he was safe, I made no effort to speak to him. I just left him to scream and shout and kick until I could stand it no longer. I went to pacify him, but he would not acknowledge me, it was as though he was in a trance. So I just left him to wear himself out, after which he came for a cuddle, during which time he remained silent for about fifteen minutes. This was the pattern now as he continued to experience tantrums over the next five years. We eventually found that the best way to help him was to hold him firmly and rigidly, if possible until the screaming subsided. After the tantrum he would usually be left with a hoarse voice because of the long concentrated screaming session.

Matthew appeared to be very destructive as boys often are. But it seemed to be more than the usual boisterous male behaviour. He was quite violent at times and attacked furniture and scribbled in reading books without mercy. Rarely did he play with any toys. He would simply line them up, often spending a long time and much effort ensuring that the line was precisely accurate and perfectly straight, and then he would neatly put them away. My aunt took him to a local park one day and was amazed to see that he just spent ages lining up lollipop sticks, twigs and stones in neat symmetrical patterns. He seemed to have an obsession, not just with touching things, as most young children do, but also in moving things in order to tidy them. Everything had to be sorted.

Keith also liked order, everything tidy and in its correct place, hence his insistence on putting toys away as soon as he returned home from work. One thing I always found odd was that we shared a bedroom together but once the wardrobe door was closed and drawers shut there was no trace of Keith. His watch and car keys were always left on his study desk each night and even his hairbrush lived in the study. While he was working in there he had files and paperwork all over the place, but when he had finished, the room was neat and tidy – everything had its own home. He didn't like the children going into 'his' study in case they disturbed anything. He had a telephone in there and if I was in the bedroom or bathroom it was quicker to answer the ringing phone in the study rather than walking down the corridor to the family phone in the lounge. These were invariably business calls and it was a much more convenient place to write messages for Keith. He always seemed to know when I had used the study telephone, as Matthew would be touching and moving objects all the time I was taking the call. I tried to put everything back to normal, but he always knew when we had been there. One day Keith got so cross with his things being disturbed that he stormed off to the garage. After a few minutes he returned with a strange looking lock in his hand. *"Matthew will not be able to wander into my study now,"* he said forcefully. I had never had locks on internal doors and felt uncomfortable with his statement. But I could see that it was obviously causing some distress to Keith that his study was being invaded. He showed me how to use the lock. It could be placed on the outside of any internal door in seconds and could be attached high enough so that it was safe from inquisitive little hands. This worked well for a while despite my reservations about using it. Matthew often tried the handle but he could no longer open the door and wander in. On one particular morning I was helping him to build towers with Duplo bricks in the bedroom when the phone rang. I ran to answer the study phone and Matthew followed me as he always did. But instead of entering the room he just played with the door, eventually slamming it shut, and then there was silence. I quickly ended the call and went to investigate. To my horror I discovered that I was locked in the study and try as I might, I could not open the door. What should I do? In less than two hours I had to collect Jonathan from school, but more importantly my toddler was on the other side of the door. I tried forcing it but there was no way the lock was going to give. I started to worry. It would be fruitless ringing one of the neighbours as the outer door was locked and they would not be able to get into the house. After several minutes of panic, clear thinking set in and I climbed out of the window. It was a tricky operation but I made it. What next? I thought. I felt I needed some tools to break in so I headed for the garage but somehow instinct told me to try the outside door of the house. I usually kept it locked during the day, but you never know and to my amazement and relief the door opened. I ran into the kitchen, through the house and found Matthew standing in the hallway looking bemused. I picked him up and hugged him and then burst into tears. I began to think of what could have happened if I hadn't managed to reach him so quickly. Suddenly this was all in the past as Matthew started a tantrum – we were then into the rest of the day. After I calmed him down, I took the lock from the outside of the door and put it into the dustbin. I had never trusted it in the first place, so now it was banished forever. When Keith came home he was frustrated that I had put his lock in the dustbin but I insisted that it stay there, as it was dangerous. Following that incident I never again felt comfortable in the study. As all our bills and household accounts were in there, I had no choice but to go in occasionally, but otherwise I kept out, which, of course, was quite acceptable to Keith.

One particular night Matthew woke up with a very high temperature. His body was shaking but his eyes were closed and he was shouting for his mummy and daddy. We knew this was not a tantrum because these only occurred during the day, and it did not cause a high temperature and his eyes were always open. So this was something different. We both talked to him independently and quietly but he continued to ask for his mummy and daddy. He was obviously too upset to recognise our voices. The shaking continued for a further thirty minutes, during which time we continuously wiped his face with cold flannels in order to reduce his temperature. Once the shaking had stopped I gave him a large plastic tumbler filled to the top with fresh orange juice. He gulped down the entire contents in one without pausing for breath. He then settled immediately and fell asleep. He was shattered. The following morning he was fine, just as though nothing had happened. In fact, as far as he was concerned, nothing had happened. But we knew differently and we suspected it was some kind of fit. Ten nights later the same thing happened, almost a carbon copy of the first incident. I had read several articles about certain additives in foods that could trigger hyperactivity in children. These additives were usually colourings identified by specific E numbers. Because of Matthew's tantrums I had removed the foods that contained E numbers from his diet and, although this action had not stopped the tantrums, they had become less frequent. Because I had not given him any new or different food to eat recently, I was racking my brain to try to recall what else could have caused the two night time incidents. I began to wonder if his recent course of cough medicine could have had something to do with them – after all, the medicine was bright red in colour – but there was nothing on the bottle to confirm the colouring was one of the usual suspects. The next morning I took him to see our GP. After I had given the doctor a detailed description of Matthew's behaviour during the two traumatic sessions, he agreed with me that he had probably suffered from a fit, but could offer no explanation as to the cause. I asked if it could have been the cough medicine. He disagreed but despite this I was convinced about the colouring and immediately poured the offending medicine down the sink. I had recently read about colouring dyes being used in medicines and the fact that they were probably just as harmful as the E numbered colourings used in food. From then on I always made a point of asking for medicines that were free of these harmful dyes, although I had to be persistent as they were difficult to get at this period in time.

Matthew's frustrations at life and everything around him, was overwhelming. When he was frustrated or having a tantrum he would kick anyone near him, which was usually me. If no person was standing near to him, it would be the closest object. But he didn't seem to be developing an awareness of danger. He was never able to judge whether an object was heavy or light, dangerous or sharp, and consequently had some very narrow escapes from serious accidents. He was fiercely independent which was good, however he was extremely indecisive. He would often ask to go out into the garden and I would get his outdoor clothes. If I made any attempt to help him to dress he would get very frustrated and aggressive. Firstly he would want his coat on, then off and then on again. His decision making process was very poor – he would take a long time to get to the point of being ready and then he would often change his mind and decide not to carry on with that particular pursuit. Matthew's greatest pleasure and release came after he learned to ride his bicycle. Despite his poor co-ordination he had mastered his two-wheeler bicycle, without stabilisers, before he was three years old. He always raced around the garden at great speed. We tried to explain that it was dangerous, even in our own garden, to go fast but he never took this on board and eventually the inevitable happened. Keith had come home from a working trip and as soon as Matthew saw him he got on his bicycle and started cycling around the bungalow in a circle. Keith held his arms out for a hug but Matthew continued in his quest to impress us with his cycling skills. Both Keith and I encouraged him to slow down and to even get off his bike but before we could stop him he had crashed. His head was in collision with a concrete post and consequently he needed stitches. He was always tough and did not make a fuss or create a scene when he was obviously in pain. Blood worried him but as soon as we had cleared that away, he could cope with any lingering pain. Once we were home from hospital he showed no signs of being upset and happily went to sleep straight away.

The garage was always out of bounds to our boys and to me. Keith kept all his stock in there for his job, neatly filed in specially constructed pigeonholes, which his dad had constructed for him. At the back of the garage, Keith had built a small room. He spent a week's holiday building it, enjoying the challenge, and was very proud of it – particularly the brick laying and pointing, which was perfect. As always, he put 100% of effort into the project. The freezer, the gardening tools and the children's bikes were all stored in this new room. We now had two separate areas; his and the family's. Once the construction work was finished, he thought it was logical that no-one would go into the main part of the garage where he had his stock overflow of paperwork, cardboard, metal stands and, significantly, his tools. However, as happens in every household, things would break down and because he was often away, I would need to look in the garage for tools. Also, the children's bikes would collect regular punctures, which the older boys were quite able to repair themselves. Naturally, they needed to get tools out for the tasks. Keith would find regular frustration in having to tidy and re-tidy his toolbox. So when he could no longer stand it, he made up a separate box of selected tools, which had a home in the little family area in which he said that the children were free to roam. I think he regretted these words, however, when Matthew managed to get a large hammer that one of his brothers had left on the drive, and proceeded to hit both Jonathan and Richard over the head while they were playing in the lounge. Fortunately no serious damage was done. Keith was like chalk and cheese. He used to really confuse the children and me. If he was at home on holiday or just doing a job at the weekend, he would let our boys help and they could all use and share the tools without any problems. There would be free access all around the house and garage and then at the end of the day he would tidy everything away himself. He had to know everything was in its place afterwards. However, when he was at home doing company work, he couldn't be disturbed. The main part of the garage and the study were no-go areas and his mind became a no-go area as well.

As the weeks went by, Matthew became more and more difficult to handle. He did not communicate with other toddlers. At playgroup he was always criticised for not playing well and being loud and awkward and constantly breaking things. I became embarrassed to take him but more than that, I was upset at feeling he was not fitting in and enjoying play. Shopping was also a nightmare, as he would touch anything and everything. Whenever we went to a bank they always had marked lanes that left you in no doubt as to which way you were to queue while waiting to see the cashier. In one bank we visited frequently, thick red ropes were held at either end by very shiny silver fittings and clipped to a stand in order to make a barrier marking the lanes. On every visit Matthew would run to the barrier and insist on unclipping and reclipping the ropes. I always tried to stop him, but his curiosity as to how they worked was always uppermost in his mind. I knew this, he knew this, but the others in the queue often voiced their opinion as to what a naughty boy they felt he was. If he were their son what a smack he would get. I used to stand in silence just wishing the time away until we could leave. What was the point in trying to explain that he needed to understand the mechanism? Asking him to leave them alone or stopping him with brute force would only bring on a tantrum as he was being denied the experience of understanding yet another wonder in this big world. And every time we went into the bank we had to put two coins into the helter-skelter charity box so that he could watch the movement of the coins on their way down to the tank at the base. We had to do it, come what may, no excuses accepted. There was a similar charity box in our doctor's waiting room and we also had to put two coins into this box on every visit.

I had similar problems in shops. I used to dread Friday coming round when we went into the village to do our shopping for the week. This was when Keith was working away and I did not have transport to get to the supermarket. I used to vary my time of shopping, although it rarely worked, in order to avoid one elderly lady who always used to pass comment on what she saw as Matthew's bad behaviour. I knew the curiosity which was inside him, and it was apparent everywhere we went. I had not brought him up to be like this, it had just evolved. His brothers could go with us to the shops and not evoke the same criticism. Whereas Matthew wanted to know why things were displayed in the way they were. One very frustrating problem for me was when shops would make a display from a pile of tins. He always had to touch these – firstly to see if they were real and then to understand why they were put in that specific place. Everything had to be touched and tested. This very fierce elderly lady used to talk at him as if he was some monster. She would instruct him on his behaviour in her very loud voice. In fact she used to make matters worse as he always responded badly in noisy atmospheres. He could not concentrate as he was retrieving his knowledge and would get frustrated. Buying anything in Marks and Spencer or similar shops was very difficult. It was a child's wonderland, with rows and rows of things hanging down to tug or pull. He could be seen on his back underneath dresses and skirts, kicking them so he could watch the material float by. He was trying to create the effect Walt Disney did on film. When I went to the tills I insisted that he held my hand and he found this acceptable as he saw it as an extension of holding his hand outside because of road safety issues. Occasionally I did have to let go of his hand to pay at a till or to take receipt of my goods. This was his signal to run off. He never went far and I was never afraid I would lose him in a shop, but I was always afraid of the chaos he might cause or how many innocent people he may offend. Eventually these visits just got too much for me and as with a lot of other everyday tasks I shopped only when Keith could accompany me and restrain Matthew. Visits to the dentist were quite challenging as Matthew would bite and kick the poor man throughout the session, not just on one occasion, but every visit, every six months, for several years. He just could not relax if someone was touching him. We were very fortunate that Mr Young had endless patience. Shortly before his third birthday we had an appointment at the hospital for him to see an eye specialist because he had a suspected squint. During the appointment the doctor got very frustrated with Matthew's lack of co-operation. She also found it difficult to concentrate as he tidied up items on her desk, the mail, the pencils, and the telephone. He left nothing untouched. Nothing was damaged or destroyed but everything had to be touched. Although she was frustrated, the reaction of this doctor was different to anything I had experienced before. It was obvious that she didn't put his behaviour down to simple bad parenting. She also looked genuinely concerned and suggested I take him to my own GP as she felt Matthew might have a problem. Wow! I thought. Someone other than Keith and myself has watched his behaviour and actually thinks there may be a problem. A feeling of relief swept through me. Could this be progress? I rushed down to the doctors, full of new-found enthusiasm. But once again the doctor took no notice and said his behaviour would improve if we were stricter with him. He also said, "*I have one at home just like him.*" Back to square one.

For years and years we were left to our own devices. I sought medical help several times in Matthew's younger days. I was branded as an over-anxious parent. I suppose I was, but instinct kept me going. This little being that we brought into the world and loved had a serious problem and I wanted to help him, he deserved that. At this time he always had red patches around his mouth and cheeks and also on his legs and wrists. I saw a pattern; if he had less milk he had fewer patches. Our GP confirmed that the patches were eczema, but when I discussed cutting out dairy produce with him, he said it would stop Matthew from developing in a healthy manner. There had to be something to stop his skin from getting so sore and inflamed as ointment and creams didn't help. I asked to see a dietician and fortunately, despite our GP feeling it was unnecessary, I was successful in persuading him to refer us. This was definite progress. On our first appointment the dietician, who came across as a very enthusiastic young lady, asked lots of questions about Matthew's daily diet. I had to write down a sample of a week's meals that I normally fed to him. She then went into great depth about the contents of the meals and ingredients. Her conclusion was that he probably had a much healthier diet than most other children. He was getting all the nutrients with none of the rubbish. We had long since found that sweets made him hyperactive because of the colouring; he did not have ice cream, ice-lollies or chocolate either. He didn't miss these luxuries as they were cut out at a young age and he had never developed a craving for them. The dietician felt he was getting enough calcium from other things in his diet and thought it was in order to cut out dairy produce completely. She did say that if I was worried at all we could introduce baby-enriched Soya milk as a replacement for cow's milk. I took her advice, the new diet worked and the eczema disappeared. But not entirely, because it would return if the slightest traces of dairy produce got into his food without us knowing about it. I had to study labels very carefully. Very innocent looking baking products could often contain things like dried milk powder, whey or lactose that would all affect him and of course, well meaning friends and relatives would often give him biscuits, cakes and even sweets when I was not around, despite me giving them a precise list of dos and don'ts beforehand. Sadly, they thought I was just a very fussy mum and that one biscuit or one sweet couldn't possibly do any harm.

I was deeply disappointed at what appeared to be a lack of support on Keith's part. Only later was I able to analyse this and understand that his first priority as he saw it was to help me become well again. He thought it was my problem, not ours nor Matthew's. After months of trying to support Matthew on my own when Keith was away, I tackled him and said that I could not cope with him on my own, I needed help. Keith shrugged his shoulders and dismissively responded, *"Hundreds of thousands of women cope very well with families and with a job. I don't know what you're complaining about. You don't have a job. You only have the children to look after."* This hurt immensely. Although he knew very well that Matthew was totally different in character to our other boys, he just didn't seem to have grasped how hard it was for me, especially as my health was in a poor state. But I carried on and the days became darker and darker for me as Matthew became a constant challenge. He was unhappy and yet I could not unlock why he was unhappy. Each night when he went to bed I would sit over him when he was asleep and watch his angelic face. I would analyse what had happened that day and resolve to try much harder the next day. I loved him so much. This was a pattern I followed for a long time, but tomorrow never became better, just more of the same.

Matthew was in bed early each night and Keith worked away a lot, so he saw little of him during the week. At weekends Keith always had paperwork and household jobs he wanted to get on with. If I asked for a chance to get on with things in the house on my own, Keith's solution was always to put Matthew in his pushchair and take him to wherever he was working and let Matthew watch him. This caused Matthew terrible frustrations as he was used to his freedom and my attention during the week, and he objected strongly to being trapped in his pushchair. Keith nearly always used to end up putting him in the bath, as this seemed the best way to cool him and calm him down after the inevitable temper tantrum.

This situation continued for months until one evening I had had enough and I decided to confront Keith again with the problem. I demanded his full attention and made him sit and listen to me. I told him powerfully, *"I need more time and support from you."* He was genuinely shocked as he felt he was giving all the time he could spare and felt he was a good dad and husband. He came back at me almost immediately with an indignant reply. *"Why can't you cope? You've brought three children up, so what's the problem with one more?"* He stormed off, back to his study. I felt hurt and totally isolated.

During this period we were often given invitations to visit friends. Most times it was inconvenient as it interfered with Keith's plans to decorate or concrete paths or repair items. This I understood as Keith's time was limited and he always wrote himself a weekly timetable of intended actions. I felt torn as I wanted more than ever to visit friends because I spent such a lot of time deprived of adult company but I also understood Keith was doing his best in a difficult situation. He tried to keep all the balls bouncing while I tried to keep the peace. When I asked for support and it was obviously not forthcoming I got upset, very upset. I had been using all my energy for months just to get through each day. Our other children were great. They helped and did not complain but I knew it was not fair to them and long term it was not going to be good for Matthew to always be the centre of attention. It was one thing saying, do not spoil him, just ignore him, but ignoring him didn't help. He could continue a tantrum for hours and explanations never seemed to help. I'd already tried our family doctor whose answer was, "*Oh he is the youngest of five, he is spoilt.*" I had looked for help from the health visitor who tried her best, but had given up at an early stage as she had no hands on knowledge of children herself, and our son did not fit the textbook theory training that she had been given.

It was obvious to me that Keith realised there was a serious problem, but the trouble was he did not understand what the problem was. He still felt it was my problem rather than our problem. So he put his logical problem-solving mind to work and came up with a solution. But he didn't sit down with me and discuss it in a rational way. He just threw the solution at me one day in retaliation, following another of my desperate attempts to get him to take notice. When I heard his words my body froze, as I could not believe what I was hearing. This was a solution? I felt sick inside and I also felt very alone.

"*We should think about having Matthew fostered.*"

He had said this in a very matter of fact way. Here was the man I would give my life for, as I would for all my children, talking about giving our baby away to strangers. How could he say this? How could he even think it? This little fellow already had lots of problems, not least the fact that although his family all loved him, many of them had great difficulty coping with his tantrums. How was another family going to get close to him and help and support him and most of all grow to love him? Here was my best friend in the entire world saying to me that we should have our son fostered. My mind went berserk. Instead of arguing and protesting with Keith I just went quiet. I was numb. I was frozen. I was also very frightened. How could I get help for our little boy and protect him at the same time? I loved Keith – I didn't hate him for what he had just said, but I knew that I could not let it happen. From that moment on and for several years to come it was my problem and mine only as I had refused Keith's support by ignoring his solution. I looked after my family and contained Matthew's tantrums as best I could. I cried inside so often it made me very tired and very low. I just felt completely alone in a desperate world.

Throughout all this time I loved Keith, as I knew he loved Matthew, he just could not perform miracles as he felt I needed him to do. Even though I took on the responsibility of sorting Matthews's problems on my own, Keith and I always talked enthusiastically about our life together, often at length. I still trusted Keith. He was always honest and truthful. It was only in later years that I saw that in his eyes, his solution had been the correct one at the time, albeit not for me and certainly not for Matthew. I was constantly asking for help and he saw this as not fulfilling my side of the partnership. He worked full time and my role was simply to look after the family and the home. However, when he was home, he was always a 'new man' He would change nappies, read bedtime stories, wash up and carry out other household tasks without objection. But I always felt that he thought I should be able to cope. Why couldn't I cope? Perhaps it was because of my own health problems, which continued to plague me. No longer taking injections to suppress the effects of an allergy to dust mites, I now appeared to be developing asthma. I had been prescribed three inhalers to be taken daily, which did keep my breathlessness in check, but I continued to lose weight and strength and suddenly I had problems in another area.

On a visit to a local museum I found that I could not reach the top of a flight of stairs, without pausing several times. I was not out of breath; the problem was a severe pain in my leg muscles that was impeding my progress. Over the next few weeks I found that any stairs or inclines created the same difficulty for me. A number of tests could not show any medical reason for the pain. Was it all in my mind, as my GP and other specialists suspected? Eventually I reached the consulting room of a young doctor in Wakefield. He listened to my story, and told me he understood. He felt my illness was genuine but unfortunately there were no tests available at that time. He could not give me a cure, but what he gave me was the hope that one day the condition affecting me would be recognised, and that somebody would then be able to help me. And so I soldiered on.

Our involvement with the church was gaining momentum. We would take all five boys to the Sunday morning service regularly. It was quite an ordeal to get them ready in time and an even bigger ordeal to keep the younger ones focused on the purpose of the visit and, of course, the biggest problem was Matthew. He wanted to talk and ask questions throughout the service and eventually I had to admit defeat. I had to take him into the children's area, which had been constructed within the old consistory court at the back of the church, well out of earshot of the congregation. Well, in theory it was out of earshot, but in reality the sound of Matthew racing up and down on the resident bikes and cars did manage to pierce the quietness of the vast church building. Both Keith and I had been involved in setting up this crèche and naturally we had to be seen to be supporting it, but it was to prove somewhat of a millstone for me as I got lumbered with child minding duties every week and couldn't take part in the normal service. More importantly, I felt cut off from the rest of my family. The young people's area was just one of a host of church activities that we were involved with at the time. The magazine was now on a firm financial footing and we were involved at every stage from editing right through to distribution. On top of that we seemed to be continuously busy with committees and fundraising events. It was hard work, but very rewarding. I was amazed when Keith accepted a request for him to stand at the lectern at the front of the church and read from the bible. And yet I shouldn't have been. This was one of his strengths, his professional, public side. He could read out aloud to an audience, with passion, with inflexion, with clarity.

Oh! if they could only see the other side of him, I thought.

When an idea for a cookery book was mooted at a fundraising meeting that I attended, I immediately voiced my approval and this was yet another project that I could get involved in; a means of keeping some sanity in my life. It was also my first real chance to try out my newly learnt typing skills. I worked alongside two good friends from church, Joan and Ann, to produce a book made up of favourite recipes from local people. Once all the material was collected, we met to agree a good cross section of recipes and tried to use at least one from each person who had contributed. When we had the list of recipes to be used it was time for me to go away and type them and then came the first problem. We only had Keith's old portable typewriter, which failed to print out the letters e and f clearly. This was no good, because for the printer to do his job we needed a clear original copy. Gareth, our vicar, came to my rescue by bringing me his typewriter. I could only have it for a few days, as he would need it for the weekend to write his Sunday sermon and his weekly order of services. How was I to find the time to do all the typing and hand the typewriter back later in the week? This was to be a united project. Keith understood the significance of the problem and decided to sort out a plan of action. This firstly involved us working on the project together and then, over a two-day period, he would entertain the children and I would type. So for two full evenings we poured over the handwritten recipes looking for spelling mistakes. Fortunately it was school holidays and also Keith's two weeks of annual leave, so he wouldn't be away. The next morning we packed a huge picnic for the day and Keith took all the children to the National Motorcycle Museum in Birmingham. I typed tirelessly all day and converted a lot of the recipes to print but I just couldn't get the layout right. I couldn't get them to fit on the page properly – they seemed jumbled and I was getting very frustrated, as I had no experience of layout. Previously I had only typed letters and so this was a new area for me. I carried on typing until the family arrived home. The boys were full of enthusiasm about the bikes they had seen. We ate, we talked and then we relaxed. After the younger boys were in bed I told Keith of my frustration over the layout of the pages. With the help of Karl and Darren, Keith started to sort the pages and between them they categorised the recipes into short ones and long ones and divided them into relevant types. Eventually, after several hours work, there were neat piles and a clear plan of action for me to tackle the next day. At six o clock the following morning we were up again putting together another picnic and, after a hearty breakfast, the family were all in the car and off again. I went straight into the study and started my typing. I was already feeling more productive and more confident this morning. I had a strategy thanks to Keith. I was not just typing endless recipes; they now blended well on the page among the correct categories. By 6.00pm I had completed my task and prepared a meal for the weary travellers. They came home tired but very happy and yet again they had enjoyed another exciting day out, which they told me all about as we ate together. That evening Keith and I worked out the index and before going to bed I typed this. My first part in the project was complete and the typewriter could be returned safely to Gareth. A day or two later, our little team of three met with the printer to discuss details of the cover for the book including the colour and to agree on the number of copies. We had not thought about a specific quantity. Our intention was to sell them at the forthcoming garden party and any remaining books would be kept in church and sold from there and at any future events. We decided on a conservative number of 500 copies. Two weeks later, the printing completed, we met in church to assemble the pages. This part was easy – it was just like putting the magazine together, which we did every month. The three of us spent a happy chatty afternoon assembling and stapling the cover to the books. My mother was at home looking after Matthew. She had come over from Bradford for the day so that I could help with the book. Because of Matthew's behaviour, the only babysitters that we felt comfortable with were our parents. We had tried the occasional outside babysitter but they were never prepared to come a second time. Once the task was finished the books were packed into boxes and stored safely in the church. We said goodbye to each other and all walked home separately in different directions.

I felt very pleased with myself as I headed for home and I'm sure that I had a smile on my face. Suddenly I felt myself being thrown against a brick wall. I remember a gentleman coming to my rescue and a lady saying to him, *"She must have been standing near the edge."* Well yes, you do stand near the edge of the pavement when you attempt to cross a road but you do not expect to be run over. The lady was actually the driver of the van and as she had come round a bend she had mounted the pavement and at the same time hit me. I was stunned and in pain and blood was flowing from my hand. I can remember thinking very clearly at this point that I was so glad Matthew was at home with my mum. Had he been with me, as he was most days, he would have been the one who was hit. His pushchair would have been the first point of contact. It did not bear thinking about. A neighbour of ours, a gentleman called

Albert, rescued me and helped me into his car and took me straight to the local doctor's surgery. He came back to the car saying he had been told to take me to the casualty department at Goole hospital, as I would probably need stitches. Albert stayed with me until a policeman came to take a statement. The hospital had advised the police that there had been a road traffic accident. The constable was a jolly man and soon had me smiling once the shock had worn off. My hand was stitched and put into a sling and I was told to keep my arm elevated for several days. How could I possibly achieve this? That coming weekend Karl and Darren were to be confirmed at a service in Hensall Church and we were having a family party at home to celebrate afterwards. I didn't know how I was going to bake or look after Matthew with one arm. The police constable took me home and to say my mum was surprised was an understatement. She had wondered why I had been so long. I had not rung her from hospital as I thought it would alarm her. The officer stayed a while and chatted and by this time my mother and our boys were reassured that I was all in one piece. Keith was away as usual and when he rang that evening I told him the news. Although sympathetic, it was clear that he had no intention of coming home and so I had to ask my mum to stay over and help me. As the evening progressed I was beginning to stiffen and many bruises were becoming evident all over my body from the impact with the wall.

The following day I was due to go to the same hospital for an important appointment with a urologist. My Auntie Doreen, to whom we were close and saw regularly, had offered to drive me to the hospital as she only lived seven miles away. It was a cold, frosty but very sunny February morning. There were four of us in my aunt's car as my mother was taking Matthew to playgroup and after we dropped them off, we continued on our way to the hospital. We had just rounded a bend in the village of Rawcliffe when the car went into a spin. What was probably only a few seconds seemed like several minutes. The car left the road and headed for a ditch. We went into the ditch but we were still spinning and appearing to rock up and down. It was a very frightening experience and we came to rest in someone's allotment. I remember just looking at my aunt who was doing her best to hold the car, hoping to limit the impact. I clearly remember waiting to see and hear all the glass smashing, but instead we came to a very abrupt halt with all the windows still intact. In an instant there were two men by our sides, unfastening our seat belts and lifting us both to safety. Once on steady ground, they were able to put us down and guide us to their van. The gentlemen had been behind us, seen what had happened and rushed to our rescue. They had quite a laugh when they asked where we had been heading and we told them that we were on our way to the hospital. They kindly took us to casualty where we were both checked out. We both had severe whiplash and I ended up going home not only with the sling from my previous accident but in addition a collar to support my neck, it was not a pretty sight. However, I did still keep my appointment with the urologist. We telephoned a friend who firstly took me home, back to my mum who was yet again very shocked to hear there had been another accident, and then took my aunt, very badly shaken up by the accident, home to rest. What neither of us had seen that morning was the black ice on the camber of the road as we turned the bend into Rawcliffe. There were two more accidents in the same spot that morning before the ice melted. That evening when Keith rang I was sure he would come home to be with me. In two short days I had been in two road accidents. I could now not even dress myself and I was in such pain both from my hand and now from my neck. On top of that I ached in every possible spot from being thrown against the wall in the first accident. I just felt I needed his support. I needed to be cuddled and reassured, as I did not want to go out of the house ever again. But he didn't come home that evening. He listened sympathetically to my news but he couldn't possibly break his planned activities. My mum kindly stayed over yet again to look after us. She was shattered after her few days nursing us – she had only intended to visit for the day originally. After these incidents, the next time I went out I was very cautious whenever I walked on the pavements. It took me several months to get over the fear of traffic noise and even to this day I still get very nervous if I am in a car when the roads are icy and whenever possible I will try to avoid going out in these conditions. Friday evening came and Keith arrived home. Once back with the family and away from work, he was very attentive and very sympathetic towards my injuries. As soon as he saw me he realised I was not very well. Saturday arrived and because of my limitations, I felt like a spare part. Keith was great as firstly he helped me to bathe and dress, and then he did the shopping and organised and prepared some food for the following day. Not all on his own, of course. I was there the whole time giving him instructions.

The confirmation service the following day was a happy occasion. We were very proud of Karl and Darren who were part of a large group of youngsters and adults who were all being confirmed. At the house afterwards there was a veritable feast. After a day at home, my mother had returned with meringues and quiches, Keith's mum had brought apple pies and almond tarts and John and Janet had arrived with homemade pizzas and cakes. In addition, of course, Keith had cooked the meat and vegetables. Even our friend Hilda from church had baked a mixture of goodies for us, which the children tucked into with great enthusiasm. So overall the family day went well. It was another good time for us. Keith coped well with the day, mainly because he had a role. I was able to do very little physically so he became my right hand man, or was it my left hand man? Being busy kept him out of the spotlight and he was quite comfortable. Only one incident spoiled the day, and yet it made a strong point. Matthew had been good all day and into the early evening and then suddenly he changed. He became flustered, belligerent and loud. He was starting with a tantrum. This was the first time it had happened with so many people around. In a fit of anger he kicked out at the person next to him. It was Keith's Mum. She was horrified and embarrassed. With one good arm, I was able to hold him until the shaking subsided. As I looked around the room I noticed that one of his brothers was eating and enjoying fruit pastilles. On the table nearby was an empty sweet wrapper from the pastilles. As I picked it up to throw it in the bin, I smiled and then held it out to show Keith's mum, and said, "Well at least he didn't have any of these or he would have been even worse."

"Well!" said Keith's Mum sheepishly, "Actually he did have some." She saw my astonished face and hurriedly qualified it with an excited exclamation, "But only a couple!"

There it was. We had the cause. We had told everyone on numerous occasions to beware when feeding him but when you are sharing things out with a group of children it's easy to forget. That day had provided a perfect example of his reaction to colouring. We had few problems in that area from that day forward, as we avoided all foods that included artificial colouring, and we ensured that whoever he was with also did the same.

During the summer following Matthew's third birthday, we decided to take a family holiday to Devon. On one particular day we planned a trip to the zoo at Paignton. We thought that the various animals would enthral Matthew, but we were wrong. We all tried to raise a spark of interest in the animals but it was in vain. His attention, all the time, was focused on inanimate things. He would study the locks on the gates, the motorised trucks used by the staff, the various mechanical contraptions used to feed the animals, the merchandise in the shop and so on and so forth. Matthew constantly asked questions about these things. As far as animals and people were concerned, he didn't want to know. It was hilarious for the rest of that holiday to hear Karl and Darren trying in vain to get him to recognise basic animals such as cows, horses and sheep that were dotted around the fields as we travelled through the countryside. And yet if the latest model of a car drove past, he could recite umpteen facts about it with unbelievable accuracy. He couldn't tell the difference between a cow and a sheep but he certainly knew the difference between a Lamborghini and a Pininfarina.

We came to the end of 1984, not quite what George Orwell had predicted, but for me it had been a very demanding period. Added to the frustrations of Keith's continuously strange behaviour and my poor health, I now had Matthew's equally strange behaviour to cope with. He had literally taken over my life. His demands were incessant. We couldn't go anywhere without his presence being felt. He would talk constantly and loudly even at the most inappropriate times and he would challenge everything. One question kept going round and round in my head: Why has all this happened and why has it happened to me? I didn't know the answer. All I could do was keep the show on the road.

Chapter 5

A TIME FOR CHANGE

As we moved in to 1985 I was determined to improve things. When I had changed my life five years earlier, I had given up my job at Midland Bank (now HSBC), a job that I loved. Because of Keith's constant trips away and his strange behaviour when he was at home, I felt isolated. I mixed with friends less as Matthew always caused problems in group situations and he was always classed as a bully. I did not know this at the time but it was because he pushed children away from him when they came too close. He could not deal with anyone being in close proximity. This continued throughout his school life with parents and teachers classing him as a bully, whereas in fact, at both primary and secondary school, Matthew was the one who was bullied.

But my major frustration was trying to cope with my 'six' children in a small bungalow with effectively only two bedrooms. So I set myself three goals for that year.

To get a job.
To get a car.
To move to a bigger house.

These were very challenging goals, particularly as Keith was not fully behind my plans at first, and also because he was having a tough time at work since a recent takeover.

One of the goals was achieved early in the year, with the support of my parents, when I became the proud owner of a new car. Well, proud may not be the correct word, as the car was a Lada, very basic, very heavy to steer, but really all we could afford at the time. It used to sap all my energy just trying to turn the steering wheel, after getting used to the power assistance in Keith's cars. What it did do was give me the independence to go places with our boys when Keith wasn't there.

The job came next. I was interviewed and given the job of receptionist / nurse at our local dental practice in Snaith. I was back in the world of work. I got my teeth into re-organising the filing system. I enjoyed meeting people and working with a professional team. One thing I never quite got the hang of, however, was the complicated names and positions of the teeth, which I still find confusing.

What the job also gave me was the credibility and authority to take over our household finances. Keith was extremely well organised when it came to paying regular bills such as utilities and had set up a simple system so that everything was divided into neat monthly chunks, which he could deal with. After that first 'expensive 'Christmas, he had insisted on us setting up a Christmas present fund and putting aside a set amount each month. The same went for birthdays, school clothes and in fact everything. He was so organised it was frightening and everything was meticulously recorded in a little red book. But there was a flaw and it was a huge one. He hadn't told me that we were, in fact, suffering from Mr McCawber syndrome. I hadn't realised that we had a credit card debt at all, let alone one that was in four figures. I couldn't understand how he had allowed this situation to happen. I vented my anger at him for several minutes, and then I saw the expression on his face. He obviously didn't appreciate the problem. He didn't see the exorbitant interest rate or the heavy monthly repayments as a problem. I realised that he had done what he thought was right; he had tried his best. He wasn't being dishonest or underhand, he was just being what he was in so many situations – naïve and thinking it would all come right in the end. I realised that I was going to have to take the management of our finance away from him and now was the perfect time. Two of my goals had been achieved and I wasn't about to let number three slip away. It was just a matter of planning.

Persuading Keith that we should move and more importantly that we could afford to move to a bigger house was not going to be easy. He had set his mind on extending the bungalow in order to create the extra space we needed. He took me to see other bungalows in the area that had been altered in all sorts of imaginative ways. He drew up plans himself and actually took them to the council offices for outline approval, but he hadn't assessed the cost of all this nor the implications. Because of two takeovers in the past year at his employers, he was feeling uneasy. He was finding it extremely difficult to adjust to the culture of the new organisation. It was now a fast moving, youthful culture built on a background of networking and socialising, which was very uncomfortable for him. With such an uncertain future he feared any sort of change in his home environment. His extension project for our bungalow was a kind of smokescreen for him. Eventually, as in so many situations, his initial resistance to change, which was usually based on fear of the unknown, gave way to logic. He realised that the bungalow extension was not really an option both practically and, more importantly, because whatever we did to it, it would still be the same basic unit, which by now we had physically and emotionally outgrown. He could also see the landscape changing at work, there was a route back, and he just needed patience.

And so in December, we moved into our current house, four bedrooms and much more room generally. The house was built on the site of the original Snaith telephone exchange, which had been demolished around 1975. The builder had secured the plot of land next to the secondary school and built three detached houses of which ours was the largest. For some reason the houses were not allocated house numbers and so we had to give it a name. We decided on Reeth House in memory of the village where we had fallen in love with each other. Once again Keith swung into action with his well-practised removal skills. John, my brother, helped us, and so did Karl. Darren was away at a bowling tournament and their younger brothers were too young to help. The distance of the move was far shorter this time – less than a mile in fact. But the quantity to be moved had increased dramatically over the previous five years, and John pleaded with us never to move again. Enough boxes of stock and samples and files from Keith's work to fill a small warehouse supplemented the normal household contents. They had been stored in the garage, in the study, in cupboards, in the hallway but mostly in the loft which had been carefully floor-boarded by Keith especially for this purpose. We had a large loft and because it was in both our natures, we hoarded everything of any significance that had passed through our hands since we had come together and before, including all the boys' school reports, exercise books and outgrown toys and games.

At the end of one particularly busy day of bringing boxes down from the loft in preparation for the move, Keith had appeared with an old briefcase. He handed it to me with a nervous grin. I peered inside and there in the battered old case were the men's magazines that we had collected including the very first one chosen together on our honeymoon in Stratford upon Avon.

"Shall I burn them?" he said.

" No," I replied forcefully. *"They are part of our history; they have to go with us."* Then, after a moment's thought, I added, *"But do mark on the front of them Pat's Books. If anything were to happen to the two of us I would hate them to be found and people to think they were your secret stash."*

They were unwanted and obsolete, but they were duly parcelled up and earmarked for the new loft.

For the most part the day of the move went without a hitch, with one major exception. Keith had hired a van for the day and Karl went with him to return it to the depot on the Saturday evening. They stopped for fuel on the way back. Keith assumed it was a diesel vehicle but unfortunately his assumption was incorrect, and the poor vehicle limped along and only just made it back to its home. Keith would have been quite happy to keep his error under wraps but Karl later described the horrific journey to all of us in graphic detail. I caught the wrath of the owner, on the telephone, after he had discovered the plight of his van when he tried to move it on the following Monday morning.

In line with my more positive attitude I decided it was time to throw out the pyjama case, as it had now become so scruffy. I did not realise how important this object was to Keith at the time, and I did not realise the significance of my actions. Later in life I would learn to do things like this in a different manner. I kept on about how scruffy it was and that it was unnecessary as he actually kept the pyjama case under the pillow. Wasn't it just as easy to keep the pyjamas under the pillow during the day and throw the case away? Over a period of about a month I mentioned this three times and on the last attempt I saw a frustration that I had never previously witnessed. Keith developed a temper and he began to shout, not at me, but at the situation. He did not know what to do. Here I was making him part with one of his trusty possessions. He got so frustrated that in the end he opened the bedroom window and threw the pyjama case onto the path and said, *"There, let the dustbin men take it if that's what you want."*

He had a very restless night's sleep. It was only looking back years later that I could see why he was so frustrated. Keith has never been a worldly man in experiences or possessions. He is very practical, does not like to see waste and puts no value whatsoever on jewellery or ornaments. I was making him throw away one of his childhood possessions but more importantly to him it was the place where he kept his pyjamas in a tidy fashion. It was all part of an important bedtime routine and I believe I both confused and hurt him.

His regular barber had ceased trading in 1981 and that had confronted him with a major problem. Too scared to go elsewhere, he had approached me. I had trained as a hairdresser in my early working life, before I went to the bank. Because of this, and in order to save money, I had cut our sons' hair all their young lives. After the closure of his barber, Keith had asked me if I would cut his hair. With reluctance I had agreed and I could see the anxiety in his face change to relief when I did so. This became one less social situation for him to cope with. I carried on cutting his hair during the following four years but now I felt it was a time for change. Karl had now moved on to professional hair stylists and I knew his brothers would follow, as they got older. When I told Keith that it was time for him to have a much more professional hair cut than I could manage, we had the same problem as before. He said he was more than happy with the way I cut his hair. I had a difficult time convincing him that it was not because I did not want to cut it, but that I felt that the cut needed to be of a higher standard. Reluctantly, he said he would find a barber but it was several months before he settled with someone he trusted. He would peep in the window of several establishments to gauge the atmosphere before he would dare to enter. If one of the hairdressers was a woman or there were 'too many' customers waiting it would get the thumbs down. There was no way he would try a modern style unisex hairdresser, as he knew he would totally freak out with embarrassment. I tried to explain that he might find it easier for a woman to cut his hair but he would not take the risk. Old habits die hard. If someone could start up 'drive in' haircuts and you could press a button to say *same again please, just shorter*, he would be a very happy man. The style was the same as he wore at school only the colour had changed. The boys, of course, would change their hairstyles frequently. We would never know if they would be sporting lots of hair or next to none. Like their clothes, this was an expression of who they were. They were simply statements of youth. Occasionally I would get upset with Keith when he felt a style was unsuitable in his eyes. He would voice his opinion to me but fortunately not generally to the children, although he did lose his temper with Jonathan and Richard one day because they were invading his workspace and he used his dislike of their hairstyle as a way of verbally scoring points against them. In later years he told me how silly he felt he'd been to make these comments.

With regard to Keith's lack of ability to sort out his own clothes, I decided that now was the time to address this problem also. One day I just said, *"This is ridiculous. Jonathan, at eight-years- old, would be able to advise you what to wear. It's time you grew up."*

I certainly did not realise how cruel this was of me. Over the next few weeks he tried to make the decisions, and he tried very hard to get it right. To me it was obvious that little things were causing great problems for him as he could wake me at four o'clock in the morning if he had a meeting in London just to say: *"Is it OK to wear these socks with this shirt?"*

We started to work together on this and his confidence grew. He had received a shock some two years earlier when, during an appraisal with a new boss, he had been told that he was completely out of fashion. He was still wearing multi-coloured striped shirts, which had been very popular in the 70s, but by 1983 had disappeared, to be replaced by plain white shirts. It was a cruel blow to him and made him feel even more inferior and out of step with the world. He made himself some markers to go in the wardrobe and with my help we sorted out sections: Work shirts, best shirts, casual shirts, shirts for doing household maintenance, and so on. The same sort of categorisation was applied to his suits and trousers. I knew we had cracked it together when one day I said to him, *"If it were me, I would have put the blue tie with that shirt."*

His reply was, *"But I like this one with it."*

That was a true sign of how much his confidence had grown.

Something that always worried me when our children were young was Keith's lack of road sense when crossing with them. He is one of the best drivers I know. He is always courteous, does not take any unnecessary risks but drives in a fast, confident manner. He updates himself regularly on the Highway Code and most noticeably, he never comments on other people's driving. If anyone else in the car does, he always smiles knowingly. As he says, shouting solves nothing: have patience with them. Tomorrow you may be in their town, struggling with strange roads, just as they are doing today. All this I knew about him and liked, but he used to throw me into confusion with his road crossing habits. When the children were very young he would carry them across the road. He never crossed at the last minute, always obeyed the rules. So why was I always so worried now when they were out with him in a town? I suppose because I had witnessed for myself that as the children got older and did not need their hands holding to cross the road he was unable to see the significance of being in charge of them. They were able to cross the road as separate people making their own decisions on the traffic, but they still needed guidance and most of all they needed a good example. If the boys were not fully concentrating, he could be gone and they were left trying to catch up. He had made the decision to cross and he took it for granted they made the decision at the same time, he would just set off without any verbal communication. That few seconds' delay between seeing Dad set off and them making the decision to go was the danger period. God must have been looking out for us because they always managed to get across without serious incident but a lot of the time it was more by good luck than good management. Many times did I voice my worries on this subject and each time he reassured me that I was making a mountain out of a molehill. How could I think he would take any risks with our children's lives? It was a fair question, but it did not make me feel any more confident.

Anyone who has tried to do their shopping in a supermarket with more than one child along to help will know what a complicated and frustrating activity it can be. Shopping has never been a love of mine – not even for clothes. The fewer trips I have to make to the shops the better, so we used to limit our supermarket visits to once a month. Fruit and vegetables we bought on a weekly basis but this was at the fruit market. Fresh milk was delivered to the door and we purchased meat from the same source that we had bought it from for many years, a wholesale farm butcher near to where we used to live. The Ives family ran the farm on a bleak hillside at Birkenshaw and the head of the household, Colin, would greet his customers with a deep Yorkshire "*Hello, love,*" from a cheeky grin surrounded by a ruddy complexion, probably a result of eating too much red meat.

One particular Saturday morning we entered the supermarket and collected three trolleys as usual, one for me, one for Keith, and a third one which the boys would share, taking it in turn to push it round. Normally we would follow each other round in convoy. I would be at the front taking things from the shelf. Once my trolley was full, I would swap it for number two in the line up and then I could continue my shopping. I had just made the exchange when we rounded the corner into the next aisle. Suddenly the full trolley took off. It careered down the aisle at great speed. I thought it must be one of the children but I was wrong. There spread-eagled on top of the trolley was Keith shouting "*WHEEE!*". The kind of sight you laugh at in the Beano comic. Our sons loved it and my overriding fear at this time was that they would attempt to copy his actions and we would be evicted from the supermarket. Keith made no apologies for it; he had obviously let off steam and thoroughly enjoyed it, judging by the huge smile on his face. It was only just becoming apparent to him that perhaps this was not the time or the place, when he saw the embarrassed and flustered look on my face. In my eyes here we were trying to complete a difficult task and instead of two adults doing the shopping with the help of our children we now had an extra child, six feet tall and very unpredictable. Fortunately none of the boys copied him and we made no more of it. But when we were on our own that night I did give him a lecture on how it was a bad example to the children. If they all did that in the supermarket, what chaos it would create? Not to mention the fact that he could have injured someone. He reassured me that he had taken into account that the aisle was clear of other shoppers and that at no point was it dangerous. I didn't agree with this, but I am pleased to say that he never repeated this activity.

Another incident that confused me happened at a transport museum. It was an open-air museum where there was a very large collection of trolley buses. We parked and got out of the car, four sons walking and our youngest in the pushchair. It was only later that I realised my mistake. I should have despatched Keith to push the pushchair and then he would have had a task to keep him occupied. As we walked nearer to the museum there were two rows of traffic cones separating the path for walking from the roadway. Keith was always ready to play with the children and relax with them and always ready to let off steam. On this occasion he went straight up to the row of traffic cones and he put one on his head and started to dance up and down. I can still see his face looking at me for praise or at least expecting me to acknowledge that this was funny, just as a child would do. Instead he saw me standing there with an expression of horror, watching passers-by look at him as if he had lost his marbles. I was panicking in case the children attempted to do the same. The cones were to help the drivers, not a toy for children – let alone child-like adults. Our children must have had some in built 'daddy restraints' in these very embarrassing confused moments because they never attempted to imitate him. Maybe it was just the look of sheer panic on my face at times like this, which prevented it, but I shall never know. In fact it became part of the family culture at such times to say 'Daddy being silly' and smile at him in acknowledgement that he had reached a point where he needed to let off steam. We all knew that it would soon be over and then we could return to the task in hand.

However, not all trips out were fraught. We went all over Britain enjoying as many experiences as we could. Keith would hear of an event on the radio or read about an interesting place to visit and then the following weekend we would be packed up with our usual family sized picnic and equipment for all weathers and off we would go. He created a file in our filing cabinet of interesting places to visit. He was never short of ideas and the boys loved it. Life was never dull; we were always on the move. We always tried to involve all our children and we also tried to rotate things and one by one do something which was special to one of them in particular. How we all fitted into our various saloon or hatchback cars I'll never know, but we did. 'Have picnic will travel' as often as possible and in all weathers. The seatbelt laws would have put paid to our travelling if the restrictions had come in years earlier. I must not take the glory for looking after our sons myself. Keith has always taken his role as a father very seriously. We would not have gone to anywhere near as many places without his forward planning. He always got up early to prepare for an outing and he matched any job that I did equally, helping whenever he could and always being there for the children and me. His stamina was immense. When we got home, particularly after a wet and muddy day out, our first job was to make a meal together for all of us. Then, when the children were playing or watching television, we always shared the tasks together; washing and cleaning the picnic equipment, the muddy jeans, shoes, wellingtons and pushchair wheels. The last job was always to tidy out the car. As Keith had a company car, he felt he had to keep it immaculate both inside and out when he was working. Although he was relaxed about it getting dirty when we were out and about, once back to work he had to remove all traces. He was obsessed about his cars being clean for work. On more than one occasion I can remember him getting up at three or four o'clock in the morning to clean his car before he left for London. Once it was clean, he would recite an endearing little phrase, *"No bits, no dust!"* whenever anyone looked as though they may spoil the immaculate condition of the seats or upholstery. This phrase would be used with monotonous regularity, until the car next went through its child-friendly period, when, of course, it didn't matter about a little additional dirt. After cleaning the car our next task was to prepare for the next day by peeling vegetables and putting out any items of clothing required. We then had the mammoth task of getting the younger three children, Richard, Jonathan and Matthew, ready for bed and reading bedtime stories. This could often take hours to achieve. When they had settled down we would sit with Karl and Darren and enjoy television together or talk or play a board game. This was always a special time together, all of us tired after a good day out, just relaxing before bedtime. We had a rota between the four of us as to who would make supper, often just a slice of toast, or a biscuit and a drink, something light. When we were all tired Keith would always come up trumps and do the task even when it was not his turn. One special treat, which kept us amused for many weeks, was the unpublished script of a story written by Keith's great aunt. He had acquired it at the time of the house clearance, following her death. Keith would read the story to the three of us and we all found it both enthralling and humorous.

One area, which was always a source of frustration, was our social calendar. We often socialised with our parents and my brother and sister and their families, but the outside world was another matter. If we went to the cinema it was up to me to organise the trip. The same happened with friends – it would always be at my instigation. I just wanted to be taken out and be able to relax once in a while without having the responsibility of organising. I did however get some lovely occasions with Keith through his company. At this point in time these were my treats and my only way of switching off and recharging my batteries. Sadly for Keith these events were always difficult, as he could not relax in the company of large groups of people. He even found it hard when people visited us. If he could organise some games he was fine. If he had a task to do like washing up or food preparation he was fine. What he found difficult was just plain talking to people. The preparation time before our visitors arrived could be difficult as he would be anticipating challenging situations and worrying how he would cope. One day when we were having visitors I was very frustrated at Keith's lack of support. At this time I always took time to do what I called my 'batch baking'. I could often spend a couple of days baking. This fitted round school runs and playgroup but I always found it therapeutic and at the end of it I would have several meals prepared. Included in the list would be sweets such as apple pies, cakes, biscuits, gateaux and my own version of ice cream Viennetta – a big favourite with all the family. As always I was up very early to start my preparation and as it was weekend, the boys, with the exception of Matthew, were all staying in bed for a while. My first job was always to set the table and then if the meal was not quite ready when visitors arrived, at least it looked as if they were expected. My next tasks were vegetable preparation and putting the joint and Yorkshire puddings in the oven to cook. It was then time to tidy the house. Not clean it fully, as I did this weekly on a Friday, but as we were a big family it was no good cleaning up the day before people visited and expecting it to stay neat and tidy. So it was a case of moving toys and clothes, books and papers and a quick duster over the furniture. On this particular day, I noticed a distinct lack of Keith's presence. It was not unusual for him to disappear for long periods of time – usually into his study or into the garage – but he was in neither of his retreats. I just thought maybe he had gone to the post box. I looked out of the window and was shocked at what I saw. Keith was standing in the school grounds, next door, with a carrier bag in his hand picking up crisp papers and sweet wrappers which were on the ground or had attached themselves to the hedge around the school. This was admirable and Keith often did this at the weekend. He often washed the bollards on the school crossing, as they got very dirty from lorries regularly splashing mud over them. But why did he have clear the rubbish today and why now, thirty minutes before our visitors were due to arrive? I wouldn't have given it another thought if we had not been expecting visitors but here I was struggling to finish food preparation and get the house tidy so that we could relax with our friends and Keith was doing one of his 'boy scout' jobs, as I called them. Surely this could have waited till another time? I went into the garage to get something out of the freezer and Keith had arrived back from the school grounds and followed me into the garage to put his rake away. I turned on him: *"Why did you have to do that job right now? Our friends will be here shortly and the house is still untidy. Why could you not have helped with that instead of wandering around the school field cleaning it up?"*

I didn't give him a chance to answer, instead I asked him to do a specific job for me. *"I am going to get a shower,"* was his aggressive reply. What happened next was probably my own fault but I just couldn't help myself from having another go at him. I blocked his exit from the garage and said *"How are we ever going to be able to sit and talk to our friends when the kitchen floor is still to clean? And any minute now the boys will be getting up and I will have them to sort out. Why can't you see that the home is more important than the surrounding environment at this moment?"*

I could see the tension building up in his body but I was totally unprepared for what happened next. He raised his hand and hit me across the face, and then shouted at me,

"You expect me to do everything, how can I?"

I was shocked and stunned. Keith had hit me.

He could get frustrated but he had never shown any signs of being a violent man. I was horrified but strangely I wasn't scared, just frustrated as much for him as for myself. He was just standing there breathing heavily, almost in tears. In hindsight I realise it was partly due to the fact that we were in very close proximity in the garage and, of course, I was blocking the door. He had no escape route. He couldn't storm off, as he would normally do. After a few minutes of thought he spoke to me again.

"OK then," he snarled. *"Why not just ring up and tell them not to come?"*

"And what excuse shall I give them?" I said, sarcastically, still smarting from the smack.

Although he did want them to visit, he was, as always, apprehensive beforehand. Here was a good excuse just to cancel. I realised this and so before he could answer I took charge of the situation.

"You go and get your shower and calm down."

Off he went and I had a few moments to reflect. How could he have hit me over something so trivial? It was obviously frustration. It reminded me of Matthew's tantrums and the way he kicked out at me when he got frustrated. I was not angry, not even afraid, I was just disappointed and confused. All I had wanted was for him to prioritise. I did not want him to do everything. I was only pointing out that the other job could have been done anytime. We could have even done it together. But he still had this fixation that the inside jobs like cleaning and cooking were mine unless I asked him well in advance for some assistance. Whereas the outside jobs like washing the car and cutting the grass and tidying up were his responsibility. There was nothing he wouldn't do for me, but he almost always needed some notice so that he could plan it into his mental work routine. Despite the shaky beginning to the day, we had a good meal with our friends, lots of good conversation and lots of humour. There was still tension between Keith and me, however, and this became obvious when he sarcastically remarked about the fact that the gravy wasn't on the table by the time some people were ready to start eating. At bedtime Keith was remorseful. He could not stop apologising and said that it would never happen again. Was he telling the truth? I wondered, and would I see this violent and aggressive side of him again?

He was always at ease with our boys, but he did let his work spill over into their time. Often during school holidays if he was working at home, he would flare up if one of them was demanding his time in any way. He had a very clear distinction in his mind between doing his job and being on holiday and seemed unable to mix the two in any way. Darren was a ten pin bowling champion and Keith would regularly drive him to a bowling alley for a championship match. But he would often sit in the car park completing his paperwork while Darren was inside the building working hard for the team and for himself. I am sure he would have welcomed some moral support and encouragement from his second dad.

In September 1986, I was at work and received a phone call with news that made me shiver with fear. Our eldest son Karl had taken an overdose of tablets in an attempt to commit suicide. He was in hospital and although I was told that everything was under control, I desperately wanted to be with my sixteen-year-old boy. It was ten o'clock in the morning and my employers asked me to stay for a further hour as they had a full appointment book. I can't believe it now, looking back, that I agreed to stay. I can't have been a lot of use to them in that hour, as my mind was all over the place. By the time I was able to leave I was beside myself, worrying if he was still alive. I was totally unfit to drive to the hospital but I jumped in to my car nevertheless and arrived there thirty minutes later, somehow managing to park in a safe place. I dashed into the ward, my heart pounding faster as I approached his bed. There he was sleeping peacefully. He's alive, thank God, he's alive, I said to myself, as I exhaled a great sigh of relief and pleasure. I just held his hand and willed him to get better. I spoke to the doctor who was very sympathetic but did advise me that Karl, although looking as if he had survived the trauma, could, after two or three days, go quickly downhill. His organs could fail and he might lapse into a coma. But after the initial shock of hearing that message, I had no more thoughts of losing him. I just felt that he would get better if we all willed him to recover. For the week that he was in hospital, his four parents kept a vigil round his bed. His brothers all visited him except for Matthew, who we felt was too young to be at the hospital. I tortured myself as to why I had not noticed Karl's serious depression, particularly as I was in the process of becoming more positive about my own life. My eldest child was very, very, unhappy and I hadn't seen it. I wondered if it could be the after effects of his parents getting divorced. Being the eldest son, he was acutely aware of all that was happening at the time and found it a very difficult and upsetting period.

Karl was a very studious child and always got glowing results at parents' evenings and was very popular at school with both peers and

Our first visit to REETH in 1980

Keith's very apologetic letter to me

The day we told our sons that their new brother was on the way

Our wedding day

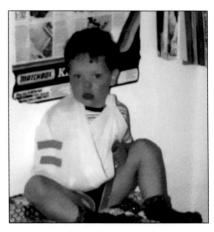

Accident prone Matthew

Darren, Jonathan and Richard
– budding hair stylists

Matthew showing Keith's
excessive project planning

Daddy being silly

We had some great days out
with our sons

Jonathan and Richard on holiday in
Wales with their Nan and Grandad

My Mum and Dad

Keith's Mum and Dad

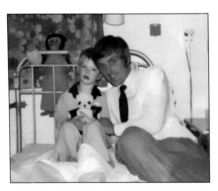

Jonathan had his tonsils removed

Matthew with his first water melon

Having fun sharing Nan's wig

Fishing at Aysgarth Falls,
Wensleydale

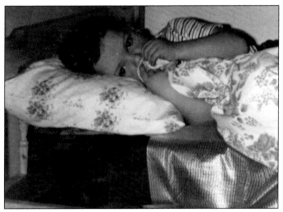

Matthew with his
'cudder'

Jonathan and Matthew with
their rabbits Fiver and Bugsy

Skiing holidays in France

Interesting sleeping arrangements
in Brussels

Matthew and me in the
Yorkshire Dales

Getting ready to go to the Moulin
Rouge, Paris for Matthew's 18th

We supported numerous fund raising events

Darren, Keith and Karl at Reeth House

Learning to ride a bike at 49

teachers. He had a thirst for knowledge and was an avid reader from a very young age. Where he felt most comfortable as a young child was in the garden and he was always happy when we were out walking and discovering the countryside. Always very fit, he loved playing football. All this changed when he went to secondary school. Industrial strikes by teachers had disrupted school life, and as they were no longer supervising after-school activities as they had once done, the football matches folded. His academic work started to suffer too and his school environment became much narrower and quite difficult for him. On top of this he was beginning to understand the adult world and its politics. Two of his closest friends had dads who were involved in the long running miners' strike of 1984. By the age of fifteen he saw limited educational possibilities and no job prospects. During the summer of 1986 he had been quieter and more withdrawn, but unfortunately I had not seen the significance. We had spent a long weekend in the Lakes in August. Jonathan and Richard had stayed with grandparents and so Keith and I grasped the opportunity to go away with Karl, Darren and Matthew. On an evening after Matthew was in bed we would go into the lounge and enjoy conversation with the owner. Darren always joined us and was eager to learn about this new area. He was always good at joining in the conversation with interesting topics and his general knowledge was vast. We just felt that maybe Karl was staying in his room to read, as he wanted some space of his own. He was always quite shy and so it was not unusual for him to want to be on his own. There were other incidents that summer of Karl being less than his usual enthusiastic self. Sadly it was only in hindsight that I pieced this together.

Fortunately, his suicide attempt was unsuccessful and he was comforted by the fact that all his family had shown their deep love for him during this crisis. He was very ill during his week in hospital but because he had been sick many times in the night after taking the tablets, not all of the poison went into his system.

When he came home we talked about him leaving school, as this was his biggest problem. He told us that he had actually grown to hate school. Eventually he made a decision to stay on and finish the year. It would mean he could take his GCSEs and hopefully get some qualifications. We had not realised, however, how far he had fallen behind. He had gone from an A student to someone who just managed average results in tests. The reason for this was that he had been skipping as much school as he possibly could, without causing concern to anybody. Discipline was not as good or as tight as it might have been and he was able to attend registration but miss most of the school day by simply walking out. It had not officially come to light that he was playing truant. Why staff had not realised he was missing for long periods and failed to act on this, we just could not understand. Because of his poor results on a day-to- day basis, several of his teachers would not even enter him for exams. In the end he was only allowed to take three exams at GCSE level. His results were two A's and a B. So he did extremely well despite his handicap. He immediately started applying for jobs. His confidence was knocked severely when he went for his first interview. Everyone was being turned away at the gate. The company had gone into liquidation that day and, of course, no interviews were being conducted. He applied for two other jobs and eventually he was successful in securing an apprenticeship in engineering. He had always been good at maths but was also particularly skilful with his hands, including a talent for art and drawing. He was a conscientious apprentice and went on to win several achievements including best improved apprentice of the year. This was the beginning of a career with a manufacturer of pumping equipment, which was to last for several years.

Naturally his attempted suicide had unsettled me and I never returned to my job at the dental practice. I just couldn't concentrate. It would take me several months to pick myself up again, but I was determined to give more care and attention to Karl and indeed his brothers, but it did worry me that I may not have the strength.

Chapter 6

LEARNING AND GROWING

I was now approaching forty years of age and physically far from well. I was using three different inhalers each day, still getting pains when I walked up gradients, and in addition I had developed persistent kidney infections. I was like a creaking gate and feeling far from strong. But despite these limitations, and for the next year, I made the house my priority. I wanted to make it more homely for the family. I decorated and gardened and re-organised. One other major area of concern I had to look at was my involvement with the church magazine. From its humble beginnings as a four-page pamphlet, it had snowballed into a 32-page booklet, of which sixteen pages were advertising. Keith had by now been sucked further into the process of helping and it was taking a huge chunk of our time. It was not only the advertising, either – we were involved at every stage. Keith would take the typed pages to a processor in Leicester who would produce stencils for us and then he would pick them up a few days later, fitting these trips around his business journeys to London. The actual printing was then completed on an old Gestetner machine housed in the church, by Ken, one of the church wardens, whose engineering training at Rolls Royce kept the wheels turning while his wife Hilda, with a marvellous sense of humour and dedication, kept us all on track. Ken and Hilda also rounded up a garrison of helpers, including us, to staple the books together and finally to deliver them to each and every household in the parish. But there was even more. The first part of the process was the collation of the material. A decision-making group including me would meet to discuss, to type, to stick. Because Keith was away a lot, the group started to meet at our house to avoid the need for a babysitter. As time moved on, our house would often be the meeting point even if Keith was home and so eventually he got involved at these meetings as well. With our involvement in the whole process, inevitably the workload was affecting our home life. On several occasions we had been forced to ignore our boys because of magazine deadlines. We had known for some time that this situation just couldn't carry on and so we decided that now was the ideal time to retire from the magazine completely.

Matthew had always been thirsty for knowledge and just wanted to learn. It probably wasn't, but it felt as though the first word he learnt to speak was "why?". He had no time for games and socialising and team events. And so he really looked forward to school. We had built it up to be a marvellous place where lots of his questions would be answered. But once he was there, he found school frustrating. Things were not moving fast enough for him and so his mind would wander and his behaviour would reflect his frustration. But, of course, other pupils, teachers and parents read his behaviour quite differently. Inevitably he was branded as difficult and odd. He did try his best to fit into everyday school life but somehow it always went wrong. On his first sports day he was so excited at being picked to run in the first race. He had been to school sports days with me before he started school, so he had watched races, but this was the first time he was actually involved. The runners were lined up. Get ready, Get set, Go! He set off at a furious pace. Immediately, ecstatic laughter from both children and parents filled the air. Realisation quickly dawned on him. He was on his own as the other children were sprinting in the opposite direction. He had completely misread the layout of the course and was running the wrong way round the track. Publicly he laughed and made light of it. However I am sure inwardly he felt embarrassed and self-conscious and I had a deep feeling of concern for him. Although he was having these difficulties at school, I knew he was in a safe environment and to a degree I could relax. Because of that, and the fact that the magazine work was behind me, I knew that I needed more stimulation. I had definitely created a better environment for myself and for the family but when Keith was at work and the children at school, I couldn't just sit around in an empty house. I knew that I had to look for a job. But it had to be a job that would give me the stimulation I needed but would also allow me the time to be there for Matthew and for our other boys. The ideal job, I thought, would be working in a school. That typing course would now prove invaluable. In 1987, I successfully applied to Rawcliffe School, situated about four miles from our village, and so began a thirteen-year career as a school secretary. It was a job I loved. It was not so much what I did on a daily basis, even though this created challenges which, with Keith's help, I overcame, thereby boosting my confidence. It was working around children that I really enjoyed; seeing their innocent faces and watching them develop from tiny four-year-olds into confident eleven-year olds was a real privilege for me.

Matthew came out of the primary school he attended one afternoon with two chocolates in his hand and gave them straight to me. He was, by now, in his second year at school. I thought that they were a present for me and said thank you.

"My teacher gave them to me today, because my work was good," he said. Oh no, I thought. Here we go again! When he had started in her class in September, I had given the teacher a short list of items Matthew must not have. It was now only October and already we seemed to be having problems. I praised him for not eating them and bringing them to me. Do I ignore it and hope it doesn't happen again? Or do I mention it to the teacher concerned? I decided it was better to sort it now. After all, it was confusing Matthew. We went back into class and when the teacher was on her own I told her that I was upset that she had given chocolates to Matthew.

"I only gave him one," was her hasty reply. I resisted the temptation to challenge her statement by producing the two chocolates. Instead I quietly tried to re-emphasise the instructions that I had originally given to her. She said it was difficult to stick to this as she found that the reward system brought good results from the children.

This was a tough one. I knew Matthew certainly needed praise as he got little of this due to his challenging behaviour.

But I started again. *"If Matthew eats sweets with colouring he can become very disruptive. If he eats chocolates, which contain milk, his skin gets very sore and irritable. Either way he is not going to be relaxed and quiet and be able to follow the lessons to the full."*

She said she understood, but it was clear from her next statement that she didn't. *"I can't leave one child out of my reward scheme – that would be unfair."*

I offered a compromise. *"If you could write a line or two of praise alongside his work, that would be a much stronger reward for Matthew than a chocolate that he cannot eat. Also the praise would be linked directly to the relevant work, whereas he might not understand the significance of the chocolate."*

She did take this on board but there were two further occasions during the year when he was given sweets. I did not speak to her about this. I did not feel it would help the situation and after all Matthew was very black and white. He knew he should not eat the sweets and he always brought them home to me. He had learned about the foods to avoid and I had been able to bake things for him using colour-free and non-dairy ingredients so that he didn't feel left out when his brothers were having treats. In fact, over a period of time, they all started to eat the same things as they thought that Matthew's homemade food tasted far better than the mass-produced items they were used to. His teacher's reaction was not unusual. Very few people were sympathetic to colour-free diets in the 1980s and if you were on any other diet, such as 'dairy free' as Matthew was, you were classed as a health freak.

We had seen the results when he had eaten these ingredients and we had seen the good results after withdrawing them. We were not on a bandwagon; we were simply trying to help our son. At the end of the school year we went to parents' evening. His teacher said she had spent a difficult year teaching him. In all her years of experience she had not come across a child like him and she was actually relieved that her time with him was coming to an end.

One very memorable day in 1987 Keith came rushing home to tell me that he had been listening to *The Jimmy Young Show* on Radio 2. There was an interview with a specialist called Dr Pearson, who had had a lot of success in dealing with people who had a number of apparently unrelated health problems. He was quite unconventional in his approach, in that he looked at the whole person. In those days this was a very unusual approach, as we had found from experience. We followed it up with our GP and within a couple of months I was in hospital in Manchester. It was a two-week period and I can only liken it to a car having a service or an MOT. They looked at everything and in conclusion, I got a checklist of faults to be corrected.

- Not allergic to any foods, but intolerant to a number of things; need to follow a strict diet regime.
- Not asthmatic in the true sense, but intolerant to pollutants: perfume, petrol fumes, cigarette smoke and others; need to avoid all these, at all times.
- Need a hysterectomy, which will correct fibroids and help in the clearance of fluids from the system.
- Chronic rhinitis (diseased nasal passages), sinuses need draining; need to learn to breathe better.
- Irritable bowel discovered; need to follow strict diet regime.
- Very tense, not relaxed; would benefit from a psychotherapy course.

I went back to Manchester for the hysterectomy and the sinus draining several months later. Keith brought Karl and Darren over to see me. He used it as a driving experience for Karl, who had just received his provisional licence. Driving home over Saddleworth Moors they encountered a flock of sheep crossing the road, which proved to be a major learning experience for both of them. After that event Keith decided that it would be safer to provide professional driving lessons for Karl – it proved to be the best course of action, and one we followed with our other four sons. They all had the same driving instructor and all passed their driving test at the first attempt.

I put Dr Pearson's other recommendations into practise immediately and did see some improvement in my health. But, unfortunately, other problems were to come into play later in my life. The first thing I tackled was my diet and the only way to do it properly was to start with a basic elimination diet of lamb, rice, cabbage and pears and have only water to drink. After that I had to add one food at a time, eliminating anything that affected me. It was a long laborious process but it proved to be worthwhile. When reintroducing dairy products and wheat I had serious problems and was advised by the dietician at St James Hospital in Leeds to stop these foods immediately but then reintroduce them again further down the line. I never did get them re-introduced. Each time I tried, they made me ill. I have since found I can tolerate small amounts of sheep's milk cheese and yoghurt and buffalo milk cheese and vegetable margarine, but anything from a cow is to be avoided. Wheat was another problem. This meant no sandwiches, biscuits or cakes. I tried over a period of a couple of years to introduce all different manners of flour substitutes. As well as pure grains affecting me, the additives in some of the alternatives were equally as troublesome. My main carbohydrates consisted of a small amount of potato or rice and rice cakes. I still have a gluten-free diet today. When I tried to re-introduce coffee into my diet I developed the shakes. This happened three times so I cut it out and I have never had coffee since that time. It seems very strange because I used to drink gallons of the stuff. I now drink water hot or cold and pure fruit juices.

There was a very interesting development from all this which was to change Keith's life completely. He had always suffered from exhaustion when faced with high temperatures. In the summer months he would almost pass out, unable to breathe and perspired excessively. It was quite noticeable after sex that he would often have to hang out of the window for several minutes in order to regain a normal level of breathing. This was quite serious but hard to take seriously when confronted by his naked backside draped over the window ledge. On a day-to-day basis, he would soon become overheated in the house. It was quite normal for him to strip off and sit bare-chested all night, even in the depths of winter. Naturally I just put it down to his usual eccentricity. Well, in sympathy with me, he decided to go on the elimination diet. Like me he cut out tea and coffee and alcohol and all the little eating treats that are nice to nibble. He still ate wheat and grains but he did cut out cakes biscuits and sweets. He couldn't believe the difference in his health. Within days he felt much fitter, less tired and the best part of all was that the heat wasn't affecting him. It was like a miracle. Like me he gradually introduced foods back in to his diet and eventually he realised that he was much healthier without milk products and caffeine and more spectacularly without added sugar products. And so 1987 was the last year he had a drink of lager or a fizzy drink or a drink of tea or coffee and the same year he stopped eating sweets, biscuits, cakes, ice cream and chocolate.

Keith had never been in the habit of buying gifts for me and I was greatly surprised, therefore, when he arrived home with a 'special present' for my 40th birthday. A large well wrapped box. When I say well wrapped that's not in the well chosen paper and fancy ribbon way. What I mean is that it was generously covered with brown paper. Could it be more coffee tables? I thought. I fought my way through the outer covering. Was it for me personally or for the house? Well from Keith's perspective it was for me. It was to make my life easier in this new world of special diets and complicated meal preparation. I tore off the final pieces of the brown paper. I had become the proud owner of a microwave oven.

On one particular Saturday Keith had driven to Watford to a football match. He was in charge of hospitality for the company box and he had taken Jonathan and Richard with him. They both enjoyed going to live football matches whenever they got the opportunity. As they were having a treat I thought I would take Matthew to the cinema. The first production I remember taking him to, was before he even went to school. Darren was appearing in a school musical. We all wanted to support him and watch his performance. Matthew was only four and in spite of his often-difficult behaviour we decided to take him along. This was his first experience in a theatre, even if it was only a school theatre. Keith and I had already decided that at the first sign of talking we would take it in turns to stay outside with him. From the moment the curtain went up he was mesmerised. The singing and dancing just held him. Darren had a singing part as well as acting and Matthew had to confirm to me that he was on the stage. That was allowed and I am sure other siblings were equally as proud to be watching their brothers or sisters. Apart from asking me about the odd sentence if he was confused about the plot, the rest of the evening went without a hitch. We had enjoyed a relaxing evening watching Darren and his friends do a very professional job with this musical. It was obvious that the school had talented and highly motivated staff, able to enthuse the pupils. Their rendition of 'Another brick in the wall' was fantastic. We also were very proud of Matthew's behaviour at the school. After that pleasurable experience we had taken him to the cinema a couple of times and on both occasions he sat quietly engrossed in the films.

So, on this occasion, I decided to take him to see the film *Three Men and a Little Lady*, which had a U certificate. He quickly settled down to watch the film. His eyes were fully focused on the screen and he watched the changing phases of the story with interest. Then the five-year-old girl, Mary, said the word 'Penis'.

Matthew immediately turned to me and said in the loudest of voices, "*Mum! What does PENIS mean?*"

It was dark but the cinema was full. Without looking up, but out of the corner of my eyes, I could see several adults looking at me and some of them sniggering, laughing, smirking. Matthew was staring at me. He had lost interest in the continuing plot. He needed an answer. At this moment, our conversation was more important to him than the film. What was I to do? Try whispering the answer to him? More than likely he would repeat the answer to me, but not in a whisper, in a very loud voice. Or, even more likely, he would ask more questions in the same loud voice. Either way we would disturb the concentration of the other cinemagoers. In a firm voice I whispered to him, "*Matthew, as soon as we get back into the car, I will explain the word to you. If we talk now we will miss the next part of the film.*"

By some miracle it worked. He asked no more questions about Penis and he was back to studying the film. It was a humorous family film and one that we both very much enjoyed. As we headed for the car, we chatted and laughed about what we had seen, but he made no mention about the penis question. The minute the seatbelts clicked, he said, "*Mum! You said you would tell me what a penis is.*"

I did, and that set a pattern for the future. It became obvious to me that once he had a specific point in time in his mind he could focus on that point and park his question until then. If Matthew ever asked for an explanation to something he did not understand and it was not convenient, which was quite often, I would use the same tactic. Provided I could give a sound reason for not explaining it there and then, and as long as I gave him a time when it would be explained, he always accepted it. He wouldn't accept being fobbed off with statements like, "I haven't time now," or, "I will tell you later". These only brought on tantrums. But when we struck up our adult deals we were both able to share some knowledge and I could get us out of a sticky situation.

However, although it was easy to give a credible answer to a question like

"Why has that lady got fat legs?" it did prove a trifle embarrassing, as the question was always delivered in his usual loud voice and in close proximity to the person in question. And my whispered retort to him of *"I'll tell you when we get outside."* somehow made me an accessory to the abuse. Like most children, he did eventually learn to be more tactful, but not until he was well into secondary school life.

On another visit to the football ground at Watford, Keith decided to take Matthew as well as Jonathan and Richard. I also went down to London, but they dropped me off first so that I could take a gentle stroll around the shops on Oxford Street and Regent Street. We had already booked some accommodation for the evening so the plan was to meet up for a meal after the match and then find something to do in the evening. As I was passing a newsagent's stand I spotted a poster advertising a musical at one of the theatres in the West End. It was 'Buddy'. Keith and I enjoyed the music of Buddy Holly and the boys had developed a keen interest in all types of music. So they were all excited when we met up later and I told them that I had booked. From the opening scene we were all hooked, tapping our feet and singing along at the appropriate time, as were most of the audience. Before long a number of people started bopping in the aisles and everyone was encouraged to clap and sing to the choruses. The atmosphere was electric and the temperature was rising. It was a warm September evening and the theatre had already put the heating back on for the winter. Matthew was really getting into the spirit of things and it was obvious from his red face that he was getting overheated. He was like Keith in this respect, and we were used to it. When it occurred at home he would strip off his shirt and sit with a bare chest. So, of course, he saw no reason why he shouldn't do the same here; off came the shirt and he continued clapping and singing with a bare chest for the rest of the night. Despite the odd looks from a number of people including a large group who were smartly turned out in evening dress and were probably going on to a formal dinner after the show, we just treated him as if he were fully dressed. We knew that if we had attempted to get him to put his shirt back on, it would have caused chaos.

We didn't have a strong enough argument to convince him that putting his shirt back on was necessary. We had a thoroughly good night. We must have enjoyed it as we went back to see the same musical on two further occasions in the future.

There were many more instances of Matthew's inability to understand the significance of his dress code but probably the most memorable came when he was ten-years-old. We were staying in a hotel in the London area. We had gone back to our hotel after a day of adventurous sightseeing. Matthew had already finished his meal and he left us in the restaurant and went up to the bedroom that he was sharing with Jonathan. He had changed into his pyjamas and had started to read a newspaper. He had always been an avid reader of newspapers from a very young age. After a while he felt we had probably returned from the dining room so he ventured out into the corridor and across to our room, but no, we were not back. In his excitement to find us, he had not thought to take his key with him to get back into his own room.

About twenty minutes later, our meal digested, the three of us went upstairs to talk to Matthew. He was animated as he related the story to us.

"So how did you get back in here?" Jonathan asked.

"I went down to reception and asked for a key and the manager brought me back up and opened the door for me." I could see Jonathan's face scrutinising Matthew.

"And did you have your pyjamas on then, Matt?"

"Yes," replied Matthew with a puzzled expression. He could see nothing wrong with going to the foyer of a busy hotel dressed in his pyjamas. Jonathan said that if it had been him, he would probably have sat huddled up on the floor outside the bedroom door and waited for our return. Matthew saw that as a complete waste of time, in a similar way that his father, several years earlier, had seen nothing wrong with driving down to the village in his pyjamas in order to post a letter.

As far as Matthew was concerned, there were questions to be asked about life every day and he had every right to ask them. He was so full of life and wanted to learn everything. I could be trying to get a shower or a bath before setting off to work on a morning and Matthew would walk into the bathroom and in a matter of fact manner would ask me to explain the difference between simple interest and compound interest on bank accounts, how such things as income tax worked and which bank accounts gave the most interest. Some of these conversations were short lived, as I often did not have the knowledge Matthew needed. When he was young I would promise to pick up relevant details from sources he could not get to. When he was older I just had to point him to the information and he would retrieve it for himself. So many times did he make me feel inadequate, not through any comments he made about me, but by what I felt was my own lack of knowledge in so many areas. I often felt that if I had been a mum with higher qualifications and intelligence, he could have achieved so much more, but who knows? His thirst for knowledge was vast and unstoppable. So much so that if we were watching a television programme it was very difficult to guarantee watching the climax, however interesting it was. If he had questions or problems he seemed to be unable to read the signs that we were enjoying a programme and did not want disturbing. The tactic of delaying the answer until after the programme did not seem to work. That only worked if other people were involved. If it was just Keith, and me, he demanded an immediate response. It took a long time for him to grasp the concept that sometimes you had to share with others and that sharing could mean understanding when it was convenient to ask questions and when it was better to wait. But part of the reason with regard to the television example, was that he seemed to have an in built aversion to television. When he was young he would sit with me to watch a children's programme that I felt he would enjoy but as soon as the theme music had finished he would then get up and say, "*Right, I've seen that, let's play now.*"

I had to explain that we had only heard the introductory music and the fun had not yet started. It took several months before I could get him to sit and watch a full fifteen-minute programme. Eventually he would sit with me but he asked questions all the way through and missed the thread of the story. This was a pattern that he would carry into adulthood.

On the emotional side, I decided to tackle the final measure from the list of recommendations given to me by Dr Pearson in Manchester. I started a course of psychotherapy with a lady called Suzanne in Leeds, which lasted for about twelve months. I found it emotionally very draining. I drove there and back, a round trip of around eighty miles, every Tuesday, which was my day off from school. Now I look back at what I feel was a very dangerous action, because at the end of the sessions I was emotionally exhausted. I survived the journeys, however, and the therapy worked. I was able to bury many of my childhood ghosts especially the main one, which I hadn't recognised up until then. My mother had been able to create a controlling and possessive influence over me, which had been there when I was a child, but had continued until as late as my forties. Now I knew this, I could deal with it and move on. My meetings with Suzanne allowed me to lay my thoughts and feelings on the table, and her to support me. But one side of my life I still kept secret. I let her believe that my life with my family was perfect. I said nothing to her about my relationship and my difficulties with Keith and Matthew. Why did I mask this side of myself? ; The dark side, Why? I don't know. Perhaps I did not want anyone else to know that Keith had at one stage suggested having Matthew fostered. The therapy came to a natural conclusion in the summer of 1989. I felt good about myself again, and yet I was still unhappy. What was making me unhappy? Try as I did, I could not answer that little conundrum.

When I had been part way through my programme with Suzanne, I had made a positive decision to plan a trip to visit my first husband's sister and family in the USA. We had always been very close and I felt that just because I was no longer married to her brother, it did not mean that my relationship with her had to suffer. I always wrote to Joyce on a regular basis and I would wait for news of our three nephews and now in later years, news of their families too. Joyce and Bob had left England for the USA in 1971 with their three sons Glenn, Lee and Ross, who were aged five, three and one. We had always been close. They had been back to England a few times when our nephews were young, but of late they had been unable to visit. I had this feeling that I was getting older and if I did not make the effort the opportunity would not always be there. I knew that we couldn't afford to go as a family so I talked to Keith about my burning desire to visit Joyce and asked him what he thought about me going on my own. He was fully behind me. He said he would help me to do all we could to raise the money to visit them. When it came to the time to book my ticket, my sister kindly lent me the money and we scrimped and saved until I had the rest. Half of me was on cloud nine after speaking to Joyce and firming up the timings.

She would meet me at O' Hare Airport, Chicago, in a week's time. The other half of me still did not see how I was able to go and leave my family. I set to work and shopped, baked and baked again, making an enormous amount of ready meals. I washed and ironed everything in sight and I cleaned everywhere and anything that stood still. I knew it was obsessive but I had to leave everything perfect for the changeover. Our two mums came up trumps, each agreeing to move in for a week at a time. Keith would then be on holiday for the third week. During this time both Jonathan and Matthew were going on separate school trips so I made sure all their clothes were left ready packed with notes reminding Keith to wash last-minute underpants and socks for them and add these to their suitcases.

Keith and I left home on Wednesday afternoon saying goodbye to my Mum and Matthew as they were the only two in the house. All my other goodbyes had been said the night before. I was more than ready to go but I was shattered and almost feeling as if I were not strong enough to make the trip, especially when I began to think that I was about to travel four thousand miles on my own.

Keith had appointments in London the following day and had arranged to take me to the airport first. We met up with some of his work colleagues and had an enjoyable meal that evening before going to bed for an early night. Next morning instead of feeling excited I just felt frozen. How could I be away from our children for three weeks? How could I be separated from Keith for so long? Yes, we had spent probably a third of our marriage apart, but that was usually in odd days, a maximum of four at a time. But there was no going back. Keith was so excited for me and kept reminding me that he would write to me and that he would ring me at an arranged time each week. I remembered I had written some birthday cards and left them ready to post. Keith reassured me he had a note of this and that it was time for me to stop thinking of home and get into a relaxed mood ready for my trip. After we kissed goodbye at the airport Keith gave me one of his big beaming smiles. These he always saved to use and reassure me that all was well. But I was not fully reassured. I did not want to go – three weeks was a lifetime – and how would I survive without all my boys? I had not been a single person for many years and even then I was a sister or a daughter. Here I was, going all the way across the Atlantic on my own. After Keith left I cried all the way to the plane.

On the flight I sat next to a lovely elderly couple who were on their way home to Chicago. They told me all about their visit to England and Scotland. They insisted I had the window seat as they had made the trip several times before and wanted me to enjoy my trip to the full. My first fantastic experience was the view over Greenland. It was just beautiful and unique. I read my book most of the time but I did stop to watch the film *Rain Man* which was a new film at the time. I found it mesmerising; A young man with so much talent and yet no social graces. The film gave me a lot to think about. At this point I did not realise how many times I would watch this film in the years to come. On the descent into O' Hare airport my new friends pointed out all the major landmarks. I was fascinated by how straight all the roads were. Here was a place I felt I would not get lost, even with my poor sense of direction. And then the vastness hit me. We were over the city and yet I could see so much greenery and so many swimming pools. It was all so new to me. I was trying to take it all in. I just wanted the plane to hover forever. In no time at all, I was in the airport and I knew I would soon be reunited with Joyce and her family. No such luck though, because it took almost two hours to get through customs and collect my luggage from the carousel. Once this was done I turned the corner in to the arrivals area and there in front of me were Joyce and my nephew Lee. My heart was pounding as I hugged both of them. We went for a drink and then they loaded my luggage into the car and we were heading for Janesville in Wisconsin. Once again I was struck by the vastness of the place, the roads and the wide-open spaces. It was very exciting and I was full of questions. When we arrived at Joyce and Bob's apartment it was so cool. I had not experienced air conditioning in houses before. Being the middle of August, the contrast from the heat was so welcome. Bob came home from work, and then Ross, their youngest son, arrived to greet me and we all had an evening meal together. No sooner had we finished than the phone rang. It was their oldest boy, Glenn, who was checking to see if I had arrived. Glenn was five when they emigrated and I had enjoyed many happy hours babysitting and taking him out for walks when he was young. This was my first day and already I felt at home. At midnight, Joyce who had been working hard preparing for my visit, started to fall asleep. We hugged and she went to bed. Bob and I managed to chat for another three hours before finally retiring ourselves. They both had to work the next day but I was able to sleep in and catch up on my jet lag and sleep in I did. I was awakened by the phone ringing and was surprised to find that it was almost lunchtime. Joyce was ringing to see if I had surfaced and to invite me out for lunch.

For me it was a very leisurely three weeks but for Joyce and Bob it must have been hectic having a houseguest as well as running a business. They could not take breaks from the business to be with me all the time and this I appreciated, but they always took me out at the weekend to visit places and friends. We also went out some evenings either for a meal or to watch a football game. These took place on Wednesday evenings and also on Saturday mornings and were part of Bob's very busy training schedule as coach for a local high school team. Opportunities like this gave Joyce and me lots of time to talk and catch up on the years we'd not seen each other. The rest of the time my nephews entertained me. It was mainly Lee, as he was home from university for the holidays and he took me to a place called 'the house on the rock' which I can only remember as the other side of Madison, their state capital. It was a wonderful home of treasures: we spent all day there, and then stopped off in Madison for a meal on the way back. On another day, Lee and his girlfriend Penny took me to Milwaukee Zoo. Both of these trips were both enjoyable and memorable. They spoilt me by showing me different places, explaining so much of American culture, but most of all treating me as a member of the family. It felt like being home with any of our own sons. These were their cousins who had been brought up on the other side of the Atlantic, but they were so much alike. Some days I stayed in the apartment in the morning and then met up with Joyce and Bob on their lunch break. Then in the afternoon Joyce would drive me to the shopping area and I would mooch round bookshops or occasionally the shopping mall until she came to pick me up again when her work was completed. My favourite afternoons were spent at the factory with Joyce, sewing and talking. The hours flew and I felt so relaxed. She was working on an order for sports T-shirts and taught me how to sew one of them on the machine. It was fun but it would take me a while to perfect. I was very proud, however, when I successfully sewed a dozen serviettes on one of their industrial machines from some Christmas material that I had purchased in the mall.

One afternoon, when we were busy sewing at the factory, a news bulletin came on the radio. Joyce always listened to the world service while she was working. There had been a disaster on the River Thames with a large number of young people killed. A dredger had ploughed in to a passenger boat. The boat was the Marchioness and it made us both very sad to hear of this tragedy happening in London while we were here happily sewing away in a little building in a small town in Wisconsin.

I enjoyed hearing about the American school system and how children were almost six by the time they started school. Because of the climate, they played sports of different types all the year round. The youngsters seemed to be heavily committed to school life and that included a lot of sport. Most evenings they would attend out-of-hours classes of one type or another. I also told Joyce about my experiences in my role as a school secretary and how I enjoyed using my banking and typing skills. But more than that, I explained how I enjoyed my additional non-teaching assistant position, which I had been lucky enough to gain and by this time I had enrolled as a school governor. I had made lots of new friends and one in particular stood out. She was a teacher at the school and I remember telling Joyce that had she been my teacher when I was young, I am sure I would have understood subjects such as art, english, literature and poetry much better. I was impressed by the way she taught through her enthusiasm and skill and the children always wanted to know more. She was to become my closest friend.

When Keith rang me I was so excited to hear all about the family and how they all were. Of course they were fine. Grandmas were looking after them and they were all busy. Keith was finding it a strain having overall responsibility as well as working and was looking forward to finishing work for the holidays. We said how much we loved each other and when I put the phone down I had a few tears. I was so homesick – I'd never been away from home like this on my own. On the other hand, everyone was making me so welcome and I was part way through a fantastic experience. Keith's regular letters helped and especially the one I received from Karl. He was working by now. But he made the time to write, which meant such a lot to me. It was great to hear how positive he was about things, especially as I thought back to the dark days three years earlier.

Glenn and his wife Jackie took me to the Annual 4H Fair along with their twin daughters. They were not identical twins, totally different in fact, but both of them were beauties, one blonde and one with dark hair. The exhibits were the results of hard work from school children who had grown produce specifically to exhibit at the fair. Some children also reared calves and trained horses to show at the 4H. Wisconsin is a farming community and the community spirit was very prevalent here. It was great to see children learning invaluable life skills and working together. Without doubt, the highlight of my stay was the first birthday party for the twins. I took lots of photos of everyone – especially Marlina and Sonja with their birthday cake all over their faces. They were so happy. Yet life was tough for Glenn and Jackie. Glenn worked for the tractor company John Deere and they lived on a farm. Jackie worked the farm as well as looking after the twins. They had sheep and goats and several horses and they also had many dogs and cats. Their days were long and they certainly packed a lot in.

My visit came to an end all too quickly and it was time to fly home. Joyce and I took the bus down to Chicago leaving ourselves time to have a couple of hours together. It was going to be hard for both of us: shortly we would be separated again and had no idea when we would be able to meet up in the future. We were like sisters and we would keep that bond through writing to each other until fate decided it was time to meet up again. This had been a very emotional trip for both of us. It had taught me a lot about myself and it had renewed my energy, but more than that, it had made me feel more confident about myself, more independent, and more grown up.

The emotion of the goodbyes in America was really nothing compared to what I felt when I saw Keith's beaming face and frenzied waving as he waited for me at the arrivals gate. We held each other tightly for several minutes and then he gave me a gift. Not an expensive gift but one that I still treasure; A small teddy-bear with the name of Harry Heathrow. I knew he wouldn't have given a lot of thought before deciding to buy it. And yet, it was the perfect gift.

Chapter 7

INTO THE 90s

As we moved into the 1990s the love between Keith and myself continued to grow. Although his behaviour still amazed me, I had adjusted myself to cope with it. All our boys had provided us with the usual cocktail of happiness and problems that parents have to face. If there was a problem with one of the children, it became our first priority; we worked together to help and supported whenever we could. At other times, we sat back as all parents do until the problem is solved or you are called to help. This became the pattern over the years. We had lots of ups and downs in this period, but we were always there for each other. Keith was not good at spotting a potential problem or even an actual problem. I had to point it out to him. Once he grasped it, however, he would be there to support me, as long as it fitted in with his work plans. I got used to knowing when it was the right time to ask.

It was an enjoyable time for him at work. He had a good relationship with both colleagues and his manager and he found that he was developing a natural affinity for training. He had developed a sales training course for his division and now he was rolling it out to the industrial sectors of the business. It was great to see him happy and settled; particularly when I recalled the trauma he had gone through five years earlier. The downside for me was the fact that he spent so much time away from home. I should have been used to it by now, but I hated it when we were apart. He too found the nights away a strain and when he did eventually arrive home from a three-day event it was late and he was tired; but as tired as he was he would feel the need to talk to me about the training. His enthusiasm was electric and it took patience and cuddles and understanding to bring him down to earth. Eventually we could both relax together and graduate to the bedroom for a well-earned night of passion. This would often be followed in the wee small hours by a 'virtual training session' as he demonstrated to me how to sell. It wouldn't be the products he was selling, it would be a washing up bowl or a whole new range of garden equipment or any number of things. This would carry on until, eventually, we drifted gently in to a deep sleep. Conferences had always had a similar effect on him; every time, he would return full of enthusiasm, full of passion. New products, new projects, he loved it.

One of the best examples of his commitment and single-mindedness was his determination to proceed with a three-day training course in Cheshire despite the fact he'd broken his arm in an accident when we had taken the boys to an ice rink. As far as he was concerned the course had been booked, everything was organised, he had to be there. Despite my protestations, he was determined to go ahead. The show must go on. And in the end I gave in and volunteered to drive him as the alternative had involved a lengthy mixture of train, bus and taxi. How he would have managed all the equipment that he took, including a very large television that required the services of two large men to carry it into the hotel, I will never know. I left him at the hotel for three days and then returned to collect him. He was over the moon about the way the course had gone. It was wonderful to see his excitement and apparently he had managed everything except his tie. I had pre-knotted them but he couldn't tighten it up to his neck and so one of the delegates had helped him with that task each day. This then was his pattern. At work, the cool calm professional that got things done. After work, a bit of an accident-prone 'bumbler'; this is why he ended up in the hospital after playing about on the ice at the skating rink. Keith told me later that the broken arm had, in fact, given him a great excuse; A reason not to be part of the social gathering at the end of each day. After all, he needed to rest his arm didn't he? Any excuse to avoid a social gathering and he would grab it. But that didn't stop him involving me whenever he could. If there were a chance for me to meet his colleagues and their partners, he would willingly accept because he knew that it was good for me and I always enjoyed meeting new people. On one particular occasion we were in London enjoying a very special night at the Grosvenor House Hotel, Park Lane. It was a fabulous night out with a group of Keith's business colleagues and friends. We both went off together at a convenient interval to find the toilets. It was a huge place and they took some finding. Keith was dressed in evening suit and I was wearing a long sequined strapless dress. I already knew he found the dress quite exciting. In our struggle to find the toilets in the very 'posh' place, we uncovered a behind the scenes room. It resembled a very large broom cupboard. We both laughed, as it was obviously not our destination. Off we went and eventually found the toilets and, as often happens, Keith was in and out quickly but I was in quite a queue. He has always been good to me in strange places as he knows I get nervous wandering about on my own and he always waits patiently to escort me back to our table or to seats if it is the theatre. We were on our way back when I saw a twinkle in his eye.

"*Let's go to our little cupboard and have a cuddle,*" he said with excitement. Well that dress certainly did the trick and I returned to the table more than a little flushed. We took several photographs that night but insisted that one of our friends took one of us together against this beautiful white and gold circular wall with its hidden secret.

After four difficult years, we made the decision to pull Matthew out of our local school and transfer him to the school I worked in, where we felt he would have a better environment in which to learn. It was a good decision. The structured approach at the school was very helpful for him and his academic work improved. I was teaching groups of children in baking and needlework and Matthew became one of my pupils. If he was kept busy he was not a problem and he was always very proud of anything he'd made. So much so that he wouldn't part with it; even if they'd made gifts or greetings cards, he wouldn't give them to the intended person. He couldn't get his head around this concept. He had made them, so he wanted to keep them for himself. I was now able to observe him for myself in the school environment. All the problems from his previous school had come to me second and third hand and they didn't know him as I did. I watched him in the classroom, I watched him at lunchtime, and I watched him in the playground. It was the same pattern. Keep him busy and structured and you wouldn't have any problems, but at lunchtime and in the playground, he became a different person. At lunchtime he wanted to eat his food quickly and get back to school. He couldn't cope with sharing and chatting and playing. And I would watch him in the playground as he stood in a corner on his own, often reading books such as 'The Railway Children' and 'The BFG' in which he was totally engaged and desperate to finish. When other children went up to him, he put his hand out to push them away. It was easy to see how this could have been misinterpreted as aggressively hitting out at other pupils.

In an effort to help his development, we encouraged him to develop interests outside of school. Activities that involved him pursuing things on his own, rather than as part of a group, were of most benefit to him. Firstly he took up horse riding which he thoroughly enjoyed, but he did have great difficulty interpreting the instructions from the trainer and usually had to be told over and over again. For four years he struggled to learn to play the piano. This activity was a real challenge for him, as he did not appear to have a natural ear for music and would spend hours sitting at our home piano going over the same piece and making the same mistakes. Keith spent a lot of time helping him even though he himself could not play the piano or indeed any musical instrument.

Matthew persevered and was successful in passing Grade One piano examinations in both theory and practice, which was a major achievement for him. He also went for regular swimming lessons but found it very difficult to follow the instructions and put them in to practice. His progress really came not from the lessons, but from regular visits to the pool with his dad. Activities, which were based on team events and co-ordination, he found to be a real struggle. Tennis, athletics, gymnastics and dancing were all tried, and he did join the Beavers. But although he didn't progress in any of these activities, the very fact that he was involved in them was helpful in keeping him active and stimulated. All of his 'bad behaviour' came at periods when he wasn't active or stimulated.

I was very proud of him when he went on the school trip to Northumberland. I was one of the accompanying staff members. He had a happy trip, because he was kept busy all the time. He found that he could interact with the adults away from the pressures of normal school life. He found it much easier with the staff than he did with the other children. He shared a bedroom with three other boys, and he took control of keeping the room tidy and was elated when they won the award for the tidiest room. Outside of school he was just the same. If he had a project he was industrious, confident and determined. Without a project, he was lost, unsure of himself, and very insecure. He was also very vulnerable to suggestion, and easily led into mischief by other pupils. We had discovered that what we needed to do was keep him busy. We didn't yet know why this was so important, and, of course, coming up with ideas was not always easy.

Looking back, there were two memorable projects that he created and developed himself and both were built in his bedroom. One morning Keith and I woke up to find Matthew at the side of us urging us to get up, which was not unusual. But then we had strict instructions to walk towards his bedroom door, which was closed. On the door it said 'Museum' and an admission price of 20p per person. We were both amazed at the tidiness of the room and the organisation that had gone into it. All across his desk there were various items and beside each item there was a postcard on which Matthew had written a simple explanation. He had also used lots of photos, some of which he had taken on a school trip and some he had borrowed from our family albums. There were fossils and stones and a whole variety of other things, all neatly labelled. He insisted we go round separately and read each individual label. It was the least we could do after all the work he had put in. It was his second year at school and he was using all the skills he had seen the teachers use when displaying the children's work. He has always been very good at imparting knowledge to others and I used to say he was a born teacher.

His next and more adventurous project was The Snaith Pet Club. One sunny day I was in the garden when I was greeted by a group of six children and three mums. One mum explained that she had brought her sons to the Pet Club and wanted to know what time she should come back to pick up the boys. After a little quick thinking I organised the children in a half circle on garden seats and gave the mums an appropriate time to return. Then I quickly went to find Matthew who seemed to have expected these boys. I wish he'd informed me first. He said he had organised a club for some children at school and it was about pets. At that time we did not have any pets and it was obvious

Matthew knew little about the subject but that did not put him off. He was a born organiser. While I made the children refreshments Matthew asked the first boy to talk about his pet. This went round in turn until they had all talked about their own pets. I don't know what Matthew thought would happen after that but he was ill-prepared to take over the meeting and carry on the discussion. At this point I stepped in and organised a few games. The boys all enjoyed their afternoon and were all quite happy when mums came back to collect them at teatime. After the children had gone home I asked Matthew why he had not mentioned the club to me, but he could not give a satisfactory answer. Maybe he felt I would not support him if I had known. He showed me cards he had made which were to be marked each time the members attended his meetings. They were all neatly ruled with spaces for a name and with date columns. Even at six years old he was very organised and very self-motivated. But after the event he realised that he did not know enough about pets to run such a group and so that turned out to be the first and only meeting of The Snaith Pet Club.

During the same period he had also been planning a much more adventurous project, which again he kept secret from us. It was only in the later stages that we got wind of it and Keith had to work hard to convince him that it was not really feasible. His plan called for the construction of a separate building within our rear garden to house a magnificent museum. He had worked out where the power was coming from, was planning to install an alarm system and was already at an advanced stage in terms of knowing which materials he would need to ensure it became a reality. His actual idea was fantastic and the amount of thought he had put in to the whole concept was really commendable. But, of course, he had not considered things like planning permission, developing a business plan or even the simple basic of raising the necessary finance. That said, it was one more example of his creative skill.

When he was nine my parents rang to ask if they could take Matthew to Malta with them for a week's holiday; we knew he would be elated. He had heard his brothers talk about holidays abroad but up until then we had only taken him on holiday in England. He was dying for the day when he would go out of Britain. When we told him only days before the trip his little face lit up with excitement. His dream was to come true. He always had difficulty getting off to sleep at night but for the next few days it was even worse. He had so many thoughts and questions going through his head. He was up and down the stairs most of the evenings during that week telling us ideas or asking questions and then eventually he would fall asleep exhausted.

The day they were due to fly we took Matthew and my parents to Keighley before our trip to the airport. This was a special visit for all of us. We were visiting my brother and his wife, their two-year-old son Tom and especially their new baby Joe. We took it in turns to nurse him. Matthew was always respectful of babies and liked to nurse them. He was also good at playing with younger children. It was people of his own age that he had difficulty with. I think it was probably because there was no social structure with toddlers – you just got in there and played with them – whereas with older ones it was more difficult. You had to take turns, you had to share and there was a structure to this, which Matthew could never follow.

He had a very special holiday in Malta with his grandparents. They spent time on the beach and by the swimming pool, went on endless trips and had regular meals out.

When we picked them up at Manchester Airport, he just told us story after story as his week had unfolded. His grandparents had given him a very special experience and it was obvious he was very grateful to them for this. He still remembers this holiday with much affection.

One sunny afternoon, Keith, Matthew and I were on one of our regular Sunday walks. We had started out at the nearby village of Airmyn and our intention was to walk in the path of the new bypass that was under construction. It had been started eighteen months earlier and we thought it was almost completed. It was a beautiful sunny day and we were enjoying walking and talking when it became obvious to Keith that we would have to change direction. The work was not as far advanced as we had hoped and the bridge over the river had not yet been completed. It would be impossible to get home going any further in this direction. Matthew immediately sat down and would not walk.

"Why not?" Keith asked him.

"Because you said we would follow the bypass all the way home and now you want to go back in the other direction."

"Yes," said Keith, "*but we have no choice, short of swimming across the River Aire. We cannot go any further in this direction.*"

"*You promised,*" was all he would say.

We explained the situation again and Keith and I started to walk, thinking that he would follow us. We walked for several minutes but he still sat in the same position with his head down. We could see him clearly as we were walking in a straight line at the side of the river. So we decided we would walk a little further. Surely he must realise there was only one way forward and he would follow us. Eventually it was obvious he was not going to follow us. What could we do? He was ten years old. We could not pick him up and carry him home. We walked all the way back to him and once again tried to reason with him. Keith explained the situation quietly. We had to retrace our steps part way as this was a dead end. We could not yet cross the bridge, as it had not been built. We could still enjoy our Sunday afternoon walk and we were, after all, just exploring the work that had been done on the bypass as part of our walk. I explained that projects did not always get completed on time and that we could have another walk and see the finished project later that summer. But he kept his head down and nothing we said would make him move. We had promised a certain route and now we were re-arranging it. It was almost thirty minutes later when he stood up and started to walk in the direction of re-tracing our steps. Good, at least he was mobile. But it was a silent walk home. He never spoke another word and on our arrival home he went straight to his bedroom. He had a short sleep and then came downstairs again as if nothing had happened. He was back to normal again. We had many incidents like this where for reasons beyond our control we had to change routes or outings or sometimes even the day of the outing, and, every time, there was always an inquest on Matthew's part before he would lodge his strong disapproval.

Darren was what I call a 'born student'. He had always achieved good marks at school, and had joined all the out of school activities he could fit into his busy life. These various activities included pet clubs and violin lessons but most of all in his early teenage years he had found ten pin bowling – or rather, it had found him. One of his tutors had run a bowling club at the school and Darren was eager to join. It soon became obvious he had a natural skill for this. His agility at the bowling alley was a sight to behold. Quickly we all jumped on the bandwagon and whenever we could, we would organise a family session. Looking back it must have been very frustrating for Darren because instead of being able to practise his skills he would spend all evening coaching each of us in turn. Even down to me who had no sense of balance or ball skills. He never gave up on me, though, and his patience always shone through. He was a good tutor and spent the much-needed time with all of us. On the tournament circuit he was unstoppable. He and two other young men from his group would usually walk away with most of the available trophies between them. They would travel throughout Britain and Holland with their school coach, attending numerous tournaments. Sometimes Keith would go along as an extra taxi if needed but most times Darren followed his hobby quite independently from the rest of the family. We went to school presentations and we were always very proud of his achievements.

On the academic field he was also doing very well. He studied hard and was very self-motivated about this. He had always had this burning thirst for knowledge. One time I remember this being very obvious was on a trip to London. We had spent a long time in The Natural History Museum. Karl had taken in everything he wanted to see and the others being younger were ready to go as soon as we said we were on our way. But we couldn't find Darren. He was just soaking it all up. Six o' clock arrived and one of the attendants had to ask us to leave as they were waiting to close. Darren could have gone on all night taking in new knowledge. He was always easy to go shopping with. I remember when we went shopping for his ski gear for his trip to Austria. We tried things on in shops and had a laugh more like two best friends than mother and son.

From an early age it was evident that he had quite a serious temper born out of frustration and this continued, as he got older. But it was always short lived and quickly he would be back to normal. He never held any grudges. I can recall one day when we were all out walking in the Lake District when Karl had made some comment that touched a raw nerve with Darren. You could cut the atmosphere with a knife. Darren just flared up and stormed off into the distance. But it was soon over and they were soon chatting again, as good friends; He and Karl were just so close. If there were a problem Darren would support Karl with undying loyalty, always.

After taking his GCSEs, Darren went on to Sixth Form College and completed his A-levels. Throughout this period he continued his bowling and went on to achieve many more awards in his league. For a period of time he was even running the club as the regular coach was absent from school due to a serious illness. They communicated by telephone and Darren did a very good job of holding the club together in his absence.

At eighteen, and after achieving his chosen A-levels, Darren announced he no longer wished to go on to university. This was a big surprise to us all as he had sailed through school and college achieving good results after the necessary studying. It was a surprise but it was not a shock. He had been at school since the age of four. Karl was already there, and clearly enjoying it, and Darren had been eager to follow him. He enjoyed everything about school life with the exception of school dinners. A very abrupt and frightening address about discipline and manners, delivered by the headteacher to the assembled new pupils in the dining hall on day one of his school life, had had a marked impression on him. He never went near that dining hall ever again.

It was not easy getting work straight away. Had he left school at sixteen, perhaps it would have been easier to get a job but here he was at eighteen with good qualifications. Employers could employ a sixteen-year-old at a cheaper rate than they needed to pay him. He was in a catch 22 situation. He was well qualified academically but at eighteen was two years behind others who were already in the workplace. He did temporary jobs and part-time jobs and eventually he went into trainee management. This went well for a while but he began to feel frustrated that he was not using his brain enough. He was not using the gifts he had, and was becoming disillusioned. We discussed with him the possibility of university. It was still not too late if this was a path he thought would be more productive. After careful thought, he decided he would go to university and secured himself a place in Hull for the following academic year on a business communications systems course. He carried on working right up to fresher's week and then we swung into action to help him. We packed with methodical precision;

I tried to think of everything he would need right down to plasters, sewing kit and powdered milk. He told me later how his friends always stopped off at his room if they needed a screwdriver, a needle or other items as they were sure he would have one. Even though he would be having his meals in the dining room he had a box of back-up food stock, which probably would have supported him and everyone on his floor. In fact it was not many weeks into term when he jokingly told me that his room was the first port of call if any student had a problem. He was almost always able to help out.

It was a bright sunny day when we packed the car ready for the journey to Hull. It was full to the brim, no spaces, just packed to capacity. We arrived in the university car park and the atmosphere was electric. There were groups of students all huddled together chatting and laughing. There were piles of boxes and rucksacks and suitcases everywhere, and there was music. It felt really special to be among all these young people. I was sad that Darren was moving away but excited for him at the endless new opportunities. I waited in the car while he went to enrol. This was a long process because of the large number of new students but eventually he arrived with a room number and a map of directions. We made endless trips from the car to his room carrying in clothes, books, and possessions. His collection of books had always been enormous – very much like Karl's. He was and still is an avid reader and it was nothing for him to read a couple of hardback novels in a week as well as his study books. He has never been able to part with books and often returns to a book a second time and even again if he has really enjoyed it. Eventually the car was empty and we were faced with a mountain of boxes in a small room with frugal storage space. I had visited other university rooms and this was no different. I knew we would manage somehow. Then he surprised me and said, "It's OK Mum, I can unpack this lot later."

That was my cue to be dismissed. OK, so I wanted to see him settled in, I wanted his induction to be smooth, but here was my outgoing Darren eager to go out in the university grounds in search of new friends. I knew at that point he was OK. He would not be sitting in his room fully unpacked and afraid to go out and make friends; here he was eager to get started. We hugged and I gave him instructions to ring home if he needed anything. I am sure I probably gave him lots of unnecessary instructions as well. He strolled out to the campus, turned and gave me a smile and a big wave. I knew he would be churning up inside but he was halfway to settling in already. I got out of the grounds and drove through the city. I'd joined the main road home before uncontrollable tears began to flow. I pulled in to a lay-by. I felt a little better so I set off again but took a further rest at the next service station. I knew I had to calm down before I finished the rest of my journey. I was upset that Darren was living a long way from home but deep down I knew he would take everything from this experience and put it to good use in the future. It was the right place for him to be at this stage of his life.

And so Matthew's primary years came to a close. It was a challenging and frustrating time for him and a challenging and frustrating time for me. I look back at this time now as the humming period. It had started just before he first went to school and continued until the latter end of his time at Rawcliffe. Why humming? Well, that's what he did on a very regular basis. If anybody told him off or said something he disagreed with – or if people simply seemed to be ignoring him – he would start to hum while displaying an air of nonchalance. It came over as a very rude and offensive gesture, indicating a lack of respect for those around him at the time. If anybody challenged his behaviour, the humming would just get louder. We found from experience that the only way to stop it was not to challenge it, but to walk away and leave him to it.

But despite his difficulties, he did enjoy his time at Rawcliffe and I remember feeling very proud watching him at the front of the hall, collecting his books at the leavers' service. It was a tradition that the trustees of the school donated some books to every leaving pupil. I had always enjoyed the leavers' service. It was a very emotional time for me, seeing children leave the school full of hope and optimism, but that particular year it was, of course, very special and extremely emotional. The secondary school now beckoned. How would he cope with it? None of us could know the answer to that.

Chapter 8

ADOLESCENCE AND FRUSTRATION

Matthew started his secondary school period in September 1992. From day one he found it very different from the primary school. In that environment he had felt safe. Although he had found it difficult to fit in to any of the various social groups that developed, he had enjoyed the structure that the school life had provided for him. His teacher had not understood him fully, but at least she had made the effort to help him and guide him, and this meant a lot to him. But now it all seemed very different. Firstly there were more pupils, many more pupils, and they all seemed to know the system at once. They seemed to know where to go and what to do. They very quickly formed themselves in to little social clusters, none of which seemed inviting to Matthew. And although there was a structure to each day, it appeared much more fragmented than he had been used to. There were different teachers for different subjects. How was Matthew going to cope with them all? But he settled down to the new challenge and, as with most children, he soon found the teachers he liked and the ones he didn't. He felt most comfortable with the teachers who stimulated him with their passion for their subject. When he encountered a wishy-washy person, he quickly turned off and became non-compliant, as he was frustrated. His behaviour pattern was much the same as we had seen over the past seven years but because he was now taller and more articulate, he was more noticeable. If he was given a project to do, if he was kept busy, he would conduct himself very positively and would be very single-minded in completing the task to the best of his ability. A stranger seeing him for the first time would admire his persistence and praise his diligence. But, of course, life isn't like that. There are long periods in between where as children we play and socialise and as adults, well.... we play and socialise. This is where Matthew found it hard. He didn't know how to play and socialise. And so now in the secondary school environment, where everyone was growing up fast and forming their social liaisons, he felt out of place, awkward, a misfit. That same stranger seeing him for the first time could easily see him as an oddball. He would come home every day, telling me how his day had gone. This was not just a brief report. It was very detailed with nothing hidden. He would tell me of his frustrations and often would take his frustrations out on me when I couldn't come up with a panacea to his problems. I found this very hard as I could listen but could not help. When I had no solution he would accuse me of not listening, of not understanding. It was as though he was living in his own little world. How could I possibly understand that concept?

When Keith came home, I would relay it all to him. But sometimes this was a few days later and it all seemed irrelevant. And yet it was there all the time. Keith could not always see it, because he too was in **his** own little world. The strange behaviour that Keith first started to display, as our courting turned in to our new life together, was still very prevalent. Now, Matthew's strange behaviour had moved in to a new phase. Not only did I have to witness his daily antics, he was now forcing me to analyse him and he was expecting me to make sense of it.

One confrontation with a teacher, which sticks in my memory, was when he was asked by the RE teacher to draw a picture of God.

"But I don't believe in God," was his reply.

"Don't argue," said the teacher, *"just draw a picture."*

"But how can I draw a picture of someone that I don't believe exists?"

Needless to say, he was forced to draw something in the end, which didn't really help their future relationship.

Tae Kwondo was the next extra-curricular activity that Matthew decided to try.

A group from Doncaster had just opened up a class in the village hall in neighbouring Cowick and he was eager to get involved. He found the co-ordination difficult but seemed to enjoy the challenge it posed for him and he persevered for quite a while. But, looking back, I would say that it was more than the challenge. I would say that it was also a link in his mind to another world, to another culture without realising it; he was probably laying the groundwork for what was to develop in his life, a love for travel, for investigating different lifestyles, for understanding the world and its wide variety of people and cultures. Whenever he got the opportunity to travel, he welcomed it with open arms. He would continuously encourage us to arrange trips around the country on a regular basis. He would often organise the trips himself and, with true military-style precision, would give us a list of instructions and timings.

Matthew had always been fascinated by water. He would always put his foot into water to test it whether it was a puddle or a stream or the sea. As a baby, on trips to the seaside, he would crawl out into the sea if we let him, and even the incoming waves did not put him off. On his own he would have drowned, as he just kept going deeper and deeper into the force. And as he grew bigger, if he came across a puddle, he could never walk round it, he had to jump in and splash himself all over. What we didn't yet know was that in later life this interest in water would develop into an obsession.

On one occasion when we were in the Dales we visited Aysgarth Falls. Matthew wanted to see where part of the film 'Robin Hood, Prince of Thieves' had been filmed. It was the scene where Robin meets Little John for the first time. They fight with staffs and Robin ends up in the water. We were walking on the pathway that runs alongside the falls. Matthew just looked into the water, which looked very calm and not too deep. He then looked at Keith and me and smiled. I had seen this look many times. It meant he was going to put his foot into the water; he could not resist it. I was horrified. Here we were at the top of the falls, not exactly Niagara, but had he fallen in there would have been a strong chance that he would not have come up again. I looked at Keith but it was too late to stop Matthew as in the next few seconds his foot was in the water and he was losing his balance. I was frozen because I could not stop this happening. Someone was obviously looking after him that day. Instead of falling forwards into the waterfall he fell backwards and on to the grass bank. I was so frightened that tears of joy flowed as he fell to the ground – the relief was immense. Keith and I both started to talk at the same time and we voiced how dangerous this act had been.

Matthew had no understanding of why we were so concerned. He just said. *"It's no big deal. I just put my foot in the water."*

I think he was trying to understand why we were coming down so hard on him. We explained that he had had a very close shave and could have lost his life.

"No," was his dismissive reply. *"You are exaggerating."*

To this day he still doesn't believe how lucky he was to escape as he did. We always had to have our eyes open and be alert. Just as he had been as a very young child, he was now a teenager who had very little perception of danger.

The Rector of Snaith, a friend of ours, organised a trip to Germany for a small group of young people during one of the school holidays and for Matthew this was a trip he could not miss. He thoroughly enjoyed it, but his obsessive behaviour did raise a few eyebrows. The rector told us afterwards that he was never in danger of losing Matthew. He could hear him at all times, talking loudly, shouting, bouncing a ball during a quiet period, the list was endless.

But the events that really gave Matthew a buzz during his years at the secondary school were the February excursions to the European ski slopes. He went on five of these trips and thoroughly enjoyed the experience of both the skiing and the foreign travel. Because these holidays were activity based, it was exactly what he needed. Even the social periods were organised and structured and left little room for him to get into difficulty.

However, fantastic as these adventures were for him, there was one country that evolved, in his mind, as the epitome of all he believed about the development of the human race. That country was the United States of America. He was determined to go there, particularly after my visit, and after I said that we couldn't afford to go, he decided to work his passage. He set about earning money in any way he could. His first job was as a newspaper delivery boy. He was very conscientious, always on time, never missing a day. But he had to give it up through frustration. The problem was that people would change their order, or cancel for a week due to holidays, or something else would be different. Despite being given a note, he couldn't get his head around these changes, and he would regularly end up with papers left at the end of the round or a lack of papers with several doors still ahead. Quite often, he would have to go and buy additional papers to complete the task.

The main source of his income came from a car washing service. He typed up some small notes advertising his venture and posted them around the village. This gave him a regular group of customers, and word of mouth and on-the-job discussion increased his clientele. In addition to the car washing he would do other odd jobs for people such as gardening. Each and every penny went into his bank account together with money that he received as a gift at Christmas and his birthday. He led a very frugal existence and worked hard and saved hard. He even got some income from Jonathan by charging him 20p every time he walked from the lounge to the kitchen to get him a drink of water. And Jonathan also became a good source of income for him when he came home from the pub after having a few too many. Matthew was always quite willing to clean up his sick or other mess and to keep it a secret from the parents, for a price. But he didn't always need paying for cleaning up. After family parties, inevitably, he was there tidying up, washing up and putting things back to normal. Not only did he like to see order restored as quickly as possible, but these actions seemed to help him by providing a structure and a clear role for him.

During the school holidays he was given the opportunity to spend a week at my sister Judith's house in Buckinghamshire. My father used to go to house-sit and look after the animals while my sister and her husband were away on holiday. Matthew had stayed there with his grandfather on a number of occasions. It was good for Matthew to get away from home for a few days and my Dad would always find Matthew plenty of jobs to do to keep him busy.

This particular year was different, however, as my sister and husband would be at home, as well as her two grown-up children and my mother. The house would be full of people. Part way through the week, I got a phone call from Judith asking me to come and collect him. She was unable to tolerate his behaviour any longer. A whole list of incidents was read out to me. I told Keith about it and his reaction was far from helpful. He felt that I should sort it out, but I couldn't. Going into school to sort out an incident there was one thing, but having to apologise for his behaviour to the family was another. I was just so upset I couldn't deal with it. I needed Keith's help on this one. But he said that he wasn't prepared to discuss the situation with Judith but more particularly with my mother. She had become very difficult to communicate with in recent times and he felt that it was probably her presence in the household that had contributed to Matthew's actions. He said he would sort it, but didn't want to discuss it with me anymore. He was very aggressive in his manner. His reaction surprised me and upset me, but I had to accept it. He spoke to Matthew on the phone about the incidents, but didn't communicate with me about the conversation except to say that he was collecting him the following day. The next morning he was off at the crack of dawn and they both arrived back in the afternoon.

When they had spoken on the phone the previous evening, Keith had told Matthew to be ready and dressed with all his things by six o'clock in the morning, to let himself out of the house and then to come on to the street where he would be waiting in the car. All went to plan except that Keith sent Matthew back to post a note through the letterbox to Judith giving some sort of reason for the clandestine operation. Matthew had also left his own note in the house to Judith. It was written from a very confused and disappointed young boy, and those emotions were expressed quite forcefully in the note. They had then made the journey to nearby Slough, to a house that Matthew had visited during the week with his granddad. It was his cousin's house and they had been doing various jobs there every day as part of a renovation process. One of the incidents that Judith had told me about related to Matthew apparently throwing soil over the garden fence, thereby polluting the water in the neighbour's swimming pool. Keith was determined that they should apologise for any inconvenience and, in fact, offered to rectify the problem there and then. Matthew explained to his cousin's neighbour that he had been turning the soil in the overgrown garden. He had found it very dry and dusty and was sorry that some of the soil had drifted on to his swimming pool. The neighbour, although upset by the incident, wasn't making a big thing of it, and was happy to accept the apology. Keith said to me that he had probably realised that it was not done in malice and that it was simply a consequence of the very dry state of the ground during that extremely hot summer of 1995 when reservoirs were empty and nationwide hosepipe bans had been imposed. During the journey home they discussed the other incidents but Matthew was very tight lipped about what had actually happened. He was really upset by the whole chain of events and totally confused by it all. I felt that Keith had handled it badly but he was adamant that he had done the right thing. His actions were to cause a rift between myself and my sister, which lasted for several years.

I had been worried before these events about Matthew's determination to get to the USA. I was even more worried now. Where would he go? Who would he stay with? We had talked about our nephew Glenn, and I knew that he and his family would welcome him but they lived too far out in the country for him to get about on his own. But, more importantly, his idiosyncrasies were also a problem. We were used to them and understood why they happened and could often anticipate and avoid trouble, but as this week's events had highlighted, other people didn't understand where he was coming from. I felt that he was too young and more importantly too naive to just thrust him loose and expect him to survive for two weeks in America on his own. But he had a determination and a passion to get there, come what may. Eventually I broached the subject with Keith. Matthew must be encouraged to go on his trip but it must be under our supervision. Keith's first question was how could we afford it. I suggested we get Matthew to postpone his impending trip until the following year while we save the money to accompany him. We talked to Matthew and while he was disappointed that he would not be visiting America that year, he was pleased that we had recognised his desire and accepted the situation. He knew that if had he gone on his own, he would have only been able to visit one area but now with us he would be able to go to several areas.

With renewed enthusiasm he made a plan, listing in detail what he intended to wear on the trip. Then, he set about saving additional money in order to buy an extensive selection of shirts, trousers, T-shirts and footwear. We planned what we could afford to save and we made lots of cuts in our spending. It worried me several times that we would not reach our required target but perseverance paid off. Keith and I discussed the possibility of including Jonathan in the trip, but the difficulty was that he had not saved as Matthew had. Therefore we would not only have to pay for him, but we would have to explain to Matthew that we were paying for him. We needn't have worried though, because Matthew was delighted to learn that Jonathan would be going with us.

The following August Jonathan, Matthew and Keith and I flew to California for our two week trip – one week in Los Angeles and one week in San Francisco. Keith and Matthew did the planning. Jonathan said he was happy to visit any of the places they wanted to go to as it was all a new experience but asked that Alcatraz be included in the itinerary. This was somewhere he had always wanted to visit since taking up a keen interest in murderers and their methods. For the first week we soaked up the atmosphere of Los Angeles, staying close to Disney Land. Unlike most of the people we know that have made a similar trip, a few hours round the amusement park was enough for all of us, and the three-day pass that we purchased at the beginning of the week became redundant after day one. The highlight for all of us was the magic of the Electric Light Parade, a procession of various Disney characters that snaked through the park in the warm summer evening. But Matthew did surprise us when he enthusiastically hurried over to the spot where 'Mickey Mouse' was signing his autograph. The pleasure on his face was a treat to see as he showed us the autograph in his book. It was the innocent smile of a young boy, but, of course, he was in a fifteen-year-old's body. When he could see our approval, he raced off again to get additional autographs from 'Donald Duck' and other 'personalities' who were there. We did the usual tourist trips such as Universal and Paramount studios, Griffith Park, a journey around the houses of the rich and famous in Beverly Hills and a window-shopping experience in Rodeo Drive. We visited Las Vegas but resisted the temptation to gamble vast amounts of money – not that we had any available money anyway. My father and his sister had made me promise to gamble $1 for each of them and so I decided to add $1 each for the five boys, plus Keith and myself, making a grand total of $9. Both Keith and Matthew refused to entertain the idea of gambling at all and so Jonathan and I shared the $9 and tried the machines. Needless to say it wasn't a long process. We had been told that the temperature would be unbearably hot during the day but it would plummet at night. It was obviously duff information as we recorded a staggering temperature of 100 degrees F sitting by the pool at our Holiday Inn Hotel at one o' clock in the morning. On the middle Saturday of our holiday we headed up the coastal route towards San Francisco.

Keith did all the driving. Matthew was not old enough and I just didn't have the courage to have a go. Jonathan did have his British driving licence but was disappointed to find that at eighteen he was too young to drive a hire car in America. But he was even more disappointed when he was unable to purchase an alcoholic drink. He did try but was rejected, so I took pity and volunteered to make the purchases on his behalf while the rest of the family all waited outside whichever liquor store we had chosen. We drove steadily up the coast and the journey lasted all day. The spectacular views of the Pacific that had been promised in the guidebook were disappointingly few and far between; a cloud haze persisted throughout much of the trip. When we arrived in San Francisco it was raining, it was dark and it was foggy. All these elements together with a challenging battle to understand the one-way systems in the city found us tired and disillusioned when we finally landed at our chosen hotel. And to add to this the receptionist was having great difficulty in understanding our rather blunt insistence that no, it wasn't OK to put Keith and me in a room on floor one and Matthew and Jonathan on the fourth floor. After a while our protest was listened to and although we did not get adjoining rooms we were at least all on the same floor.

The following day the sun was shining, our energy was restored and we set out to learn about the city in the bay. And the more we saw, the more we learned, the more we loved it. The highlight of the holiday for me was the vastness of Yosemite National Park. We rode on a small open truck with about fifty other people at midnight under the glare of a full moon, keeping warm with a hot drink and a blanket and listening to the distant cries of wolves and bears and other animals, punctuated by the occasional human sound of mountaineers scaling the sheer tree-lined precipice, by torchlight, some two miles away. But I also felt very comfortable in San Francisco and I know that the three of them had the same feeling. Once again we visited all the well-known attractions including the little cable cars and Jonathan did get his trip to Alcatraz. I found it a very moving experience as we walked slowly around the prison being guided by a personal Walkman machine. The feeling of horror standing in the prison cells, which were no bigger than six feet by six feet. The claustrophobia and the stench in those cells must have been terrific. The view from the prison dining room window was breathtaking. You could see all the wonderful buildings – the small, medium and skyscrapers. Glass, brick and metal – take your pick – all types of architecture could be seen. This must have been punishment enough for the inmates to see this beautiful skyline, particularly as, with the exception of meals and an hour each day if permitted, the rest of the time they were locked up in a tiny cell.

I know that one of the highlights for both Keith and Matthew was to cycle across the Golden Gate Bridge. They hired the bikes for a few hours and took in as much as they could. Jonathan and I went at a more leisurely pace on that day, mainly just strolling about and people watching on the boardwalk. For Matthew I know that this, his first visit to the States, lived up to his expectations. It certainly reinforced his desire to see more of the country and eventually, possibly, to settle there.

The holiday was a great bonding experience for us all but it also threw up some gigantic problems. One of Matthew's habits at this time was grinding his teeth. It was something he did constantly throughout the day. It didn't disappear on this holiday despite the fact that he was enjoying the trip and learning so much about American culture. And he also developed a habit for twisting strands of his hair around his index finger and pulling at the roots, a habit he would carry forward in to his adult years.

On any holiday, of course, plans that are made often have to be changed at the last minute. Matthew struggled to cope with this. The itinerary had been written and it had to be adhered to. Any slight change in plan confused him and brought on a discussion that was always very heated. Several times on this trip he accused us of doing things that were not in the schedule and perceived that we were changing the itinerary in favour of someone else's choice. The reality was we fitted in everything we had planned but sometimes because of things beyond our control we had to juggle with the timing or duration of an outing. At several points we had long talks with Matthew who was getting very worked up about any slight change. It had to be *the plan* or nothing for him. He had no conception of us trying to move things to fit everything in and to keep all four of us happy at the same time. Psychologically, I found it a very difficult holiday. I was always afraid to state what we were about to do each day in case there was a change and Matthew's wrath would be upon me. I am like his partner or his best friend. When you fall down in the world or all goes wrong, who do you take it out on? Your nearest and dearest – it's human nature. You know that most times they will support you and be there for you, and this was no exception. Jonathan had been my calming influence both at home and now on this holiday. Keith did not create any confrontations as Matthew did but he also had a need to stick to the schedule and if it meant driving an extra 100 miles that day that is exactly what we did, even though it might be very late at night. We had to be in the right place on the day planned. I regularly pointed out that we were not on a public tour and could please ourselves with what we did. Sometimes the travelling was quite gruelling just so that Keith could keep to his targets. Heated discussions with Matthew were getting more frequent and were happening sometimes several times each day. If I could have waved a magic wand I would have transported us all home to Britain at those times. I found these constant confrontations very stressful as I was trying to keep this an enjoyable holiday for all, and indeed overall it was, and we all have some fantastic memories from the visit.

What it did demonstrate to Keith and me was that Matthew's daily struggle to understand the world was constant. It did not go away just because we were on holiday. In fact new situations could often magnify the problems. We found out later that, although he thoroughly enjoyed the holiday, it was a huge struggle for him, and obsessive thoughts were a constant threat to his stability.

His adolescence period was peppered with a number of incidents, which were all, in some way, related to misunderstanding. Matthew would make a decision about something and would act in a certain way. But time and again the way he chose was not perceived to be the 'correct way' by other people. He had misunderstood their intentions or expectations and they had misunderstood his reasoning, and in doing so branded him as odd, out of step, weird. This left him frustrated and confused. He was subjected to bullying on many occasions because he was an easy target.

But for Matthew the most damaging reactions came not from his peers, but from a number of teachers and other adults who not only misunderstood him, but took the decision to isolate him by branding him with labels such as 'troublemaker' and 'an undesirable'. Because he would stick to his guns even if he was out of step with normal behaviour, he was seen as arrogant and rude.

On one particular occasion, Matthew had been accused of inappropriate behaviour. He had denied the charge and was duly forced to stay confined in the teacher's room until he changed his plea. When he came home he was heartbroken that he had told a lie. After several hours of trying to comfort him, it became evident that he was innocent. He had, in fact, confessed to the teacher so that he could be released. He didn't see any other way out of the dilemma and had, quite simply, told a lie in order to escape the confinement. Matthew had a number of difficulties with that particular member of staff, and I was called into school on several occasions for an update on my son's latest misdemeanours. But this was not the only teacher he had problems with. His form tutor found his behaviour quite intolerable and, after consultation with me, it was decided to switch him in to a different form group with a different teacher. His new teacher was of a stronger personality and Matthew had respect for him. This new situation worked well.

Matthew had always been very frugal and careful with money, but he had also been very generous where charities were concerned. He had supported a number of causes, most notably a collection in support of a local young girl who was suffering from a serious life-threatening disease. A trip to a special hospital in the USA for an operation was the only answer; Also, and while still at primary school, he and a friend had organised a jumble sale at the top of our drive, raising money for the NSPCC. So it was with surprise that we heard his reaction to a collection at school for the sixteen primary school children murdered at Dunblane in March 1996. He refused to contribute.

"Money won't bring those children back to their parents," he said. He was told that he was the only child who had not contributed, but he wouldn't change his mind. And it is incidents like this that gave him the reputation of being a rebel. Another notable example was the school's policy of having a non-uniform day in support of Comic Relief. All the pupils thought it was a great hoot to be able to ditch the dreaded uniform even if it was only for a day; But not Matthew. No, to him school meant wearing a uniform. He could see no logical reason for following the crowd. Being seen as the odd one out didn't faze him. To him, they were the odd ones out. Out of 750 pupils only two wore the school uniform on that day. The other boy had simply forgotten

and spent all day feeling embarrassed. Matthew, however, felt proudly independent.

His individuality and stubbornness would often bring him great pride in himself. A good example comes from a quiz that a teacher at the school had put together for the pupils. The quiz was made up of questions about the school itself and the winner would receive a prize of £25. When it was announced, he was determined that he would win it. He lost no time in getting hold of an entry form and his first port of call was Mr Lawrence. He was the former headteacher of the school, now retired, and they knew each other from church activities. Mr Lawrence was very helpful in supplying answers to a large number of the questions. Matthew then quickly worked out the others by 'walking' the school buildings looking for the clues. His completed entry was handed in before many of his fellow pupils had even decided whether to bother participating. He was confident that he would win and he kept badgering the organising teacher for the results. As with most competitions, there was a closing date for entries, but because Matthew's sheet had been returned so quickly, he found it frustrating that he had to wait so long for the decision. Eventually the results were announced to the school. In third place... in second place... and the winner is … Matthew Greenwood. He was number one. He was over the moon and, of course, we were as well.

Our involvement with the church had, by now, reached a natural conclusion. What had started, back in 1981 as a re-affirmation of our beliefs and a subconscious need to establish our roots in our newly found community had travelled through a variety of experiences and had now left both Keith and myself with a feeling of emptiness. It was, for both of us, a feeling that the return on the investment was no longer an attractive option.

There had been some memorable events, most notably our blessing in church for our marriage, which had been a civil ceremony at Bradford registry office six years earlier. Then there was the visit to Snaith of a group of pilgrims from St Laurence Church Northfield Birmingham who, in celebrating their church's 900th birthday, were visiting other St Laurence's churches across the country. There was the arrival on a canal barge at nearby Rawcliffe Bridge of the Archbishop of Sheffield, with our boys playing and wresting with him after all the formalities were over.

But a visit that touched all of us, and Matthew in particular, was a group of some 100 young children from Uganda who had been orphaned as a result of wars and civil unrest in that country. They had been formed into a choir and were on a singing trip around Europe. Two of the boys, Moses and Farouk, stayed with us, together with one of the adults in the party, Emmanuel. The youngsters were full of energy and we had some great fun with them over the five nights they were with us. They slept in Jonathan's room and on one of the walls there was a poster of James Dean. Farouk spotted the poster and asked if he was a Christian. After hesitating momentarily, I replied *"Yes, I believe so."*

His reply shocked and intrigued both Matthew and me. *"No, he can't be,"* he said. *"He has a cigarette in his mouth."*

There was no credible answer that I could possibly give.

We indulged them with games and bible stories while Emmanuel was out with the other adults but we all had to quickly clear everything away and make it appear like a normal child/babysitter arrangement when we heard him insert the key that we had loaned him, into the door. When we eventually had to say goodbye to them, it was a real tearjerker.

We attended special services at various places, most dramatically at Doncaster Racecourse where thousands of people had congregated to celebrate Pentecost.

There was the magazine, and the church council, and the endless round of garden parties and other sales, all of which saw us all heavily involved at every stage. All five sons had a role to play when we staged our first flower festival in church. Karl and Darren worked tirelessly all day on the Friday, fetching and carrying for the flower arrangers who were busy preparing their arrangements. There were lots of activities over many years, which gave us enormous pleasure, but the biggest benefit was our introduction to so many wonderful people, all with their own stories to tell, all with their own peaks and troughs. Some of those people have moved away and we have lost touch, some have sadly departed, but many are still our friends today.

But that warmth, the magnet that drew us and kept us involved with the church community for so long, was no longer there for either of us for some inexplicable reason. For the boys it was a time of growing up and they had been involved in church life because we were involved. When they reached an age of independence they pulled away as young people often do. But for Keith and me it was just an evolutionary process.

And so time moved on, and I was more heavily involved with both the governorship at my school and as a member of the school committee at Matthew's school. In both cases it led inevitably to involvement with fundraising events. At all these occasions Matthew's commitment was outstanding. He would work tirelessly to ensure that we got the maximum benefit from each event.

But now here we were with Matthew, sixteen-years-old and struggling to fit in to a society he didn't understand. Still with the same difficulties he had developed at an early age but now with them compounded by the hormones of adolescence. Unfortunately, my enforced visits to school were increasing. The last straw came when I was summoned to see the headteacher regarding an alleged incident of serious inappropriate behaviour. I went home from that meeting feeling useless and ineffectual. What was the problem? Perhaps it wasn't Matthew after all, perhaps it was me. Other people had said as much over the years – school staff, doctors, friends, family. They may not all have said it, but you could read it in their body language.

"What that child needs is a good spanking!"

But Keith and I knew that somewhere out there, there was an answer.

This latest incident highlighted that the stress was getting to me. I really needed Keith's help. No longer could I cope with him keeping a safe distance both physically and psychologically. He would always listen and offer advice, which was invariably good advice, but I needed more, I needed a more hands-on approach, I needed his full involvement. He was very concerned when I told him about today's incident and, despite his workload, assured me that he was committed to supporting me and more importantly Matthew. He promised he would be there for him in the future.

But despite his many problems Matthew continued to surprise us with special treats that he planned and organised for us. From a young age he had loved birthday celebrations. He always liked to be in charge. He would spend hours colouring posters he had drawn of letters spelling out happy birthday. He would blow up balloons and trim both the walls and the table. Everyone appreciated his hard work and he always made these occasions special. He liked to be involved in the choice of food and would also make menus and place names for everyone.

When it was my fiftieth birthday I opened the card that he had sent to me. Inside was a fax message. It was a confirmation of a booking he had made for two rooms, for one night at the Hilton Hotel in Berlin. We had already promised to take him to Germany for a week in August in recognition of the enormous effort he had put into revising for his GCSEs. We had planned to stay in Cologne on our first night and then travel on to Berlin on the Saturday. So Matthew had saved hard once again and was treating me to a special night during our trip.

The weekend of my birthday he and Keith had invited our family to join us, our sons, their grandparents and my aunt and my cousin Caroline who is also my Goddaughter. We had lots of fun and it was a very good party. Keith and Matthew had been up at the crack of dawn cooking and putting up trimmings. They had shared the cooking between them and also planned the menu together.

The following morning started as normal but then I was told to get dressed as we were going out. I was given an approximate time to be ready. All was quiet in the house. I realised I was the only inhabitant; Keith and Matthew had obviously disappeared somewhere. They had told me to give Jonathan a ring and ask him to come home, as he had stayed at his friend's the night before. He was as surprised as me when a minibus pulled into our drive. Keith and Matthew's faces were a picture with their big beaming smiles. I was told no more than to get into the minibus.

"*Where are we going?*" I asked.

"*You'll see,*" was the answer, with no more information than that. We drove to our first destination in Castleford, where Darren, Richard and his girlfriend Sarah all climbed into the bus and hugged me and wished me happy birthday. Still no wiser, we continued on our journey. Next we arrived at the flat of Karl and his partner Kath. I was ushered out of the bus by Kath to look at their new edition, a rabbit that they had adopted and that lived out on the patio and looked like a gorgeous ball of brown fluff. Back into the bus and after some more happy birthday wishes, we were on our way. I was racking my brain to think why we were all travelling together and where we could be going. Then, thirty minutes later, we arrived at the Cedar Court Hotel in Bradford. We were having a family meal as Keith had wanted us all to be together with none of our sons having to drive. That is why he had secretly hired a minibus. This reminded me of the school annual trips I used to go on. I could look out of the window at a perspective you were unable to enjoy from a car seat. The meal was superb and the conversation even better. As the meal was drawing to a close the waiter brought out a very distinctive birthday cake that Keith and Matthew had ordered from our favourite cake shop in Selby. On the top of the cake was an icing covered model that represented me as a harassed school secretary. It was wonderful, and although I couldn't sample the cake due to my gluten-free diet, the rest of the family tucked in ravenously.

When our visit to Germany came round we were eager to explore Berlin. We soon found our way into the city but it took a further three hours to get to the Hilton Hotel. Not only was it full of people enjoying a bank holiday carnival, but most of the city was taken up by one-way traffic and the worst thing of all was that there was an enormous amount of building work going on. New pipes were being laid all over the city and scaffolding was everywhere. It was all part of transforming Berlin in preparation for its re-instatement as the capital of a united Germany. After many dead end and one-way streets, we finally got to our destination. The hotel was beautiful inside and despite being right in the city centre, at night-time the view from the dining room was stunning. The scenes of the floodlit churches and old buildings were breathtaking. We had a lot of fun on this trip, too. Matthew used his German language skills on many occasions, especially when it came to finding accommodation for us. Our final night of the trip was in Brussels. Matthew booked us in to an Ibis Hotel and asked for a family room. We entered the bedroom and set down our suitcases. Something was wrong. One double bed but there was no sign of a single one. We looked everywhere, under the double bed, in the wardrobe, even in the bathroom. Keith was shouting, *"Come out, come out wherever you are."* Matthew suddenly looked up and then looked at both of us. *"You haven't spotted it have you?"*

We then saw a sight we had never seen before or witnessed since. About four feet above the double bed was a single pull down bed flat to the wall. We had seen fold down beds before, but this was one with a difference. It ran at right angles across our bed and he had to stand between us to get up into it.

"*How does this work?*" said Matthew. "*If I roll out of bed in the night I will crush you both.*"

We all got ready for retiring but we had the giggles for ages and it was another hour before we were able to settle down to sleep.

Despite having lots of laughs on this trip it did have a very serious side. On an evening Matthew often wanted to have deep meaningful conversations about the problems he was experiencing with his thoughts, and whereas I would always reciprocate and join in, Keith would stay quiet or reply abruptly creating an atmosphere. It was very frustrating for Matthew. These were the opportunities when we were together that he could relax and put the world to rights as lots of young people do. Keith, on the other hand, also wanted to relax and in an evening was not going to be bogged down by conversation, which would challenge him. As I tried to draw him into the conversation to make more of a balance he would back off or be awkward. This often created an atmosphere and left Matthew in a state of wondering how he would ever be able to communicate better if we were not fully prepared to sit and talk at length with him.

Mine was not the only fiftieth birthday to have had a surprise element to it. Keith had turned fifty the previous November and Matthew had wanted to make it special. When he had told me what he was planning, a night in a luxury local hotel, it came as no surprise that he had chosen Oulton Hall, where he had done his work placement from school. He had enjoyed his time there and the manager had praised his hard work and diligence.

He asked me to go with him to check out all the suites and then he booked the Lyttondale Suite for the night of Keith's birthday for the three of us. He also booked a meal in the dining room for the same evening.

When Saturday arrived we went to the cinema in the afternoon. Matthew did not want Keith to be doing any jobs at home, and so planned for him to relax. After we left the cinema I drove to the hotel. We started to get out of the car and Keith said, "*Oh, this is a lovely surprise,*" as he thought we had just arrived for a meal. Matthew answered, *"It will be,"* as he took two suitcases out of the boot. Keith was bewildered and it took him a little while to realise we were here to stay and not just having a meal. We had a wonderful time, swimming, walking, dining and generally relaxing together. Back at home on Monday morning, the actual day of his birthday; complete with all his birthday cards and presents, Matthew presented Keith with a mountain bike. He'd also bought one for himself so that they could go out together to cycle and keep fit. That evening was another trip to a restaurant with all the family to celebrate Keith's birthday together.

Matthew has always been a traveller and just loves new experiences. But at this time of his life he was finding that special outings, while creating fun and enjoyment for him, usually also threw up other challenges. New situations proved difficult for him even when he had been looking forward to the experience. One such time was when we had taken him, together with Jonathan and his girlfriend Beccy, to stay in London so that we could take them all to Drury Lane Theatre to see Miss Saigon. This was to celebrate Matthew's sixteenth birthday. Keith and I had enjoyed it several years before and Matthew had always expressed a wish to see it. Although it was clear that he was enjoying the show, there were times when he seemed a little distant. On our return home he was obviously upset about something. He said he had enjoyed his trip away, but the main event that he had been excited about, the visit to the theatre, had been spoilt for him. He started to tell me that all the time he was watching the action on the stage, he had images of one of his teachers in his mind. He had encountered problems with him that week and had become quite upset about it. We had thought that it was now behind him, but obviously it wasn't. He also said that he felt guilty that we had taken him to see Miss Saigon as a treat and that he had spoilt it by not enjoying it, all thanks to these thoughts running through his head. I tried to explain to him that nothing in life was ever perfect. Sometimes when we look forward to something for a long time, the reality may not live up to our expectations, and we may be a little disappointed. I didn't really help because he felt that I didn't really understand. It wasn't the musical that had been a letdown – far from it. It was his thoughts that had been the problem. I related to him an experience when we had taken him to Harrogate the previous year.

We had visited a theatre to be part of the studio audience during the recording of a radio comedy programme called 'I'm Sorry, I Haven't a Clue'. We were near the front of the theatre and had a very good view of the stage. Suddenly I saw Matthew twitch his nose like a rabbit several times, then push his lips out as far as he could, followed by him tilting his chin towards the ceiling.. He would then settle back to watch the show, but every few minutes would repeat this cycle. I must admit it did worry me that we were right in front of the stage and that, Matthew being over six feet in height, would be seen by all. I thought someone might make a fuss and comment but luckily no one did.

Now, one year later, he was telling me that his obsessive thoughts and obsessive compulsions left him feeling enslaved and powerless and that they probably caused the contortions. I told him that when I had pointed it out to him, he had stopped for a few minutes, but then it had returned, probably because he couldn't control it. He also told me about his paper round, when he was thirteen. He said that was probably his first experience of obsessive thoughts. Every morning he had a recurring image of pulling a knife out of my chest. Try as he may, he couldn't shake the images from his mind. Eventually the thoughts disappeared, but he was still very worried. It took many years before he realised it was due to him subconsciously wanting to protect me and getting upset if he felt I was vulnerable. In hindsight, it was no wonder he had problems with which door to put the papers through, particularly as the list was constantly changing. He could do the round from memory but the regular visions in his head made him forget to look and see if there were any changes.

Because of these obsessive thoughts, he had some very troubled times and was unable to concentrate fully throughout much of his secondary school life. He didn't socialise much during his secondary school years and, although I would have liked to see him with more friends, I was actually quite relieved that he didn't go out much. I always had a fear at that time that he would disappear. He seemed very vulnerable and I felt that someone with ill intentions could have easily led him astray. Or he may even have just decided to go off to London, on his own. So, I was always very uneasy when he was out. One day in particular had me extremely worried. He had been missing for hours. I was frantic. Where could he be? Fortunately Keith was home and he went off round the town looking for him. Panic over! Matthew and a friend had been playing in an old building close to the high street. Well. Playing is the wrong word. They were planning to turn the old building into a shop and had spent all day working out the logistics of the exercise. It was the same building which would later see him in extreme pain when a piece of glass pierced the sole of his shoe and embedded itself in his foot. He simply hopped all the way home, a distance of about a mile, and calmly told me what had happened. No drama, no complaints of pain, just a matter of fact report. A few weeks later he had another incident with his feet. After school one day, he and the same school friend walked into the village together on their way home. They started to be silly, jumping about and pushing each other. Matthew suddenly kicked one leg in the air and his shoe went flying into the distance, and out of sight. He came home to tell me and seemed totally unaware of any pain in his shoeless foot. He had walked on gravel, stones and pavement and seemed unaware of any discomfort. His mission was to tell me that he had lost his shoe. He put on some trainers and we returned together to the spot where he had been messing about. How could it have just disappeared? Was it stuck in one of the many trees inside the nearby walled garden? It was obvious we were not going to find the shoe in this alley. We would have to look in the garden beyond the wall. I knocked on the door and explained our plight. The lady inside smiled and asked us to come through and that she would help us to look. We searched and searched for fifteen minutes but it was in vain. This was going to be an expensive lesson for Matthew to learn – the price of a new pair of leather shoes. And although we wouldn't expect him to pay, he had somewhat of an obsession about money and was already quite critical when we bought anything that he didn't consider to be necessary. Suddenly, as we were on our way out of the garden, a big beaming smile appeared on his face and the missing shoe was in his hand. He was delighted. It was as if he had been given a surprise present. The mystery was now solved. The shoe had been hiding just behind an open water butt. Fortunately it had not fallen in, or it would have been ruined. Matthew always responded the same way whenever anything was lost. He would become very upset and confused, but that feeling didn't kick in until it was virtually certain that the item was lost. Like this shoe, when he came to tell me, he was grinning, because he felt that we would easily find it.

When it looked as though we wouldn't, that's when his mood changed. But now he was happy as he had retrieved his shoe. It was lost no more.

Matthew's obsession with money also extended to insurance. And this was heightened following a burglary at our home. Someone had broken the glass in the side door, climbed through the opening and then searched through cupboards and drawers. It was suspected that they were looking for cash, jewellery and other easily disposable items in order to generate money for drugs, as these were the only things that were taken. Matthew had counted the loose cash in my desk only the previous evening so he was able to be accurate when we started to complete the insurance claiming documentation: £73. And after helping us to complete the forms, he took charge of things, insisting that we carry out a full itinerary of our possessions to ensure that we were fully insured. He was also very persistent in ensuring that Keith had the door replaced with a solid one and also arranged for a burglar alarm to be fitted.

They say that you often have to wait for a generation to change before you can see any progress in human co-existence. The older generation gets too entrenched in ideology and past beliefs. The new generation attacks a problem with an open mind and youthful enthusiasm. Well, we had to wait for such a change to occur with our local doctors before we could get the help we needed. Our new and youthful GP actually listened to me when I poured out my tales of woe and my distress at my inability to understand my youngest son's behaviour. It was so obvious to him that it wasn't me that needed to visit a psychiatrist. It was Matthew. At last, someone was listening. But we would be back.

Appointment after appointment came round and we visited one professional after another. We got nowhere. Matthew was a highly intelligent young man and he could see right through their questions and knew that they had no idea how to help him. Eventually we arrived for an appointment at a place called The Retreat in York. We had heard some encouraging reports about a particular psychiatrist there. Keith had taken some time off work so that the three of us could attend the appointment. The Georgian building looked severe and harsh as we approached. Once inside, we saw much the same. The corridors were dark and dreary; the furniture looked old and well-used and there was a sense of despair in the air. After announcing our arrival at the reception desk, we were given directions to the waiting area. We headed down one of the corridors, passing through two enormous thick wooden doors that creaked noisily as they returned to the closed position. At every corner there was a chair and on every chair there was a patient. Without exception they would be staring into space and were apparently totally unaware of our presence. The place was generally quiet, as you would expect in a hospital building, but every now and then the air was pierced by involuntary shouts and screeches – presumably from patients. These were people with serious problems of the mind. Was this really the place we'd get help for Matthew? Our doubts were increased when we were told that the psychiatrist that we had come to see was not at work as he was suffering from depression. Wonderful! His locum arrived and Matthew was shown into his office. We carried on thumbing through the faded Reader's Digests that adorned the fake Regency table. After about thirty minutes we were summoned to the consulting room to be part of the therapy. We listened, we answered questions, we listened again, but at the end of the hour's session we knew we hadn't progressed. Matthew hadn't given the answers he had expected and it threw him. He said he didn't think he could help because Matthew was not co-operating. Clearly he didn't understand how this young man's brain was working. He didn't know how to unlock him. As Matthew said later *"He was barking up the wrong tree."*

We didn't say a lot to each other for the next hour. Keith drove to the village of Naburn where we strolled beside the River Ouse in order to think and chat and decide on our next move. Matthew was clearly getting more and more frustrated as we did the rounds but he trusted us. He knew we were doing our best to try to discover why he did things and thought things in the way he did. We didn't really have an immediate plan, except to carry on our research to try and find the answer. We didn't have long to wait. I was scanning a women's magazine one day when I came across a letter from a reader and in turn a reply from a professor. The reader described her son's behaviour and the reply suggested that she took a particular course of action. I read it again and again and again. I couldn't believe it. She could have been describing Matthew rather than her own son. So what was the advice from the professor? Well I don't know if that reader took his advice, but we certainly did, and so began a whole new chapter in our lives.

Chapter 9

THE DIAGNOSIS

So what was the advice from the professor to the magazine reader? Well, it was simple enough. Talk to your family doctor about Asperger syndrome. He explained in the article that this was a condition linked to autism and referred to children who had difficulty in communicating and fitting into the normal pattern of society.

Yes, Matthew fitted the description. However, it was devastating to think that our son had a syndrome; that he was not normal, and yet, I knew instinctively that this was the answer that I had been searching for all along. I knew his behaviour was not due to him being spoilt as the youngest of five by ineffective parents as the world had been telling us for sixteen years. I felt sure that it had to be something medical and that once we knew what it was, we could begin to tackle it. Although the professor hadn't directed his advice towards me personally, I took it, and confronted our GP with it. He listened carefully but admitted he hadn't heard about Asperger; I simply couldn't understand how he could not have heard about this condition. But he wasn't dismissive and he promised to look into it and, true to his word, he came back to me with more information.

The human condition known as autism was first recognised in the 1940s. It referred to people who clearly had a noticeable degree of difficulty in communication.

In 1946, Hans Asperger, an Austrian pediatrician, first wrote his theory that there were many children in the world who also had a difficulty in communication, but unlike autistic people their difficulty was often masked by higher intelligence and apparently 'normal' appearance. In 1962, The National Autistic Society was formed by a group of concerned parents trying desperately to help their children to cope with every day life. Sadly it was to take another thirty years before anyone in the UK picked up on Hans Asperger's research and it wasn't recognised as a separate condition until 1994.

Now I understood how it was possible for the doctor to have not known about Asperger syndrome. It was only three years earlier that it had been recognised. He was intrigued by the information he had unearthed and keen to help us. He had genuinely shared my frustration over the past months in trying to find an answer to our son's strange behaviour. The next logical step was to go back down the psychiatry route but I didn't feel comfortable re-visiting any of the specialists that we had seen up to now and felt that it had to be somebody new, and I was confident that Matthew would welcome this. They say that a little knowledge is a dangerous thing and that is what we found. Three consecutive psychiatrist appointments took us exactly nowhere. Two of the professionals had little or no knowledge about Asperger syndrome and the third one became quite aggressive towards us when he realised that we knew far more than he did about the subject. I had continued to find out all I could about this condition and my knowledge and understanding was growing. Keith, had been a little sceptical when I first found the article, but was now fully on board with my approach. We could have been wrong about this, of course – we realised that these guys were experts in their field and yet instinct told me that we were right. So it was back to our friendly practitioner again, armed with more knowledge and even more determination to succeed. He was noticeably frustrated and couldn't believe that there was no-one out there able to help, but it did seem that that was the case, at least within the scope of the NHS. Fortunately Keith had a private healthcare package with his company so we made contact with them. Did they know of anyone who understood this condition? Initially we received the same unhelpful replies to our questions, but persistence paid off and eventually they came up with a name. I rang up and made an appointment.

By this time Matthew had left the secondary school and was about to start at Selby College. When he first went to the school his goal had been to complete five years of 100% attendance. Although he had difficulties at school, he couldn't understand how anybody would not want to go and learn things. His first year went according to plan but then he had a setback in year two. He was out on the school field participating in a football game, which was not one of his favourite pursuits. He suffered a severe injury to his eyes as the ball hit him full in the face and he was hospitalised for four days. I stayed with him throughout this time because he had burst blood vessels in his eye. The nursing staff kept him under observation because of the risk of haemorrhage. During this time he was unable to read or watch television so we told each other stories all the time. I was concerned for him, but he was more upset by the fact that his attendance record would be broken than by the injury itself. Year three was a tough year as his mind started to play tricks. An added complication was migraine. At the start of the year he would go into school to get his mark for the day, even though his head was throbbing. He would then come home to lie-down, in the hope that it would clear by lunchtime, allowing him to attend a full afternoon session. It usually worked, but towards the end of the year the migraine attacks were getting stronger and more persistent and he felt less inclined to fight them, particularly as the incentive of a clean five year record was no longer there. When he returned to school in year four he had a change of heart and decided to set himself a new goal of 100% attendance in the last two years of his school career. This he achieved, making a grand total of three absence-free years.

He had found the final year quite challenging because of the amount of unsupervised work required to pass the GCSE exams he needed. He found great difficulty in organising himself to study or carry out projects. Working at school after a task had been set was smooth sailing, but left to sort it out for himself and he struggled. Keith went to special maths lessons at the school one evening a week in order to enable him to help Matthew in his studying. He also assisted him with a number of other projects, which formed part of his home study brief. It paid off and although he didn't get all the results he needed, what he did get proved to be enough to take him to the next stage of his academic development.

The day of the appointment arrived. It was exactly one month after our last visit to our doctor. It was ten minutes to ten and the three of us were in Sheffield. The location had obviously been a rather grand detached house in its former days but it had been converted into offices and now formed part of the University of Sheffield's research department. We were directed up a narrow staircase to a tiny waiting room on the first floor. At precisely ten o'clock the receptionist collected us and we were shown into an office, which was full of character and charm, but at the same time was very business-focused. Professor Digby Tantam greeted us with a beaming smile, which was made more evident as it was surrounded by a large, bushy, jet-black beard. Although quite relaxed in his manner, he soon got to the point by asking a few well-chosen questions about why we were there. He had received a very persuasive letter from our doctor – now he needed to hear it from us. He then moved quickly to a series of questions directed at Matthew. Then there were more questions for both Keith and myself. The consultation lasted about two hours and then we were asked to go to the waiting room. Five minutes later he declared that he had completed his assessment and now needed to study what he had heard and consult with a colleague before he could give us the benefit of his experience. We all came away with mixed feelings. It was different from all the previous encounters with professor-type people we had experienced. On all those occasions we had come away with no follow up, no next step in sight. With this one, at least he had said we would be invited back when he had reached a conclusion.

Once on our own, Keith and I discussed the appointment in great detail. We were both of the same opinion. He hadn't really heard the full story. He couldn't possibly understand all the heartaches and frustrations from a brief interview. The major factor, we both felt, had to be Matthew's performance in the interview. How had he dealt with the professor's questions for instance? If that was his basis for determining whether or not Matthew suffered from Asperger syndrome, we feared his answer would be no. This caused us to dig deep into our hearts again. Surely any parent would want a doctor to say no, your child doesn't have a medical condition which renders him abnormal. And yet here we were getting upset because he might do just that. We wanted the opposite. Could this be right? We agonised over these questions and in the end decided we had to, at least, ensure that the professor had all the facts at his disposal, and we had to act quickly. So the two of us sat down together and for the first time we put everything on paper. Everything that had happened during Matthew's life that appeared to be less than normal. We filled six A4 pages – too much we thought and perhaps with too many negatives. So the six pages became three pages, which we divided between strengths and difficulties. I hurriedly addressed the envelope to Professor Tantam and rushed to the village to catch the last post. I can remember clearly putting my hand into the gaping mouth of the post box but still clasping the letter for several seconds before making the final decision to release it. The next week we received details of a follow-up appointment.

There we were there again in that tiny waiting room on the first floor of the house in Sheffield. This time he firstly saw Matthew on his own, then me and Keith without Matthew and finally all three of us together. My heart was pounding as he looked at his notes and then momentarily gave eye contact to each of us in turn and then returning his gaze to his notes he began his summary. The statement,

"*I can confirm Asperger syndrome,*" was lost somewhere in a whole host of much longer, more complicated words, of which I have no recollection. Keith and I had fought so long for this day and now the fight was over. I came away from that meeting feeling that at long last someone in authority had acknowledged what I had believed all these years. And yet what Professor Tantam wasn't able to give us was a clear way forward. He had told us it was broken but couldn't help us when we asked how do we mend it. We would come to realise that it couldn't actually be mended. All you could do was to learn how to manage it better. In some ways it felt like a bereavement. On that day we lost our little badly behaved boy. We now had a bright sixteen-year-old with a label and a whole new set of needs and difficulties and it was quite frightening. It was Matthew's reaction to this turn of events which really surprised and confused me. All the way through he had trusted us as we went from one appointment to the next and even when we started to talk about the possibility of his problem being related to autism, he seemed to trust us. But when it came to the crunch, he wasn't able to accept the diagnosis – naturally he didn't want to be labelled.

As our intake of literature regarding this subject increased, both Keith and I poured over the details with interest and amazement. Matthew, however, refused to show an interest, dismissing it totally from his mind, as if the problems had all gone away. The more we read, the more we understood and it seemed that each new piece of information further confirmed Professor Tantam's diagnosis. But Keith and I were still the only true believers. We shared our findings with his brothers and with his grandparents. His brothers only half-believed us at the time and his grandparents were totally dismissive. It didn't take long before we realised that there was little help and support around. Most of our help in those days came from other parents that we met at support groups. Keith and I attended these groups together and I always came home in tears at the negativity and uncertainty of Matthew's future as painted by these people. They would talk about being unable to work, unable to have friends, unable to have loving relationships, unable to drive a car. It was a nightmare. He would not die from having Asperger syndrome – it was not a life threatening disease – but his quality of life was going to be totally different from that of most children. I really couldn't accept this negative look at the future. We tried really hard to inject some sort of positivity into the various groups we were involved with, but in the end I asked Keith if we could stop attending as I felt it was doing more harm than good. We had got to this point in Matthew's life dealing with the ups and downs as they came along, but now it seemed there was a danger of mourning for a son who was actually still very much alive and very healthy.

Matthew did come along to one of the meetings, held in a room above a pub in Doncaster. This particular group was not just for the parents and carers of young people with Asperger; young people with the condition joined in too. After only a short time in the group meeting, Matthew slipped away and Keith spotted him through the window loitering outside. When he went out to talk to him, it was obvious that being in a group of people who had similar problems was not the right way forward. He felt stifled and he felt that what he needed was stimulation from the normal world, not isolation and confinement with a group whose only common ground was their so-called 'illness'.

I was able to fully empathise with this view. When my allergies had been at their worst in the early 80s, Keith had found a hotel in Northumberland that specialised in creating an allergy free environment. There were no carpets, no curtains, feather free pillows and allergen-free fabrics and the menu catered for every type of allergy. It sounded like a heavenly retreat from the dust and formaldehyde of everyday life. It was, but of course all the guests had problems. So what was the topic of conversation at every meal? You tell me your problems and I'll tell you mine! We all had a common bond but surely we had a life beyond the allergies. It was totally depressing and we were glad when our weekend break came to an end.

Selby College now came into the picture and I felt that we had to inform the college about the diagnosis. With the history of school problems behind us, my feeling was that if only they had known about Matthew's condition while he was there, it would have been so much easier for him. This was, of course, wishful thinking, because in reality, even if they had known, the staff generally would not have had the knowledge to understand his condition. I was not surprised when Matthew came out strongly against telling the college. Although he was moving towards acceptance he was not about to broadcast it to a wider audience. He was still very unhappy with me for sharing his diagnosis with other members of the family. What I was surprised with, however, and not a little confused by, was Keith's reaction to my thoughts. Since realising that I needed his full help and support, he had given me exactly that. We had agreed the way forward together and he had pulled me through a very difficult few months. Why then was he far from supportive with regards to the college? Why couldn't he see that it would reduce the risk of our son failing in the college environment? He tried to explain his reasoning, but his argument really had no foundation, which I found intriguing. However, he didn't back down immediately. It took a lot of persuasion and determination from me to convince firstly Keith and then Matthew that the college had to know. Once Keith realised that we were going to see them, his organisational skill kicked in and he set to work on planning the meeting. I felt that we should just go in and tell them straight: "*Matthew has Asperger syndrome.*"

But he said to me calmly, "*Yes, that's what we want them to know, but it's more than that. What the staff will want to know is: What does it really mean? How will it affect his studying? What can we do to help?*"

He typed up a number of pages that presented the answer to all these questions and more, in a logical and clear way.

One of the key things that he had picked up in research was that a professional such as Professor Digby Tantam could diagnose two children with Asperger syndrome, and yet they could project different behaviours. So it wasn't good enough just to say that the person has the condition – it was necessary to explain the impact of the condition on that individual. He seemed to have really got underneath the clinical jargon that we were facing on a daily basis. He seemed to have a gained very real insight into the subject in such a short time. We saw both the student support manager and one of the head tutors at Selby College. The reception from them was excellent and they committed both the college and themselves to their full support for Matthew, so much so that they agreed to let him sit for A-levels. His original acceptance had been on the basis of taking a GNVQ course, because of his GCSE results from school. But now they were prepared to grant his wish to study A-levels providing he agreed to re-sit his English GCSE at the end of the year. The meeting had produced a good result, which did transfer into a very good academic experience for him, including a B for that English re-take.

While at school, Matthew had been away on five ski trips, visiting France, Austria and Italy. He had followed the example set by his brothers who, with the exception of Karl, had all gained enormous enjoyment from this sport. He was therefore disappointed that the ending of his school life would also mean an end to skiing. Graham, one of the teachers who gave up his break each February to take young people to ski resorts and give them the experience of winter sports, ran the trips. But there was a chance because Graham was now running an additional trip at Christmas for former pupils and their families. Matthew was delighted at the prospect of continuing these winter activities, but his hopes were dashed when he was told that the former pupils had to be over eighteen to qualify. However, there was a way round it. If Matthew could persuade his parents to go on the holiday as well, as he was still a minor, then there would be a place for him. Well I didn't take much persuading, though as usual, I had to work on Keith. I could see how disappointed Matthew was at the thought of not going and so there was no way I was going to lose on this one. There was a problem though in that neither Keith nor I were able to ski. I had never been able to balance, even as a child, which meant that roller-skating, ice-skating, even riding a bike had all eluded me. And every time Keith went near an ice rink or a dry ski slope he ended up in hospital. So when Graham assured us that we wouldn't be forced to take to the piste, we agreed.

The resort was Valoire in France and the scenery was breathtaking. We enjoyed simply walking along the various snow-covered footpaths that snaked through the village. We were also able to experience for ourselves Matthews's passion for skiing. He attended all the instruction groups arranged for him and joined in each casual session with the group, never missing one. One day the group had to be bussed to another resort because of lack of snow on the main ski run, so we hitched a lift on the bus and found new areas to walk and new scenery to marvel at as well as watching Matthew in action. Matthew had tuition in a morning and we met up and ate together at lunchtime. This was a new experience for Keith and myself, dining in a beautiful area halfway up a mountain, wearing only our T-shirts and ski pants while relaxing with snow on the ground and blazing sun above us. It was a very happy experience for us and we regretted not having had enough money to have experienced it earlier in our lives with all our children. Evenings were spent firstly dining and then Graham had arranged activities ranging from outdoor events such as ice-skating, bum boarding and snow-karting to swimming and ten pin bowling at local centres. Sometimes it was just simply quizzes and games around the fire at the hotel, which was always my favourite as I found the other events a bit too challenging. Keith joined in most of them, except, of course, the ice-skating. This was an ideal holiday combination. Matthew was following a sport he loved during the day and he and Keith were enjoying activities together each evening. I had my little relaxation slot in the early evening when, after we showered, the three of us would sit together to talk about the day and then I would have an hour reading my book while they caught forty winks and then it would be on to our evening meal.

On New Year's Eve the three of us squeezed into a phone box, intent on ringing England to speak to all our sons one at a time. The lines were engaged for hours. We should have realised it would be like that but in our naivety we just thought come midnight we would ring home. Obviously we wanted to wish all our sons a Happy New Year. It was a new experience for us as we had never been out of the country on New Year's Eve before and we needed to be close to our sons. Matthew had just said to me. *"Mum, do you think Sarah and Richard will have had the baby yet?"* The baby was due in January and casually I just said that we would probably be home before Sarah went into hospital as first babies can be up to two weeks late. Little did I know that our first grandchild was being born as we talked about her. The following day we spoke to Karl who wished us Happy New Year and told us we were grandparents. Other than that he did not have any details. We rang Richard who was at the hospital and could not take a call at the time, so we rang Darren who, after we had exchanged the season's greetings, proceeded to fill us in on the much sought after details of the new baby. It was obvious to us all that this little girl had not just made her parents very happy but that she had some very delighted uncles as well. Her other uncle, Jonathan, was unaware at this time because he was celebrating the New Year in Holland with his girlfriend Beccy and her two brothers.

We were holding hands walking in the crisp white snow when Keith suddenly picked me up and kissed me. When I said, *"What was that for,"* he said that he had had a flash from the past and remembered me telling him how silly he was to think about giving up on Richard all those years ago. *"If it hadn't been for you,"* he said to me, *"I would not have had a relationship with him and there would be no chance of building a future which included him and his daughter. Thank you,"* he added, as he kissed me again.

The ski trip was a new experience for me and for Keith and one which we very much enjoyed. So when Graham approached us the following month about attending the ski trip the following Christmas, we eagerly signed up for the three of us to go to another French ski resort, Alpe d'Huez. Graham was the one teacher who had witnessed Matthew's behaviour both in and out of school and he seemed to empathise with him even though he was unaware of the diagnosis at that time.. He was a strict disciplinarian both in school and on the ski trips. Although his pupils did not always welcome this approach he did seem to command their respect. On the mountainside he expected and encouraged them to have fun but he made it very plain that there were certain rules that had to be obeyed for safety. Matthew had always done much better when his boundaries were set for him, and so he found Graham's approach to teaching quite helpful.

After years of battling I now knew why our son had behaved in the way he did and why he still needed my help. On top of that I had a husband who still flitted between professional Mr Cool and Little Boy Lost, although by now I usually knew when he was going to make that switch. But strangely I could actually see a change coming over him. Following the diagnosis, Keith seemed different. I would catch him on numerous occasions just sitting, staring in to space, lost in thought. When I asked him what was wrong, he quickly dismissed my concerns as unnecessary. Had he realised at last how hard he had made things for me? No, I think he probably realised that fact a long time ago. What I could see was happening was that he was just starting to piece things together in his mind. He was on the verge of a great discovery about himself, and after more discussion, I was able to persuade him to write down his thoughts.

Chapter 10

REALISATION FOR KEITH

Why had I made life so difficult for Pat? It wasn't intentional. I loved her to bits. I had done my best to help her, but she didn't seem to realise that I had to go out to work to earn some money. She expected me to bring home the money and yet she had expected me to be there all the time. I didn't understand compromise and balance, I had just done what I thought was right.

I didn't have her insight when it came to Matthew. It took me a long time to come to terms with the fact that there must be a medical reason for the way he was. When Pat found the article on Asperger syndrome I was lukewarm at first but I trusted her instinct and gave her my full support. The more I read about the subject and began to understand it, the more I knew it was right. And then when Professor Digby Tantam gave his diagnosis my emotions went haywire. I started to read more and more on the subject. It was as though something or someone was driving me, and yet when Pat told me that we should inform our parents and his brothers and even Selby College I just froze. No, that can't be right. It's a personal thing; it won't serve any purpose. It will just open him up to ridicule. Why I was thinking like this? I just didn't know.

Eventually I snapped out of it and agreed with Pat that we had to tell people but only certain people and only those that could help. I knew instinctively that, when we told the college, we had to tell them specifically about Matthew and his difficulties, not about Asperger syndrome in isolation. Otherwise they might give him the wrong kind of help and that could be disastrous for him. How did I know all this? Had I read it somewhere? I must have done! I kept having flashbacks about my life. Something was throwing my thoughts around like a small boat negotiating the giant waves on the edge of a hurricane. It was as if my life was flashing before my eyes, reminding me of my weird behaviour and the strange emotions that I had experienced both as a child and as an adult.

Until my teenage years, I was probably just like any other young boy of the post-war baby boom generation. I did have friends although I recall being at my happiest in my own company. I created my own little world inside my head. I was involved in the world outside but I never really felt part of it. I was always tall for my age and developed the nickname 'big lad'. But the size belied the person; inside I fell small and became an easy target for bullies, of which there were several over my years at school.

In the early teens, sexual thoughts developed as they do with all boys, but I found girls difficult to relate to. People would say I was shy but inside I knew it was more than that. It was self-doubt and inferiority. But the sexual feelings were there all right and rude pictures and masturbation were the order of the day. I found the female form fascinating and developed a fetish for stockings and suspenders, corsets and garters and frilly underskirts. But all I could do was look and wonder. I did not have the confidence to strike up a conversation with the girls I fancied. I would catalogue pictures that I collected into different sections to aid my masturbation agenda: One section for big breasts, another for lesbian, yet another for up the skirt shots and so on. The need to catalogue things spread into other areas. I listened to the Top 20 Chart Show on the radio regularly every Sunday, but I actually created my own Top 20. The Keith Greenwood Top 20 would reflect the movement of my musical taste on a weekly basis. The chart was displayed on my bedroom wall alongside a small selection of pictures of sexy women. I would run a chart programme in my bedroom with an audience of one. Also on the wall were the football league tables, which I would religiously keep up to date on a game-by-game basis. I knew nothing about football, hated playing it and yet I kept this list up to date. I don't know why, maybe it was simply because it was factual. I used to love factual books and would study them for hours on end, but I just couldn't get into novels and I found English literature boring.

So now you have a picture of this young person, somewhat of a loner, spending hours in his bedroom studying, creating catalogues and lists, living in his own little world, and wanking. But it's important to note that when I was at school and with my friends I probably came over as normal. I didn't have a problem in a crowd because I could hide my identity. The outside world was always something slightly sinister and I never really felt totally comfortable. I suppose I didn't know who I was and how I was supposed to fit in.

At school I enjoyed the subjects that were delivered by teachers who I felt commanded respect – teachers who had a structure, a discipline, an order to their subject and who made the subject interesting and relevant. With teachers who didn't fit these criteria, I played up and was very disruptive. I have lost count of the number of times I was forced to stand outside the headmaster's room patiently waiting for another ten lashes across my buttocks from his cane. I remember very clearly that his cane was larger than those used by the teachers, clearly something to do with his status. In fact some of the teachers didn't use canes. The physics master used a piece of rubber tubing and the music master used one of his gym shoes which, as he was a very large man, was probably about size twelve and left a large red footprint on your skin which lasted for days. I hated team events such as football and cricket but was very good at lone sports including swimming and athletics, particularly running. One very strong memory that I have is the communal changing rooms. I hated the camaraderie with all the boys standing about displaying their tackle and I felt very inferior, awkward and unsure in this environment.

Every Saturday, at one stage of my life, my parents generally went out with a couple of friends from a nearby house. Sometimes I would be in the house on my own during the evening and sometimes I would be out for a while with my friend. He lived on the same street and our evening usually consisted of a tour of the neighbourhood, simply walking the streets and sitting for periods on benches. But whether I went out or stayed in, I was always in the house by the time my parents and their friends came home for supper and I would be included in the gathering. Sometimes their teenage daughter would also join the group after an evening out with her friends. I used to enjoy these sessions, not so much for the good humour, although this was good, but because I used to get several penis-lifting views of candid stocking tops and creamy thighs from both mother and daughter. A vision I would take with me as I climbed into my bed that night. Yes, Saturday night was a 'very special night'.

The first incident I can remember where my actions really affected other people was when I was about fifteen and staying with my female cousin, her husband and two young children, while my parents were away on holiday. They tried their best to get me to join in their family activities but all I wanted to do was to stay in the bedroom. I can't recall what I was doing in the bedroom, only that I felt really uncomfortable with them and I wanted to be alone. Why couldn't they leave me alone? Eventually they could tolerate my weird behaviour no longer and I was despatched to my grandparents' house for the remainder of the holiday.

I am an only child and because of this my parents had no comparisons to make. I was what I was. They created a stable, loving home for me. I can recall a large variety of holidays, special events and family gatherings, which I enjoyed immensely.

But something was missing. I was unable to confide in them about my frustrations, probably not least because I didn't know what they were or how to describe them.

I knew I was different, but how do you get your loving parents to accept this? That their son is somehow a bit 'weird'?

So now, in hindsight, I can see that I was creative, liked organisation and structure but had great difficulty interacting with the opposite sex and felt embarrassed, inferior and uncomfortable in many group situations. I wanted recognition but didn't know how to achieve it. Two incidents that were probably an unconscious 'cry for help' to gain recognition could easily have ended in tragedy.

The first one took place in some woods close to where I lived as a young teenager. I probably carried out this action about four or five times during one particular summer.

Once in the woods I would take off all my clothes, put them in a neat pile under my arm and proceed to run between the trees naked and screaming. Fortunately no-one saw me on any of these outings, or at least that's what I like to believe. Why did I do it? Was I just releasing my frustrations? Or maybe I hoped a girl would see me, want me, and have me without me having to go through the contact part that I found so difficult. I only had two so-called girlfriends when I was growing up. I use the term girlfriends to signify that these were girls I met more than once and that I exchanged kisses with. In both cases I was a victim of stalking, and the 'relationship' ended when I felt that they were getting too close to me.

The second incident was a criminal act involving that same friend with whom I used to wander the streets. It involved shoplifting and the illegal removal of letters from Royal Mail boxes in order to retrieve cash from the envelopes. It is probably due to us that people are now advised never to send cash through the post. Perhaps this was a subconscious cry for recognition, I just don't know, but thanks to supportive parents and a new Juvenile Liaison Department, it went no further and my criminal thoughts were confined to the dustbin of life.

At the age of sixteen I was able to buy a motor scooter. This gave me some freedom to express myself, and to a degree, I became less of a recluse. At seventeen I moved over to a motorbike and at eighteen to a car. Most of my friends graduated to girlfriends, smoking and alcohol but I was not involved in any of these. The first I would love to have been but was still unable to connect. As far as the other two were concerned, I didn't see the point. This was probably the first time in my life I actually felt slightly superior to my peers. I saw them as sheep slavishly following a belief that to be grown up you had to smoke and drink. I felt that I didn't need to do that, and yet, I did not feel grown up Far from it. How could I? They were all streetwise. They knew the latest fashions and trends and what was groovy (cool); I didn't.

I spent a year at a further education-college with the objective of gaining some more certificates but probably due to the less structured environment at the college, I failed in this exercise. Then at eighteen I went to work full time as a bread and confectionery salesman. I enjoyed the work – I was on my own, driving a van, visiting customers. There were another hundred drivers just like me but I didn't need to mix with them and I made sure I didn't. In the four years I worked there, I prided myself on the fact that at 5.30am, I was always the first to arrive at the bakery and the first fully loaded van to leave the garage. The majority of drivers had not arrived at work when I was on my way to the customers. You could set your watch by my activities. Structure, recognition, avoiding the crowds – it's all there.

It was while I was delivering bread to one of my customers that I met my first wife, Maureen. She worked in a shoe shop next door and regular smiles and waves led to a date, arranged by her friend. Not by me, you notice. New Year's Eve 1965 was that first date. I was nineteen; she had turned sixteen only three months earlier. We had a good laugh, we enjoyed each other's company and I lost my virginity. Just over three years later we were married. Our marriage lasted for twelve years and although we remained good friends throughout we didn't help each other to grow and at the end of twelve years we were probably both still as immature as when we first met.

In many ways, domestically, she had replaced my mother. The jobs that my mother did for me as a child, Maureen was still doing for me all those years later.

Although I had been quite successful in my chosen career as a salesman, I was still very insular and avoided social contact wherever possible. I would invent excuses to avoid having to accept an invitation or go out to celebrate an event. I can recall several instances where, on the odd occasions when we did go out with friends, I would disappear from the table for long periods. I would go for a walk to escape from the inner torture I was going through because I felt insecure and insignificant particularly in the company of a group of men, even scared at times.

Then suddenly in 1980, Pat came in to my life. Maureen had been my friend and my girlfriend all rolled into a wife. Now there was Pat and she was a real women and she was interested in ME. We quickly struck up a close friendship and I fell in love with her. What a dilemma.

It was an agonising period but eventually we took the decision and moved in together. And then for the first time she saw the real me. My easy life suddenly came to an end. Now, somebody was challenging my way of life. I had to grow up; I couldn't be the little boy with the schoolboy attitude to life any more. Wow, this was going to be hard. But there was no going back. We loved each other and we needed each other. We had regular confrontations about my behaviour and in the end it always ended in me storming off and shutting myself away until

I realised I was in the wrong and needed to go back to Pat and apologise. During these periods of isolation, I kept having flashbacks and the same question kept coming back to me, flashing like a neon advertising sign. Why did I make life so difficult for Pat? It must have been hell for her, dealing not only with Matthew and the other four boys, but also dealing with me and my weird behaviour. The weird behaviour didn't stop when we fell in love and united. It changed, but it didn't stop.

It was Matthew's diagnosis that had suddenly made me realise how difficult it had been for her during the previous seventeen years and I knew I had to try harder.

My first task was to make myself more available, to be there for Pat and Matthew. I had been trying much harder in recent times making sure I was there for the numerous appointments with psychiatrists and other professionals. However in reality I was still fitting both of them into the space that was left when my work was over.

It had been back in 1990 when I had first realised that I had a passion for training. And then the following year I won an award for service to the company achieved on two fronts. I had led my team of sales representatives to achieve exceptional sales figures for the year and in addition I had introduced sales skills to around fifty people representing the company in many varied industries. The following year it all changed as my boss was promoted to a sales director role in another part of the business, which meant that further change, was inevitable. So I took the bull by the horns and wrote to the managing director. What the company needed, I said, was a sales training manager to increase the effectiveness of all salespeople across the whole company – and who better to fill that role than Keith Greenwood. It didn't work and one month later I moved across to another sector to lead a different group of sales representatives. The training opportunity had gone and for the next three years I went through a period of stagnation.

In 1995, I was given the chance to develop the sales training once again. I took up the challenge and immediately saw my motivation rise dramatically. Again there was a huge downside for my family. Being away from home had been a pattern of my working life for the previous twenty years. I never enjoyed it but saw it as a necessary evil in order to get the job done effectively. This new role meant whole weeks away as I trained more and more people on their own territories. When I did eventually get home it would be late because of the distances I had to travel and then there would be phone calls and paperwork and planning for the next trip away. I had little time or energy left for Pat.

Well now we had Matthew's diagnosis and I knew that I had to make a change.

I contacted my sales director and told him about Asperger and Matthew. I said I needed a job that didn't involve travelling too far, didn't require being away from home and didn't include a high degree of responsibility. I said that I realised that it would mean a pay cut but I had no choice. Could he help me or did I have to leave the company to achieve such a position? Probably because of my thirty years loyal service to the company, he was able to help me. After a few days off, I started my new role as a sales representative working in the Yorkshire area. It seemed really strange to be back where I had started all those years ago. I had gained my stripes and climbed the ranks but now I was back on the beat. My new line manager found it quite weird to be in charge of me, as only five years earlier I had interviewed him, given him the job and trained him in the art of selling. It was funny but I didn't even consider what he and everyone else thought about my apparent fall from grace, especially as I was remaining tight-lipped about the reasons. Strange as the new role was, I was totally comfortable with it because it signified the beginning of a new journey for me; A journey of change.

Because of these changes, my relationship with Pat seemed to be getting better as I tried harder. And yet there was still something nagging me about my life and the flashbacks continued. Since the diagnosis we had collected endless pamphlets, books and newspaper cuttings on the subject of Asperger. Sitting in the study one day, I glanced at a pile of papers scattered on the floor. One headline stood out from the rest. 'No two Aspies are alike.' I picked it up and read further 'The Autistic spectrum is wide and Asperger children are spread out along one end of that spectrum; So two children can both have Asperger syndrome and yet behave differently'. Another adjacent article reflected on the fact that children with Asperger syndrome become adults with Asperger syndrome. You don't grow out of it. It's a condition for life.

The realisation was forming in my mind. Just because I behaved differently from Matthew, didn't mean that I couldn't be suffering from the same syndrome that he was. I had always known that I was different from other people. I certainly did fit the criteria as listed in many of the official books on the subject. When I told Pat about my thoughts, she smiled at me and I could see the relief literally drain from her body. Her expression said it all. She too had come to the same conclusion. Just as I had been able to self-diagnose my health condition ten years earlier, I was now able to self-diagnose my state of mind. I didn't need Digby Tantum on this one – I could write it myself. 'WITH REGARD TO KEITH GREENWOOD, I CAN CONFIRM ASPERGER SYNDROME'. At the age of fifty-one, Matthew's diagnosis had unlocked a door into my mind and now the challenge was to step through the doorway. I had discovered something sensational about myself and unless I did things differently in the future and made some positive changes, I wouldn't benefit from the discovery. More importantly, neither would my family.

Chapter 11

CLOSER UNDERSTANDING

Over the next few years I saw a change in Keith as he came to terms with his newly found condition. Although his new role of sales representative lasted for only a few months, his re-instated role as sales training manager allowed him the flexibility to train people in Yorkshire. Instead of travelling hundreds of miles to train them on their own area, they would now travel to him. At least that's how it started out.

What I found, in the main, was that he became more open-minded about things, more willing to listen to reason and more analytical about himself and his actions. It was actually quite strange because generally as people get older they tend to go the other way. Their minds close, they definitely won't listen to reason and they don't need to analyse themselves, because, of course, they are never wrong. Once again Keith was breaking all the rules of normal behaviour. His father had definitely followed the general route as he moved into old age and I know that this upset and disappointed Keith. They often had quite heated discussions about a variety of subjects. Earlier in our life together, Keith had written several letters to both television companies and publishers complaining bitterly about the fact that they had got some aspect of a quiz wrong or that something was incorrect, and he would punch the air with glee when they wrote back with an apology. In his mind everything was either correct or it was wrong, black or white – there were no grey areas and that also included me and whatever I said or did. And now, strangely, all that was a fading memory. He was beginning to analyse every situation. It wasn't all black and white; there were grey areas as well. He was learning to have patience and understanding. It was an incredible change. He started to be a little more spontaneous and he would bring home little treats such as a bunch of flowers or sometimes just a single rose. When Valentine's Day came around he actually organised a surprise for me; A dinner dance at a local hotel with a romantic night away from home. Wow. It was almost like our whirlwind courtship.

Probably the most dramatic change I saw was the lowering of his resistance to making changes in the house. Since taking charge of the household budget I had been able to buy things whenever I felt we would benefit from them. I would always make the decision but seek his approval before making the final move. I had taken the decision-making process away from him and all he had to do was to say yes. In effect, I was using the sales skills that he had taught me. Selling, he used to say to me, is about helping the buyer to make a decision. Take away all the thinking process. You do all that for them and all they have to do is give their approval. The key, of course, is to know and understand what's right for the person making the purchase, and this can often take a long time to perfect. Well I had perfected it and so in 99.9% of cases he would say yes, go ahead. Two notable exceptions had been a video recorder and a dishwasher where, in both cases he had said No! He had an inbuilt resistance to anything that smacked of 'buying to keep up with the Joneses' rather than getting something through necessity or practicality. He eventually gave into the VCR request because of pressure from the boys but it took until this new 'open-minded' period to get him to agree to the dishwasher. We were discussing our ideas for the house one day and there on his plan was a new space for a dishwasher; I didn't even have to try to sell it to him. It was amazing! In the garden he had struggled for years to cut the grass with a manual lawnmower. He just wouldn't admit that it was a struggle and he resisted pressure from me and other members of the family to switch to an electric one. Then one day he had arrived home with one and slammed the box down on the table in a very offhand way. He was making it known that we didn't really need to replace the manual one, and that he had bought it simply to keep the peace. Every time he used the new machine he complained about the poor quality of the cut and made me feel guilty because, of course, it was my fault that he had bought it.

Keith had never enjoyed the maintenance work that comes with a garden. He was not interested in the flowers and he had no idea of any of their names. We often had jokes about this as he would pretend that he had learned a flower's name but when put to the test the name he had used was not the one we were looking at. It was a name he had maybe picked up from the television as he overheard somebody talking on one of the many gardening programmes I watched. I've been a consistent gardener throughout the time I have shared a property as we have always had gardens. I love being out in the fresh air, digging and planting. For years Keith would come along and look at what I was doing and maybe help for a short time, but it was just one more job ticked off the job list as far as he was concerned and he didn't really show any interest. I had always kept the garden plain and simple when our sons were young. There's no point in having a beautiful garden if everyone is falling out, as the children cannot play due to parents being neurotic about a flower or plant losing its bloom due to a misplaced football. But now I felt it was time to carry out a major overhaul, and you can imagine my surprise when Keith readily agreed with me about the project. In fact, he was very positive and immediately starting watching Alan Titchmarsh with me. He found his style of gardening to be helpful and friendly and by watching him it helped Keith, giving him the confidence to approach jobs that he would never have considered in the past. Now he was raring to go and his first job was to design a master plan that he shared with me once completed, to gain my approval. This was true teamwork and was a refreshing change from some of the problems we had encountered in the past. And remember the fiasco with the electric lawnmower? Well after watching one of these programmes he asked me what I thought about getting a petrol mower. 'What did I think?' I believe it's what you call a rhetorical question.

The first item to have pride of place in the new garden was a bench that Matthew had made as a GCSE project at school. It was extremely well made and heavily coated in a protective varnish. Keith's plan was to create five distinct areas, which would develop over a four-year period. The bench was the focal point for the Quiet Area. The first month we started the project it looked as if our lovely new ceanothus shrub was doomed. Karl and his fiancé Kath were visiting with their greyhound, Rum, who took a liking to it and cocked his leg up at frequent intervals. After a few weeks it looked to be withering but, in fact, we think he must have given it a good start, as years on it is both healthy and beautiful. It flowers every April/May and gives us much pleasure as we look out of the window. As the project developed, I could see that Keith was really getting enjoyment from the planning, construction and experimenting with different materials, but he also took an interest in the plants themselves. Because of problems with my joints I was unable to plant any bulbs in the garden. This was something I had done every year, adding to the bulbs we already had. Keith could see that I was frustrated and as he had gained so much confidence in the garden, he enthusiastically picked up a trowel one day and said *"Show me where they go and I will do it."*

I just laughed and said, *"That's no good, the bulbs will come up in Australia."*

From the look on his hurt face I realised it was time to delegate the planting for that season at least and so he planted them in three sections in the garden and they have had many healthy seasons since. He is very proud of these plants when they show up each spring even though he still does not know if they are daffodils or tulips. I have to tell him again each year.

We spent many happy hours travelling and looking at gardens when we were at our planning stage. One thing that was very difficult to get over to Keith was that nearly all plants have seasons. He would see something he liked in a garden and say we will have that and would expect to be able to put that plant, at that shape and height, and it would be in our garden all the year round. He found the planning stage very confusing but together we cracked it. We made a few mistakes along the way but on the whole we are pleased with the results. We went around other gardens and got a feel for which shrubs and plants we wanted but then consulted our many gardening books for height and width. Keith's plan included cut-out scale models of shrubs so we could get our borders looking well stocked while ensuring that all plants were visible.

After the Quiet Area and The Borders Area were finished I let Keith loose on a tiny patch which he transformed into the Woodland Area. He liked this because it meant very low maintenance. To be authentic it had to be wild which was just right for him. I still have to keep reminding him that he does have to carry out some maintenance in this area otherwise his wild seeds are blown in to the borders, causing many problems. The Discussion Area came next and then finally at the end of the four-year period his favourite section, the Imagination Area. For this he constructed a dry riverbed running under a bridge, which leads to an impressive set of waterfalls. On the hillside, which slopes down to the riverbed, he has built up a collection of sheep. Not real sheep you understand, because after all this is the imagination area. The size of the flock is growing as each year he buys a few more and people buy them for him as gifts. The sheep do get special treatment in winter though – unlike the big fluffy ones, they go into hibernation in our garage. Our sons have all joined the project at different times, buying presents of plants, tubs, and garden animals, spotting and collecting materials and often just joining in with the general maintenance of both the natural side and jobs like varnishing and painting. It's been a very worthwhile project. As well as starting to look quite attractive and being a comfortable place in which to relax, our garden is a treasure of memories.

As a break from gardening, Matthew, Keith and I would often go off on day trips or sometimes away for the weekend. We were on a weekend trip to London when Matthew surprised us by announcing that he was not going home with us on Sunday night. He had saved some money and wanted to stay in London overnight on his own, and then make his own way back to Yorkshire by coach the following evening. This was good for his development and good for his independence; however it was not good for our peace of mind. We had no fears about him getting lost as his sense of direction was fantastic and had been since he was about six years old. I always felt at ease when he was with me in the car; if we were travelling to a new area as he could usually guide me out of trouble if I got lost. No, it was because we knew that Matthew, now seventeen, saw the world differently to others. Not everyone was as patient or as understanding as he needed them to be. This would be the first time that he had stayed away from home, entirely on his own, without members of his family or as part of an organised group. The protection we gave at home was not there in the outside world.

With my sister in law Joyce and the snake that shared my bedroom for three weeks in the USA in 1989

Keith's special gift to welcome me home

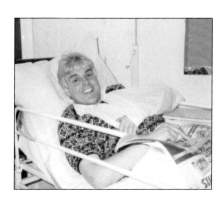

After the ice rink accident

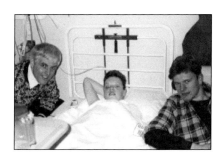

Keith and Jonathan visiting Matthew after his eye injury

Matthew horse riding

Matthew with Jonathan

And with Richard

Darren's 18ᵗʰ birthday

Keith's 50ᵗʰ birthday, Oulton Hall

Karl and Darren

Matthew entertaining his two year old twin cousins

California 1996

Forest Gump bench

Venice Beach

On Alcatraz island

Me with Elvis

At the hotel

Relaxing in Yosemite

Happy days at Rawcliffe school for me and Matthew

Darren – Ten Pin Bowling Champion

And teaching the family to bowl

Matthew leaving Rawcliffe School

Having fun with Farouk and Moses from Uganda

Darren's first day at University

Action man or child-like man?

Leah – Our first grandchild   **One of my favourite photos**

The special cupboard at Grosvenor House Hotel

Jonathan dressed by Army & Navy Surplus

And in his smart interview suit

Our five sons

We knew that it would give him life experiences that he needed so we felt that he had to do these things for himself, even though we felt far from comfortable. We had a meal together in the evening and then we accompanied him when he went to check in at his hotel. We were very impressed with the quality of the hotel to which he was treating himself. We hugged and said goodbye and agreed the time that I was going to pick him up in York the following evening. We drove up the motorway with very mixed feelings, wishing he were in the car with us but also confident that he would thoroughly enjoy his time in the big city that he loved so much. It was after lunch the following day when I received a call from him. He had done several sightseeing things already that morning and had decided to catch the tube and train out to Ickenham. He had enjoyed looking round this town which was situated not far from where his aunt and cousins lived.

He was standing in the station at Ickenham asking me what he should do. When he had arrived earlier in the day, he had checked the timetable for the time of the return train but he had obviously mis-read it, and he now realised that the next train didn't depart for another hour. That was not the problem, however. The problem was that the train wasn't scheduled to arrive at Victoria until ten past four and the coach to York would be leaving at four o'clock. The first thing I asked him was, how much money he had. He was very much like his father, in that he rarely carried spare cash in his wallet to cover unexpected expenses. He would calculate his planned costs and only carry that amount of money with him. He confirmed that he had hardly any money left. We talked about the fact that his dad was working in the Midlands on that day and hopefully he would be able to collect him from somewhere in the London area. I then rang Keith and was surprised to get hold of him straight away. I usually had to speak to an answer phone because his mobile phone would invariably be switched off if he was in a meeting. Keith agreed that once he had finished his various assignments, he could head southwards and collect Matthew. When Matthew rang me at a pre-arranged time so that I could tell him what I had sorted he said, "Hi mum," in a very upbeat voice. "I read the wrong line on the timetable. It's OK, my train leaves in two minutes, see you in York tonight. Bye."

I felt relief and sickness both at the same time. Would he really catch the train and then connect to the coach? And would he be in York when

I got there to collect him? I was never going to let him out of my sight again. And then I started to think. He was such a capable young man, with such ideas, such stamina to see things through, such a zest for life, it was just the attention to detail which often let him down. His enthusiasm for knowledge was so great that he just took any mishap in his stride, there was no panic. I rang Keith back to tell him that we did not need his emergency rescue service after all. I told him of my upset and fear in those few short moments when Matthew was stranded and also about the fact that he was always frugal with money and how I felt that the day he turned eighteen we should make sure that he had a bank account, which included a credit card. That way if he ran out of money he would have the safety net of the card and could cover the cost of any alternative arrangements that he needed to make. We both agreed that, although this would not solve the basic problem, it would minimise the effect. Matthew was in York that evening on time and it was obvious from his conversation on the way home that he had had a wonderfully independent experience. This was despite the fact he had almost had to be rescued. I was fiercely proud of this adventurous young man and I felt that he had achieved so much. Hopefully the finer details would come eventually.

Over the years we had accumulated a vast amount of stuff in the loft and it had just become chaos up there. Previous attempts to get Keith to take action had always fallen on deaf ears, but now, as part of the overall house improvement plans, he was keen to sort it. A car boot sale was our first thought but having had some experience of the pros and cons we decided that we needed something different. So we agreed that what we should have is an idea that we had seen in the USA: a yard sale. Matthew typed some small notes advertising the event and posted them around the village a few days before. On the appointed day we spread our wares all over the front garden and driveway. We tried to make the displays as attractive as possible and ensured that everything was priced. A large sign was erected on the roadside for the benefit of passing motorists. We were astounded at the response with customers coming from near and far. We sold virtually everything that we had put out, met a lot of people, and had a thoroughly enjoyable day. It was probably this success that inspired us to step up our interest in antiques and collectible items. We had often been to house clearance sales and antique fairs but now we were starting to get more serious and, in fact, learning a lot more about what to look out for. We would go to collectors' fairs and spend hours there both browsing together and then separating to check out specific items of interest. We relaxed and chatted and generally had a good day out. Whenever we were looking at antique furniture we often laughed about the time he chopped the legs off my dressing table and he would say that back then he just saw it as old furniture. We taught each other something from that episode. He learned to take more care and be more aware of other people's feelings and I learned never to put possessions before people.

We settled down to watch television one evening, and Keith picked up the TV Times to check our evening viewing. Nothing extraordinary about that and it could have been any evening, but this evening was different. It was several minutes before he spoke. Instead of telling me what he was suggesting we watch he spoke with excitement in his voice. "I could adapt this for you." The mind boggled – what had he found in the TV Times that he could adapt for me? It was a recipe. He started to tell me that it was called Green Dragon Chicken. It was a stir-fry recipe and contained flour and a couple of other ingredients that he knew I could not have.

"I could easily make some substitutions so that you will be able to eat it," he said excitedly. And so Keith's new passion for cooking began. On the Saturday he added the ingredients to our shopping list. Sunday afternoon he banished me from the kitchen while he created his new dish. Gorgeous smells were permeating the house and we were all looking forward to eating this meal. The family was very excited when we sat down to taste Dad's first attempt at solo cooking. Keith was beaming all over his face at his new success. Sadly this was not to last. He brought the steaming bowl of stir-fry to the table, placed it in the middle and then sat down. We all looked at each other and nobody dared ask the question that everyone was thinking. Where is the rice? Usually when we had stir-fry we had an accompanying dish of rice or potatoes or pasta. Keith's face dropped when he saw our hesitation and realised his omission. In his excitement to create, he had missed the line at the bottom of the recipe that said "Serve with rice or pasta". Here we were with a new dish that had been lovingly created especially for me and there was a hitch. Quickly I got up and brought bread rolls to the table.

Everyone was delighted and all enjoyed the meal. Of course, I could not eat the bread rolls but the stir-fry was very appetising. Despite the faux pas, the fact that everyone enjoyed his modified dish gave him a new confidence in the kitchen. So much so that he waited eagerly for the TV Times to come each week and he built up a repertoire of recipes, all of which he adapted for the family and cooked each Sunday. Sometimes he would just introduce a Sunday dinner which we always enjoyed. In his enthusiasm he would enjoy creating the big things but occasionally still forgot the smaller details. The first time he made beef casserole he forgot to cook the accompanying roast potatoes. He was also learning that cooking could be quite informal and was able to quickly adapt to a situation. The family saw Dad using another skill and this gave me a break from the constant round of cooking and the endless task of trying to incorporate variety into our meals. This was only the beginning. We started to share the cooking when we had friends and family to visit and eventually he was cooking probably as much as I was, which made life much easier for me as it was no longer my endless daily task. We were planning together and sharing. I still felt that my bolognese had the edge on his but his Yorkshire puddings were far superior to mine.

I continued in my task to find the answer to my health problems. Why did I retain so much fluid? Why could I never empty my bowel successfully and regularly, as most people did? I always felt so uncomfortable and in pain. Kidney infections were still frequent. While attending a hospital appointment to discuss the possibility of having an illeostomy, the surgeon suggested that it might be preferable for me to consider a new development that was called an Ace Procedure. This was an operation designed to help the patient to empty their bowel by means of self-irrigation, instead of using a colostomy bag. The procedure involved opening the appendix area to create a tube. True to form, Keith was away when I had to go into hospital so a friend gave me a lift. After the operation, I had to stay in hospital for a week to recover and to learn how to use my new opening to irrigate my colon. It was trial and error and the staff were great, particularly as the procedure was relatively new and they were still learning. I was feeling a little less feminine during this time but the stoma care staff were wonderful and raised my spirits and with it my confidence. At the end of the week I went home as the proud owner of an extra navel. Going home however was another hurdle. I had told Keith at evening visiting that I would probably be discharged the following day. I could not give him a specific time, as it was all dependent on what time the doctor arrived. So we agreed I would ring after lunch and let him know and then he could pick me up. I was discharged about eleven in the morning and, delighted at this, I rang home. There was no answer. Not to worry, it was earlier than I had anticipated. The nurse in charge said it was a good opportunity for me to have lunch and then go home leisurely in the afternoon. I took her advice and as all my belongings were packed and ready to go I sat and enjoyed yet another meal that had been cooked for me. This was the best part of being in hospital – the meals were reasonable and I didn't have to prepare them, what a treat. The afternoon moved on and I rang Keith at hourly intervals. There was still no answer. At 4pm I began to get quite concerned as to where he could be and what could have happened to him. I was most anxious, especially when the staff came to set up my tray for tea – I should have been long gone by now. After getting no response at 5pm I decided I would ring my mother-in-law who only lived minutes away from us. While Keith's dad was going through a period of ill health, we had persuaded them to move from Bradford to Snaith. She agreed to go round and see if there was a problem. An hour later he arrived at the hospital to take me home. I was so pleased to see him it seemed irrelevant why he was late. Later when I did ask him he said calmly, "Oh yes, I heard the phone, but I didn't want to get broken off."

He had been laying some flags to form a paved patio area and wanted to finish them before I came home; Very commendable, but very frustrating for me.

After the operation I needed ten weeks of rest before I could go back to work. It had come at an opportune time because I did need the rest. My joints had been in constant pain for some time and I had found typing quite difficult and there'd been a lot of it at work. I had been heavily involved with the campaign to get a new school for Rawcliffe. The current Victorian building was totally unsuitable for modern educational needs. The volume of day-to-day typing had increased dramatically. While I was in hospital I received many cards and flowers from my family and friends, from staff, governors and parents and I received some lovely cards made by the children themselves. Lots of notes and messages were included. The one that really touched me was a handmade card from a special little six-year-old friend of mine.

He had arrived in school on the first day of term two years earlier. He was tall for his age with a shock of lovely thick blonde hair. He was quite a serious child but had the most amazing smile when it shone through. He was in the school less than five days when I was drawn to watching him. There were a number of little things. How he stood on his own in the playground, making no attempt to join the other children. How the girls were drawn to him and appeared to mother him. How he liked to hold the hand of the teacher on duty making him feel secure. His method of walking could be described as a little wobbly and our uneven playground caused him several problems. There were lots of times over the following months when I heard his name mentioned. He seemed to be getting very confused and he smiled less and became even more serious. If ever I saw him in the classroom he looked to be trying his best to take part but by now he was being called disruptive and it was only his first year in school. I knew he was doing his best. I had seen the pattern before. I had seen it in Matthew. The harder he tried, the more he got into trouble. This young man started to have tantrums in and out of school. His mummy was reporting that he no longer wanted to come to school and virtually every day she found it a struggle to get him to go.

One day I heard a lot of commotion in the nursery classroom and went to investigate. He had been reprimanded for not doing as he was told and he had gone into a tantrum. When I arrived he was pulling the last of the books from the library shelves. He was bright red, tears streaming down his face and was systematically working his way through all the books, pulling batches of them down into a big heap on the floor. I stood by his side and he stopped. As the two members of staff were trying to settle the other children in the class, some of whom were getting very upset, they allowed me to take control of this confused little boy. I knew of old the best solution was to quickly remove the child from the scene, take time and then they would calm down. This I did and we sat together and he began to sob quietly until the tears subsided. He was not cross, his outburst had not been in temper, it had been in confusion.

All he had been asked to do was continue with his maths work using his coloured pencils. The children were colouring in pictures of pieces of fruit. Numbers represented the different colours. I asked him why he had not done this and he said, *"I can't do what the teacher asked because I don't have any coloured pencils."*

He knew that the point in the pencils was grey and that he didn't have any coloured ones. All he had were coloured crayons, and so he did not understand the term coloured pencils. To adults and to most of the children, it was a very simple thing but for him it was totally confusing. Worse still, he was getting upset because he could not do his work as he did not have the tools that his teacher was insisting he use. As he had upturned most of the library area it was decided that he should be punished. I tried to explain that a punishment should fit the crime and in this instance the crime had been a total misunderstanding. He would have no idea why he was being punished and this would confuse him and upset him even further. Reluctantly and probably out of respect for me no more was said. I helped him to tidy all the books and restore order to the library. How could I protect this little one? I suspected he had Asperger syndrome but I was no expert. How could I voice this to anyone? It was a serious condition and meant that once it was acknowledged he would need daily support in school and at that time there was very little support for aspergic children. I had only seen one special needs course advertised for teaching staff which referred to autism, and in this little boy's case I didn't believe it was classic autism. I had to be careful or the staff would have thought I was 'getting above my station' trying to tell them how to teach, instead of getting on with my job as the secretary. The nursery nurse and infant teacher were both caring people and were very committed to teaching the children. They put lots of extra effort into teaching the class, and the pupils were given extra outings and treats that were over and above what was expected. So I decided that I had to sit tight and watch for a while because apart from this particular incident, all the other occasions I had witnessed were not explainable in the way this incident had been. Several weeks later I could sit back no longer. My little friend was having many problems and was getting very upset on a regular basis. A lot of his behaviour was classed as disruptive to the other children. This was true, but I knew there had to be a solution to this problem. I took a huge chance and went to visit his mum at her home. I told her I was concerned. This mum knew Matthew, as her older children had been in school at the same time, and had, in fact, been in the same class. I told her that Matthew had experienced some of the problems that her son was having both at primary school and secondary school. And then I said that I wanted to share an incident with her.

I told her that one day Matthew had been working hard and doing his best to get a piece of work finished correctly, but he had been accused of playing about. He had relayed the story to me as soon as he came home and we had talked about it at length. He was so upset as he was eager to finish this work but the teacher had taken it away from him and said that, as a punishment, he would have to stay on after school and start back at the beginning again. I had stressed to Matthew that punishments were for a reason or pupils would be unruly. He stormed off upstairs with me following. As he got to his bedroom I caught up with him, but then he slammed the door in my face. He slammed it so hard that all the plaster around the door began to crack and caused quite a bit of damage. I opened the door and followed him in. He was standing there shaking. *"Nobody understands me. I am a waste of space. I might as well be dead."*

I grabbed him and hugged him and spoke to him calmly. *"Don't say that. You are a lovely person; we just need to work harder together."*

We sat together in his bedroom talking things through until he had calmed down. I didn't get to the root of what had actually happened that day, but I knew instinctively that he hadn't done anything wrong. He had just been misunderstood.

Keith and I had always backed the school in whatever discipline they had handed out. We had taught him to respect adults, especially his teachers. But from that day onwards I was much more discerning in my reinforcement of school discipline. I always listened to him and never pre- judged anything.

She had listened to me with interest. I finished talking by telling her that Matthew had been diagnosed with Asperger syndrome and that the reason I had come to see her was that I could see many similarities with her son.

I waited for her reaction with baited breath. If I had got it wrong I could lose my job because as the parent she could have complained to the education department about my interference. But I could see from her expression that she knew I was on the right track. I then went on to say that her son was a boy who was eager to learn and also eager to please, despite the tantrums I had witnessed. I stressed that I felt the way forward for him was to know that his mum would not be soft with him, because children with Asperger syndrome need rules and guidelines. It helps them to understand the world better. But he also needed to know that his mum would be very understanding and supportive. From then on his mum did just that. She became very assertive in her support for him. There were times when he stayed at home as there were problems. There were times when she was at the end of her tether, as she had to deal with him and her other children, but she never wavered in her support. Even when the school psychologist wrote a report stating he was playing up and being disruptive because he was not disciplined well enough, she calmly pointed out the help he required in order to reduce his disruptive behaviour. I too continued to support him in school. I tried to give him a quiet corner. He would come and see me on errands and we would often talk about the computer or my office equipment. He was eager to learn about new things, eager to find out how machines worked. Behind my desk in my office was a row of guitars and at one stage every time he came to my office he would ask to be able to hold one of the guitars and we would sing nursery rhymes to each other. These visits only lasted five to ten minutes and sometimes I had to make an excuse to escort him back to class or he would have been missed. I felt that if I could make my office a safe quiet place for him maybe he could cope with the overload in the classroom. His mum had already told me that he found the days in school long and always needed a sleep when he arrived home.

And so, when I opened his card I cried. I wondered how he was doing. I wasn't there to give him that safe quiet place. But hopefully, I had given him and his family some hope for the future. I had always been quite perceptive about people but now I had an added advantage. I had some knowledge of Asperger and found that I was watching people, particularly children, more closely. Both Matthew and Keith also confessed to doing the same. We watched *Rain Man* again. The three of us had watched it together on two occasions before and for me it was the fourth time of viewing. But this time it was different. This time we could identify. It was still funny, but at the same time it held a number of truths for us. The phrase 'Underpants on the highway' which the character Raymond repeats in the film was added to Matthew's repertoire of silly sayings, which he would recite during periods of total relaxation.

We started to investigate support groups again and joined one in Goole, which then led us to a group in Hull. Unfortunately the group was run on a casual basis and needed much better organisation. Eventually a small band of people broke away to form a splinter group whose interest was focused on children and young people with Asperger syndrome. Both Matthew and Keith were helpful to the group in acting as role models. They were able to share their experiences which many of the group found helpful, particularly the mums with younger children. It was amazing to find how many of them had made the decision to educate their children themselves at home, rather than have them subjected to the local school system, which at that time, had a total lack of understanding with regard to autistic spectrum disorders. Keith soon got frustrated, however, as he saw it merely as a talking shop, and felt that they had to get organised and take some positive actions. One member of the group who himself suffered from a number of disorders held very extreme views and was very volatile and quick to blame the authorities for everything. Keith found himself trying hard to steer the group along a middle path. As well as attending the groups, we continued to read all that we could about the subject. We had joined the National Autistic Society and this was a great source of inspiration and knowledge. There was a lot of debate about the causes of Autistic spectrum disorders with many different theories being bandied about. We favoured the theory that it was genetic – after all, we had first-hand evidence. Yes, it could just be a coincidence that both Keith and Matthew were aspergians, but surely it was much more likely that the genes were responsible and that Keith had passed it on to Matthew. So where had Keith got it from; from his father or from his mother? How could we tell? Maybe it was from both of them, particularly when you remember that all children with Down syndrome are born to two apparently normal parents. It's just something that happens when their genes come together. We struggled on this one for some time. We were looking for outward signs, for behaviours that fitted a pattern. Maybe the fact that Matthew's aspergic characteristics were more severe than Keith's suggested that it was a combination of Keith's genes and mine. Maybe I had aspergic traits. We were just going round in circles

On 14th November 1998, Keith was listening to the news. The Prince of Wales was celebrating his fiftieth birthday. It reminded him of his cousin, Philip. He was born on the same day. He too should have been fifty on that day but had sadly died early in life due to diabetes. His mind then jumped to another cousin, David, who had died in his early forties. The more he thought about David, the more sure he was that the signs were there.

When the boys were young, we had packed up a huge picnic on one particular day and we had ventured on one of our many trips to Sherwood Forest. Keith's parents had gone with us. On the way we called to see Keith's aunt and uncle (his mother's brother) and their son, David, who happened to be at home with them. He would be in his mid-thirties at that time and we spent a very pleasant time with them. We were a big group, nine of us and three of them, and so it was no wonder I didn't hear David speak above all the bedlam. However, as I carried empty cups into the kitchen he had helped me. There were just the two of us and he started chatting to me. He told me about his travels on the railway and how he always rode to work on a bike, about his love of music and how he had more than one guitar. He even told me briefly about his time at university. We had a very pleasant chat and I remember thinking how friendly he was. When I went upstairs to the toilet, his bedroom door was open, and I couldn't help but glance in as I passed. It was the bedroom of a child, but a tidy-minded child. Everything was precise and neat and tidy; the bed, the posters on the wall, the displays of toy soldiers and all his guitars hanging neatly in a row.

I remember that, later in the day, when we were discussing our visit, Keith's mum had said that David had always been strange and that it was unusual to see him when they visited as usually he stayed in his bedroom when people came to visit the house.

So here we were years later wondering if he could have been a victim of Asperger syndrome.

As soon as it was convenient, we arranged to visit Keith's aunt to try to get some more background about her son. Keith had been honest about his reasons for interviewing her and she answered all his questions clearly and calmly. It was clear to see that she was, understandably, a little uneasy. The picture that we were able to paint of David was uncannily familiar. He was highly intelligent, hard-working, obsessive, child-like in many ways, naïve and strong willed. There were two very strong clues to the fact that he was strong willed. Number one was the fact that he refused to have his photograph taken. His mother had no photographs of him after he left university. Fact number two was even more startling. He stubbornly refused to visit a doctor whenever he was unwell, even when he developed a swollen neck and a lump – even when he was having trouble swallowing. Sadly he died from throat cancer.

We were convinced. David had Asperger syndrome. Here was a family link. Keith started to think about other people in the family. No-one stood out quite like David. He could only make assumptions about other links in the chain from his limited memories of those people, David's father and grandfather.

He assumed for a moment that they both carried the strain and then continued the link. David's grandfather was, of course, also Keith's grandfather. And who was the person in between his grandfather and himself? Of course, it was his mother.

And so together we analysed his mother to see if there were any aspergic characteristics.

She certainly appeared very childish and naïve in many situations. Just like a child she would demand attention and recognition. Virtually every discussion would graduate to her perspective. If Keith and I went somewhere new or experienced something out of the ordinary, she would only half listen to our description because she would want to tell us what she had been doing. In many cases she would persuade my father-in-law to take her to the place we had been, at the earliest opportunity. And there was an obsession linked to this with regard to holidays. Whichever holiday she went on was invariably enjoyed, but there seemed to be a greater thrill in being able to tick the destination off an imaginary list. Once back home, the brochures were out for the next trip. Visits to shops and restaurants were always difficult as she was so indecisive. Her decisions were governed by choices of other people, rather than being based on personal likes and dislikes. If we went out for Sunday lunch, for instance, it was often like taking a young child out. She would be bemused by the choices available on the menu, and strangely she would often read out aloud her surprised discovery about certain dishes, even though they were standard dishes available in every restaurant in the country. While she was doing this, she was not making a choice. *"I don't know what to have, what are you having?"* became a regular phrase. Eventually a choice was made, but when the meals arrived, and without fail, she would look at somebody else's meal and say, *"That looks nice, I should have had that."* Then she'd often go on to complain that her dish was too hot or too cold or too much or too little or that the meat was tough or undercooked or too well done. She was very obsessive about tidiness, even to the point of spontaneously cleaning and dusting our house or other people's houses and totally misunderstanding the critical messages that this action was sending. Probably the key factor that made us believe that there was a definite link was a clue in her method of communication. We had recently read about something called 'tangential behaviour' which was a behaviour often associated with the autistic spectrum. It described a communication style in which the person often had not completed a sentence when they moved on to the next one. It is as though their brain is moving much faster than their ability to get the words out. Because of this, their eye contact is poor during this session – they are searching the memory bank for the next piece of information, as though it's connected on a loop system. When I first experienced Keith's mum talking to me in this way I was a little confused and shocked. Then I moved on to frustration, until eventually I began to play along with it and tried to end the sentences myself. I had seen Keith do this and although it reminded me of the Two Ronnies' sketches on television, it did seem to make the conversations more lively and interesting. Since Keith's realisation and our joint awareness, we both now accept it as part of who she is.

I felt awful. We had constructed a list of negative behaviours about Keith's mum which were really insignificant. It was only our perception and surely if you analysed anybody, autistic spectrum people or not, you would get a list of behaviours which you didn't agree with. The important thing, surely, was whether an Asperger person's behaviour affected somebody else, somebody close to them. It was true to say that

Keith's behaviour affected me and that Matthew's behaviour affected both Keith and me. But did their behaviour affect anybody else?; Probably not.

David's behaviour may have affected the one girlfriend he had, which could be why the relationship broke up. It seemed odds-on that David felt an inner loneliness, as did Matthew and Keith. Back to my mother-in-law; had her behaviour affected her husband? We didn't know. And did she have an inner loneliness? Again, we didn't know. But she had suffered a breakdown recently, which resulted in her confinement to a clinic. We weren't really much further forward. It was too complex. We couldn't prove anything either, but at this stage, we didn't need to. In our own minds we were convinced that Asperger is a genetic disorder.

Matthew's two years at Selby College went by without a serious hitch and at the end of it he achieved the A-levels he required to go to university. He had developed an interest in the world of business from an early age and while at college had decided to have a go and launch a small business. After lots of research he settled on children's educational videos. He found suitable suppliers, had impressive full colour leaflets printed and attended a number of local events with a display stand he had instructed a moulding company to produce for him. One of the events he attended was the annual Snaith Show where he won a trophy for having the best trade stand. Sadly, despite all his hard work the venture did not generate enough interest and he had to shelve it. He was not disheartened, however, and it was a great learning experience for him.

Another good opportunity for him to learn came when he was invited to attend the Conservative Party conference in Bournemouth. He had joined the party some months before and had attended several meetings and debates.

He was dealt a severe blow the night before sitting his A-levels. His grandfather, Keith's father, died after being unwell for some time. Although Matthew never really got close to his grandfather, he did feel a degree of empathy, and his departure did have a pronounced effect on him. He was insistent on writing down his own memories and he delivered his words at the service of cremation. It was a very moving eulogy, which was presented with genuine emotion. The whole congregation applauded in respect when Matthew reached the end.

Keith himself was comforted by the fact that he had been at the hospital bedside when his father slipped away. He had been holding his hand throughout the last minutes of his life.

After considering a number of universities and courses, Matthew settled on Guildhall, London. It was a four-year degree course in business studies. His ambition was still to start his own business and he saw this course as a way of developing his skills to aid him in that target. His reason for selecting Guildhall was twofold. Not only did it give him the studying opportunity but it also gave him the opportunity to explore London. He took up residence in a student accommodation block which had been converted from council flats. It was located in Bethnal Green, not far from the Blind Beggar pub, the infamous watering hole for the Kray twins. He soon settled into the life of a student during the day and eager tourist by night. He had taken his bike with him and would often cycle around different parts of the city including the seedy streets of Soho in the early hours, soaking up the atmosphere.

I was very pleased for him. He had achieved one of his ambitions, living in London, but I was also very apprehensive as to how he was going to cope on his own with his aspergic behaviour and his restless mind as companions.

Chapter 12

THE NEW MILLENNIUM

The new century started well. Keith and I decided to do something really different to see the new-year in. We retired at about 10pm on New Year's Eve and then at three o'clock in the morning we arose from our bed and headed for Holy Island in Northumberland.

We – well Keith more than me – wanted to see the first sunrise of the new millennium as it actually happened. When we arrived it was pitch black and we settled down in the car with blankets and pillows and duvets. At about 6.15am the first signs of light appeared in the sky and we decided to take a walk towards the sea. It was then that we realised we were not on our own. Hundreds of other people had had the same idea, and just like us were just emerging from their warm cars into the cold morning air. For the next hour or so we walked and rested and looked skyward, as the light grew more intense. At just after 8am the sun popped into view and a ripple of applause thundered through the air. We all watched in wonder and amazement as this large shimmering ball of light climbed higher and higher. I am sure that most people felt a sense of smallness, as we did, standing on this tiny island in the North Sea watching nature take its course. It was a fantastic experience and one we will never forget. All these people united and all feeling positive about moving into the twenty-first century.

Once the looking had ceased and the cameras had stopped clicking there was a mad scramble to the cars and a dash to return to the mainland before the advancing tide covered the causeway at around nine o'clock and cut off the island from the mainland. We would have loved to stay much longer but it would have meant staying until early evening and we were excited to wish all our sons and the rest of the family a Happy New Year. We had already wished Matthew a Happy New Year. He was in London for the millennium and he rang on his mobile soon after midnight. It was obvious he was having a wonderful experience, which he was sharing with thousands of people in the capital.

As far as my health was concerned I still had the daily chore of irrigating my colon, Firstly I had to put water in to a small plastic tank. The water was then heated to the required temperature and then I had to insert a tube in to my extra navel down which the water could travel. The procedure took up to a couple of hours each day and meant I was tied to the house to complete the task. I also had severe pains in my joints and muscles and this was taking some sorting. Through my GP I tried several courses of tablets, which while to some degree took the pain away, always irritated my stomach and caused side effects. The pain was more severe when I was sitting or standing, so I found relief by lying down. But I could not lie down all the time and if I did the stiffness was even more severe when I eventually started to move again. There were lots of areas of my health which were causing problems. Despite these difficulties, I had thought that I might have been back at work in January but the doctor would still not allow me to go back. We were taking it on a week-by-week basis and it soon became obvious that my next mental deadline would be Easter. Maybe I would be well enough to go back to work after Easter. After all, I was only supposed to be off work for ten weeks at the most and once Easter came, I would have been away from work for almost six months.

I had worked very closely with my head teacher on all areas of school life. Now, during my sick leave, he had struggled to keep everything contained. He had contacted me for advice on the odd occasion, but generally he tried not to worry me with anything. This frustrated me even further as I knew he had a full-time teaching commitment and the administration side was increasing weekly and had done so over the past couple of years. Since the introduction of the computer into my office the paperwork had gone up dramatically. Instead of simply working with a piece of carbon paper and sending weekly financial and academic reports to County Hall we now were accounting for everything we did in school in some kind of report. It seemed like everyone wanted hard copies of every activity in school. If you could produce a chart or a graph then this was demanded as well. The paperwork, which was introduced in a few short years after the computer arrived, was unbelievable. I loved working on the computer and the more I did the more I wanted to do, but it did frustrate me with the amount of forms that had to be completed. Some of the documents that County Hall requested were so complex that I was convinced that nobody would ever read them or refer to them once they had been ticked off a list as having been received. Multiply this by all the schools that would be sending in the same document and it would have been nigh on impossible for anyone to have checked all these documents. My role had changed from being a part-time secretary and part-time non-teaching assistant to a full-time secretary. When I started at the school in 1987 we had only a very strained and bent typewriter and I had started taking work home using our home computer. It was my choice as the presentation on the computer was far superior to the finished product on the typewriter. This left me time in school to work with the children, which I loved. I was every bit as committed as the very professional teachers I worked with. Over the years my workload at home was increasing and as well as typing in the evenings I always spent one day out of the weekend doing schoolwork. The commitment to work was high in the school and the level of staff sickness was extremely low. We all loved our jobs and we were a united team. Because of this I felt very guilty about having to take extended leave and this mental state was not helping me to recover. But I had to be sensible. My health had to be my priority and I kept thinking back in time; back to a time when trying to do too much had resulted in a very dangerous situation for me.

It was a Tuesday evening and I was preparing a meal for the family. It had been a very busy day in school. During the morning I had baked bread with a group of five-year-old children. We had had lots of fun but they had also learned a great deal. How to knead the dough, how to let it rise, how to 'knock it back', how to cover it, leave it in a warm place and see it rise again. But best of all they learned how to turn the dough into three recognisable shapes. I gave them a choice of plaits, a hedgehog or a plain bread roll.

Following this enjoyable but tiring session I headed back to my office and during my lunch period dealt with a large consignment of stock that had been delivered during the morning. Firstly I had to check the goods against the delivery note and then pack everything away in the various store cupboards while separating specific items that had been reported to me as urgently required by members of staff.

In the afternoon I had to type a very lengthy governor's report that had to be completed before the end of the school day, which meant non-stop typing for just short of three hours. Matthew and I drove home and chatted happily about our school day. When we arrived at home, he immediately went off to make a start on his homework. I said hello to Keith who had been at home all day working on a project for his job. I knew better than to disturb him for long, so I quickly went to the kitchen.

It was when I was peeling carrots that I felt the pins and needles in my hand. At first I wasn't unduly worried because I often found myself with cramp in my fingers and yet this time it was different. The pins and needles were also affecting my mouth and jaw and I could only see clearly out of one eye. It was a weird feeling and after what seemed like a very long time as I stood there checking the different feelings and malfunctions, unable to move away from the sink, I saw Matthew through my good eye, approaching the fridge.

"*Please tell Dad I am not well. I need his help,*" I said, or rather I meant to say. My lips were shaping those words, but my brain had other ideas. I did utter some sounds, even some normal complete words but they were not the ones I was trying to say and they made no sense. It must have been like watching a film where the sound is not synchronised with the picture. Matthew looked puzzled. I wasn't getting through to him. He didn't understand what was happening. What was I to do? I looked around the room and spotted a piece of paper. He obviously followed my thinking because when I pointed towards the paper, he brought it to me together with a pen. I began to write my message with a very shaky hand and all I could manage were groups of letters devoid of any vowels. Matthew must have decided by now that it was just a game and not a very interesting one, because he collected his drink from the fridge and returned to his bedroom. I had no choice but to force myself to move. I had to get to Keith. I managed to shuffle up the stairs, one at a time, on my bottom. Eventually I reached his closed study door and from the floor I was able to bang on it with my good hand. When he opened the door and saw the state I was in, he sprang in to action. He carried me to bed and I fell asleep almost immediately. It wasn't until the following morning when I awoke that I was able to tell him what had happened and how I had felt. But now I felt normal again. Whatever it was had gone and I went to work as usual.

A little over two years later I was sitting at my desk in my office at school. I shared the office with my head teacher, Dave. Because he had an almost full-time teaching commitment, projects that we had to work on together were usually crammed into the lunch period or after school hours. For most of the time I was on my own and, of course, I now didn't have the stimulation from the children, as my role had changed to that of a full-time secretary. So this was just another day like any other, not hard work physically, but very taxing for me mentally. But it wasn't just another day. The first clue that something was wrong was when I fell on the village green on the way to the shop at lunchtime. I was rushing because I didn't really have time to spare to go shopping but the office coffee supplies had run out and I knew that Dave had visitors coming to see him that evening. I hadn't tripped on an obstacle or anything; I had just sort of collapsed. Nobody saw me and I was soon able to get up again and continue on my way. But when I got back to my desk and started attacking the pile of paperwork I soon realised that I was feeling quite lethargic. I felt distant and it was hard to concentrate and consequently I was taking much longer to achieve things. I thought, perhaps I was just tired, and yet before lunch I had felt perfectly OK. I carried on relentlessly and after about an hour, Dave walked through the door. He had been coaching a group of children in football skills and had popped into the office to sort out a few bits and pieces. He studied a few papers on his desk and then asked me about some forms that were due to be completed and sent to County Hall that day. I answered him but just like the incident with Matthew two years earlier; the words came out in a complete jumble. He was very alarmed and did not know what to make of this strange woman. This was not the calm, take-everything-in-her-stride secretary he was used to. He asked the question again and once again I answered with a load of rubbish. It was frustrating for me, but strangely I felt quite calm about it. After all, it had happened before and it had gone away. *"Pat, what's wrong?"* Dave said with a very concerned expression on his face. I tried again to speak to him and this time I did manage to make sense but only just. I eventually managed to say the words *"happened before"* and then after a brief struggle with my handbag I was able to give him my personal telephone list. *"Do you want me to ring Keith?"* he asked with obvious understanding. Keith answered the phone immediately and although he was many miles away said he would set off for home at once. He was also able to reassure Dave that I would be all right and asked him if he could take me home. Fifteen minutes later Dave and I were sitting together in the lounge. He promised to stay with me until either Keith or Matthew arrived home. He could see that I was far from well and despite Keith's reassurance, was very concerned about me. By now I had developed very similar symptoms to the ones I had experienced before. There were pins and needles in my arm, there was no strength in my leg, one side of my face was numb and, of course, I was still unable to speak properly. My brain was still working. I had normal thoughts but my body just couldn't keep up. It was a totally weird sensation. Matthew was the first to arrive and he kept me company until Keith returned about an hour later.

I couldn't brush this incident away as easily as I had done two years earlier, particularly as the effects of this one lasted for several days which meant time off work. Several tests were carried out and the specialist reached his verdict. I was horrified. How could I have had a minor stroke – no, two minor strokes – how could I? Strokes were what old people suffered from. I was only in my forties. But I was told that a combination of a far-from-healthy body and a stressful environment had just been too much for me and what I needed was lots of rest and TLC. Four weeks' sick leave and the six-week school holiday period would give me the required rest which was good, but there was another consequence of the diagnosis and that was much harder to accept. The specialist informed me that I would have to notify the DVLA in Swansea about my condition and this would mean surrendering my driving licence for a period of six months. So many places I could have gone during my enforced absence from work and so many people I could have visited but it was not to be. I was grounded.

The new term started in September and I was ready to return to work. I now felt fully fit again, my batteries recharged. But, of course, I was still without a licence. So, on day one I headed for the local bus stop, timetable in hand. I only needed the bus for that one day, however, because a kind friend came to the rescue. He was a parent of one of the children at the school and he owned a minibus. He was contracted to take children in the morning from the village of Rawcliffe to the secondary school in Snaith and back again in the afternoon. I am very grateful that he took me to work, and back home again in the empty bus. Not only did he make it easier for me, we also shared a lot of humour on those journeys.

But now my mind was back in the present, in the year 2000, and although I may not have had any more strokes, I did have many other medical difficulties. My paid sick leave was coming to an end and I would now need to be assessed by a doctor from County Hall's education department. Firstly a senior nurse came out to see me at home and completed a questionnaire. She explained that there would be a meeting at County Hall on my case notes and then I would be summoned for an assessment interview. The day arrived and I don't know why but I felt very nervous. I was unable to drive so Matthew, on holiday from university, volunteered to take me there and back. Like the other four boys, he had passed his driving test at the first attempt, but he had taken his time. We had informed the driving instructor about Asperger syndrome and, following his advice, Matthew had carried on taking lessons with him after the standard course had been completed. These additional lessons continued until both of them felt confident about a positive result.

I arrived at County Hall and was shown into a brightly decorated room and was greeted by a smart man in his early forties. He explained that he was an occupational consultant and that it was his job to assess whether or not I was fit enough to return to work. He already had my notes that his nurse had completed several weeks before. Over the next two hours he examined me, asked me questions and told me about his medical experience. Mainly he was concerned with my capabilities on a daily basis, around the house. He explained that he had had a lot of involvement in helping members of the armed forces who had developed weird symptoms following their involvement in the Gulf War in the early 90s. Gulf War syndrome, as it became known, led to affected people having fatigue of the muscles, joints and organs of the body because of pollution from chemicals. At first it had been very difficult to diagnose as the illness presented itself in different ways in different people. The side effects were very diverse. The treatment for this was lots of rest and cognitive behaviour therapy, which meant patiently learning how to manage the disability effectively. Because of this experience, he was able to identify that I was a casualty of ME and had been suffering from this condition for close to twenty years. He realised that I had learned to cope with the condition without really knowing what it was. Because it had been undetected for so long it had taken its toll on my body and there was unlikely to be any way of correcting the damage. ME was not the only thing attacking my body. Arthritis continued to affect my joints and my GP had recently diagnosed fibromyalgia, which was causing problems with most of my muscles and joints. The consultant stated that I was unfit to return to work as this would put more pressure on my system and I would probably become seriously ill. Also, I would be a creaking gate as an employee and would go from a previously very reliable worker to a totally unreliable one as a result of my illness. He said I had done very well to struggle on so far but it was unrealistic to assume I could follow an occupation in the future. He said that he would be writing to my head teacher and board of governors with his findings and that he would be recommending that I cease working on ill health grounds. He did tell me that any one of the three conditions that I had would probably render me unfit for work and as I had all three it was virtually a certainty. This was a huge shock. Despite the fact that I was ill and had been for some time, I still had this hope and wish that it would miraculously go away. I wanted to go back to school. I wanted to see the happy little faces that had made my job so worthwhile over the past thirteen years. I was not fit to be a secretary. I could accept that, even though I knew I would miss it. But surely I could manage to assist the teaching staff in some way? But the doctor had explained that idyllic as it sounded, I would soon be back in the tension and drama of everyday school life and my body was just not up to it. And when I was honest with myself I had to admit that I had trouble hearing properly in a busy classroom. I had been prescribed a hearing aid after admitting to our school nurse one day that I was struggling to hear a child read. I had no clarity of sound and against normal classroom background noises; I was failing to pick up on some words that children were saying. It was detected that I had lost about 50% of my hearing. High sounds were not too bad. I could often hear the doorbell ring at home when most others in the family did not hear it. The problem was deep sounds which were muffled and inaudible. I was prescribed a hearing aid but this did nothing to improve the clarity for me. In fact, it did not help at all, because instead of just magnifying the deep sounds, all sounds were magnified and if anything it made it even harder for me to decipher the words the child at the side of me was reading.

So finally I had to admit to myself that my school career had ended. In my thirteen years at Rawcliffe I met some lovely children and some very supportive parents and I worked with a marvellous team of teachers, governors and support staff. In that time there were three very diverse head teachers, two males and one female. They all had their own way of working, their own strengths and foibles as we all have. One thing they were all united in was their tireless striving to make sure that the children in their care got the best education that they were capable of administering. They were all passionate about their role. They would all go that extra mile to help the children and with all three it took its toll on their own health in some shape or form. I was very lucky and very privileged to be part of it all. Instead of sitting at home worrying about my body letting me down, I had been part of a very professional team. During this time I made two very strong friendships. Di was already at the school when I arrived, working part time as a class teacher. She had three sons, and that gave us a lot in common, particularly as her eldest son and Matthew moved to the secondary school at the same time. We had similar ups and downs with our children over the years, but always managed to have a laugh together and helped each other move forward positively into the future. Although a few years younger than me, we found that we had much in common and on more than one residential visit we ended up sharing a twin room. Neither of us was used to being on our own away from home without husbands or children, and we used to joke that it felt like being away at boarding school together.

As the school secretary, it was my responsibility to arrange supply teachers, and it was because of this that I became friendly with Halina who was able to help with a temporary vacancy on many occasions. She was always a bundle of energy and had a good sense of humour, which became infectious. My friendship with these two very dedicated women developed throughout the thirteen years and, happily, despite my retirement and their career changes, it would continue to flourish and develop into the future.

Keith's work threw up an opportunity for me to recuperate for a week at their expense. In February we flew to Nice and travelled to Monte Carlo and spent a very exciting week discovering the principality. We visited the International World Circus which the Grimaldi family hosted every year. On the final night, Prince Rainier, Prince Albert, Princess Caroline and Princess Stephanie and Prince Rainier's grandchildren were all there to enjoy the final performances and the highlight of the evening was the awards presentation to the winning performers. We dined in a restaurant at La Colombe d'Or, up in the mountains in a village called St Paul de Vence along the Cote d'Azure. On the walls in the dining room were priceless pieces of artwork by artists such as Picasso, Matisse, Braque, Calder and Delaunay. There were countless beautiful works of art that the owner, Paul Roux, wanted on display for the enjoyment of his guests, rather than being locked away in a museum. The majority of these paintings had come into the hands of the owner at a time when the artists were struggling. They would eat at the owner's generosity and in return they would give him sketches or paintings. At the time, of course, none of these people were famous – it was just a business deal. Nowadays, however, such works of art are priceless and no insurance company will insure them as the premium would be impossible to cover. Here we were relaxed, eating, and looking at some of the world's most famous artists' early work. Not only was the food out of this world, the ambience was incredible. Many famous people have stayed at this hotel including F Scott Fitzgerald, Charlie Chaplin, Winston Churchill, Robert de Nero, Orson Wells and Madonna. We visited the casino and we dined at the Café de Paris, which was situated beside our hotel, and also had many other experiences too numerous to list. We both enjoyed our visit although Keith was always relieved when we were on our own. He needs his 'cooling time', his winding down time and this he cannot achieve in and amongst a large group of people he knows. In family groups he has learned to relax and be himself but he still finds other groups very difficult. It was a wonderful change for me, as I never thought I would be able to go on holiday again. In order to execute my daily stoma irrigation I had to carry an enormous amount of medical stock with me. In fact I had to get a medical certificate to allow me to take the extra baggage on the plane. The process was long and arduous and I couldn't leave the hotel room until it was completed. Because of this, we had to miss out on some of the events on the itinerary. What the break did show me was that slowly I was able to return to some sort of normality. I could socialise and I could still travel if I paced myself.

What I should have done at this time was throw out the past altogether and start to live within my new capabilities. For a long time I always felt that I would regain my former energy. I would be back to 'normal'. I had not taken into consideration my immune system and how everything took so much longer to heal now. The answer was really so simple but I would not see it for a long time to come. The answer was to take each day as it came, do what I could physically cope with, and leave what I could not. In other words, prioritise the important things and forget about the rest. By ignoring this at the time, I was compounding my ill health and did not realise it. I would not allow myself to read during the day or to watch television as I kept telling myself that this was lazy and that I had to keep myself busy. I caught up on all my correspondence but this brought with it problems. Because I had lots of time to fill I would attempt to type for longer than I was physically able and then the following day I would not be able to grip anything. The pain in my hands was excruciating. I would set myself a task in the garden but instead of doing just that one task and then going indoors to recover, I would attempt to go further until I literally dropped with exhaustion. It was Keith who gave me the hard word: *"If you want to stay in bed permanently then carry on as you are."*

"But I'm not doing it on purpose," was my curt reply.

"You are answerable to yourself," he said calmly.

"But I have commitments to the family."

Keith shook his head, looked at me sympathetically and said, *"If you end up in bed permanently, the life of the family will still carry on. It may not be as good as before but life will not stand still."*

His message got through to me. What good was I to anyone if I was bedridden and people had to look after me? And, of course, what a waste of my life! Some people do not have a choice, but surely I did. I only ended up in bed when I did too much. If I could learn to pace myself, things could get better. So with much support from Keith I began to learn how much I could do both in and out of the house before making myself ill. It took a long time of experimenting, a long time of frustration. Periodically, when I felt I was improving, I would do a bit too much the following day and then swiftly went downhill again. Eventually the pendulum began to swing fairly evenly. If I behaved then I had good days and if I misbehaved, it was followed by bad days. It was up to me, I could control it.

In April we were invited to join Keith's colleagues on a trip to Sun City near Johannesburg in South Africa. I remember he rang me from the office and said that we had been invited. I could feel that he would much rather have said thank you, but we would be unable to go. I managed to convince him that we were very fortunate to be given this chance and would probably never get such a great opportunity again and at least we would be together, and it was not work. I convinced him that with his help I would be able to manage OK and that with careful planning it would not be too overpowering for him. It worked. We stayed at a beautiful hotel called The Palace. Neither of us had experienced such splendour and elegance, so much rich dark wood and beautiful materials and fabrics. We enjoyed the experience together and have wonderful memories and photographs of the game reserves, the parks and the camaraderie. The only thing that would have stopped me going on that trip would have been a vaccination. We had initially been advised that when visiting any part of southern Africa it was usual to have a vaccination against malaria and typhoid. But re-assurance followed that the risk of infection in the sanitised area of South Africa that we were visiting was very low.

Matthew was now struggling at Guildhall. He found that the course he had chosen was not presenting him with the challenges that he had expected and he was not learning as he had hoped. The course, being geared towards the achievement of a degree, was far too theoretical for him and what he needed was practical, hands-on learning. But his main difficulty was loneliness. The first few months had gone fairly well as he settled into his new environment. He had thoroughly enjoyed the millennium celebrations in the capital. He had bought over a thousand party poppers and then sold them at a very healthy profit in the streets alongside the River Thames in the hours leading up to midnight. Now it was back to reality and he found himself all alone in a big city. We had helped him to move into his flat the previous October. The car had been packed to capacity. I remember feeling very inadequate as Keith and Matthew mounted the steps two at time, all the way up the four flights of stairs. I went up much more slowly and once there had spent my time unpacking. There I stayed until it was time to leave. Once the unpacking was completed we had a picnic in one of the local parks and spent the rest of the day together. I recall being very worried about Matthew as we drove back home and once we were home, I had to ring him, but he had said he was fine and was just about to go to a party which had been arranged for freshers. We went down to visit him as often as we could. We would take him out for the day and have a good chat and a few laughs and then I would get really upset when the time came to leave him in his tiny student flat, way up on the fourth floor. Although he gave us a big smile and a wave as he looked down at us in the courtyard below, it was clear to see he was lonely. He had conversed with a number of the other students who were living in the same accommodation block, many of whom were from completely different countries and cultural backgrounds. It was this diversity of cultures that seemed to interest him and excite him about London. Occasionally he would team up with some of his fellow students and join in their social activities. On one of these occasions he went to the Tottenham area with two young women who had heard good reports about a nightclub there. When they arrived at the club they were disappointed to find a long snaking queue of over a hundred young people. The girls had expressed their disappointment and suggested they should go elsewhere, but Matthew had persuaded them to join the line. What he hadn't realised was that their disappointment was enhanced by a high level of discomfort and to some degree fear. One of them quietly asked Matthew if he had noticed anything unusual about the people in the queue. He admitted that he hadn't, and so he stepped out of the line in to the dark passageway and quickly surveyed the mass of people in front of them. Surely, it was just a queue of ordinary people? And then he realised that because of the gloom, all he could see were lots of bright eyes and white teeth. Every single person was black. Although this fact didn't have any significance for him, and he would have been quite happy to stay there, he now understood why both of his companions were feeling a little uneasy being part of a trio of the only white people in the neighbourhood, and so they headed for the nearest tube station and a different venue. Despite trying very hard he had not made any real friendships during his time at Guildhall and it was so obvious that he was desperate for someone to confide in. Virtually every night we would talk to him on the phone. We had bought a new telephone that was equipped with a microphone and loudspeaker so that we could have a three-way conversation. These sessions would continue for hours as we listened to him and tried desperately to console him. They were desperate times for him.

Darren decided that the time had come to move out of the family home and seek his independence. He and a friend had found a suitable house in nearby Castleford. They decided that they could share the rent and associated costs and divide up the household chores on an amicable basis. So for the first time in our history Keith and I were on our own. All our birds had flown the nest, although we knew that it wasn't for long, as Matthew was due back home from university for the summer holidays in less than three weeks. We would have to make the most of this short period but as it turned out, it was shorter than we thought. Matthew decided to come back earlier and so our quiet house was only quiet for four days. And then in late August Jonathan and Beccy moved in with us. They had been living in a flat in Hessle for a year and a half and had decided that they wanted to have a year in Australia. In preparation for that trip, they needed to sort out their affairs and the best way of achieving that was by vacating the flat. Once again the house was buzzing with people.

In September 2000 we joined family in Barcelona for our nephew Ross's wedding. The wedding ceremony was at the Basilica and the reception at the Palau de Musica. Matthew was able to join us on this trip and we all thoroughly enjoyed exploring the city and surrounding areas. I had passed through the city many years before while visiting nearby holiday resorts but for Keith and Matthew it was their first visit to Spain. Keith had always had a thing about Spain as his vision was of one resort after another looking just like Blackpool but with a few more outdoor pools and guaranteed sunshine. When I reminded him of this and asked him if his views on Spain had now changed, he reminded me that we were in Catalonia and that Catalonia was to Spain what Scotland was to England, united but totally different. That reminded me about how precise he always was about the names of countries and about why various groups in the world were fighting. He had always taken a keen interest in the developments in Northern Ireland and the Middle East and always tried to understand the issues from both sides, always looking at it from the human perspective.

"Why is it always so difficult," he would say, "to get two different cultures to live side by side, to accept their differences and to learn from each other? It's such a simple formula and yet the human race keeps on getting it wrong."

Despite having had the experience of a lifetime in London, Matthew had decided to look for an alternative course. He had trawled the available courses and universities again and this time came up with a course in entrepreneurship, which was running at The University of Stafford. He had found accommodation in the centre of the town in a newly converted complex in the old education offices. He had not declared his diagnosis to anyone in London but this time decided to register with the student support counsellor. He was quite surprised when he found that it was a woman. All the professionals that he had confided in up to now had been men. He told me that he had actually found it a lot easier to talk to her. His experiences from London behind him, he now seemed reasonably settled and ready for the forthcoming term.

The year 2000 had, so far, been a comparatively good year for me. Despite the trauma of my worsening health and resultant forced retirement and the usual mixed bag of emotions caused by Keith and Matthew, I had been able to enjoy some wonderful experiences. It had started on the beach on Holy Island and continued with some particularly memorable journeys to different parts of the world. But as we moved towards the end of October, the year was about to turn sour. Darkness was about to descend on me and my family.

Chapter 13

DARKNESS

On the 23rd of October 2000 at approximately 4am, the world of our family appeared to stop. Keith was preparing for a trip to London. The house was quiet as he crept around not wanting to disturb any of us.

The telephone rang.

His screaming woke me. What was wrong? He came in to the bedroom shaking. The entire colour had gone from his face. He held me and said I needed to be strong.

The words he stuttered were, *"We will never see Karl again."*

Our eldest son, Karl, my first baby, who had just turned thirty only a week before was dead.

Karl was dead.

I remember letting out one long scream and felt almost unable to stop. My head was racing. He was away working on the oil rigs. I knew this and I had always feared something might happen. Had there been a fire? Had there been an explosion? I was unable to comprehend any information. All I could picture was our son with his long flowing hair, his long legs and, most of all, the twinkle in his smile. It could not be true. There must be some mistake. Keith did not get as emotional as he was at that moment unless something had really upset him, so it must be true. He sat and hugged me and explained that all he knew so far was that Karl had been in the woods near home shooting rabbits and foxes and there had been an accident and that he was dead. Later that morning he should have been at Aberdeen Airport to take his helicopter flight out to The Alba, the rig he was working on at the time. He would never make that trip again, but far worse than that, we would never see him again. My mind was playing tricks. No, this had not happened! Because of Karl's shifts off shore, we had seen little of him and Kath in the past year. Our only contact had been by phone, although we had been able to communicate by email while he was on the rig. I could pretend he was still 450 miles away; however in my heart I knew I was wrong.

After two long-term relationships had run their course Karl had met Kath in a nightclub in Castleford. Although a native of Keith in Banffshire, she was working in Yorkshire at the time. Her passion was horses and she also had a love for all kinds of animals, particularly dogs. This was manna from heaven for Karl and they very quickly struck up a friendship, which developed quite rapidly into something much deeper. Eventually they moved in together and then there were three of them: Kath, Karl and an elderly greyhound called Rum. At first they lived in a flat alongside the stables where Kath worked, training and looking after horses. Karl would help her at weekends and after he had finished work on weekdays. Then, later, with Darren's help, they moved to the centre of Castleford. Their new home was not ideal as they were now in an upstairs flat with a greyhound but they did have a patio so Rum could spend time outside. Kath quickly set to work to add plant pots full of shrubs to make an artificial roof garden. They were happy together but then Kath had to give up the thing that really gave her the most pleasure, her work with horses. She had been advised by her doctor to take some time out, because old back injuries were causing pain and she was at risk of doing permanent damage if she continued the heavy work involved in feeding, grooming and training the horses. She was very upset with this instruction but took the advice and looked around for something else to do and was soon working in a pet store. Karl at this time was on permanent night shift. He did not like this but was assured that continental shifts would be brought in before long and so he would get a variety of work times. Three years later, however, he was still working permanent nights. He had visited Kath's family in the north of Scotland on several occasions and was always reluctant to leave when the time came to return home. He told us how he loved the countryside in that area and how he could just see himself living there. If they could just get a cottage in the area, they could have some land and keep their own horses, but for the time being it just wasn't possible, so they would have to stay in the flat in Castleford. They both felt that Rum needed some company and they soon acquired a variety of animals – a wounded squirrel, two snakes called Hiss and Sid, two chipmunks, a pet rat, a rabbit and a gorgeous harlequin Great Dane puppy they named Murphy. By the time he was one, he weighed almost ten stones and could put his paws on Karl's shoulders. Karl was six foot three in height so Murphy was some force to be reckoned with. If he decided he liked you, he would encourage you to play with him. He was such a softy but did not know his own strength so you had to remain alert at all times. Initially, Rum viewed the newcomer with disdain. He had a settled life and didn't see why this ball of dynamite had to come and upset his peace. Just like the rest of us, though, before too long you could see he loved Murphy, who while wanting to play all the time, respected Rum. One word from his big brother and he would quickly do as he was told. Rum's regal demeanour said it all. 'He who should be obeyed'. Eventually Kath got the all clear from the doctor and they rented a stable nearby and bought a chestnut foal called Harvey. Kath was eager to look after him, but Karl feared that she would do too much and make herself ill again, so he insisted she left the strenuous jobs to him. Unfortunately, it was Karl who suffered. One day when he was helping Kath and trying to lighten her load by mucking out the stable, she spotted him slumped over the bonnet of the car, struggling to get his breath. His childhood asthma had returned and he had to be taken to hospital and it was thought that he would be kept in overnight. However, once he was put on oxygen and then a stronger inhaler was introduced, he soon started to recover and was allowed to go home, but it was a hazard he had to be aware of in the future.

His asthma attacks had started when he was four years of age and an inhaler had been prescribed which he adjusted to very quickly. He used it daily and seemed to understand the need for it and what would happen if he forgot to use it. He could become very breathless in a short space of time. When he started school, life became more stressful and he was now doing PE and playing more games and taking more daily exercise. At first he seemed to be coping with school, but often he was very breathless when he got home and it took him quite a while to recover each day. Sometimes I could see him hiding in the garden behind a bush or in the greenhouse. I soon realised he was hiding from other children as he did not want them to know he had a problem. After talking to his GP his inhaler was changed to a stronger version and he was advised to use it more frequently during the day.

Just as he had done as a child, now as an adult he knew he had to respect the problem and work with it. He always kept his special inhaler where he could get to it quickly and worked at building up his resistance to hay. It was not long before he could cope with moving it about again without collapsing.

In October 1997, four years after their first meeting, and a year after they became engaged, Karl's dream became a reality. They decided to move to Rothiemay, a village just outside Kath's hometown of Keith. Kath organised a farewell party so that they could say goodbye to friends and family. Our favourite cake shop in Selby provided a beautiful cake, which was mounted by figures of their two beloved dogs Rum and Murphy. We had left a photograph of the dogs so that the young lady could model them realistically. The cake was spectacular and the models were indeed very realistic and both Karl and Kath appreciated the effort made to make this a happy event. Later that weekend we held another gathering at our house for more family and grandparents who did not want to attend the disco-style party which they would find too noisy. Both events were dual purpose to celebrate their move to Scotland and also Karl's twenty-seventh birthday. The following weekend, Keith, Darren and Matthew helped Karl and Kath to load all their belongings into a removal van, and once that was full other things were packed into their car. I had been at the flat during the day, helping Kath to clean and once the van was loaded and they checked that no pets had been left behind Keith drove the van and Karl took his car, and we all went to Snaith to get a good night's sleep before the long drive north. We sat down to our last meal together for some time and listened to their plans for their new home. Most of the animals spent the evening in their respective cages in the van, but the snakes had been brought in to the house in order to keep them at the correct temperature. Rum and Murphy were also in the house and there was an additional animal there as well as they had by now also acquired a cat. It had been a leaving present to them from Kath's friends at work. Neither of them was very keen at the thought of having a cat with the two large dogs, so their plan was to pass her on the Kath's sister once they arrived in Scotland. It was already obvious to us, however, that they had fallen in love with this bundle of fluff and that she would not leave their family. Someone else who had fallen in love with Shaun the cat was Jonathan. After the pub that night when everyone except myself was in bed, he came back with friends and let Shaun out of the cat basket in which she was sleeping. Yes, Shaun was female! Shortly after naming the cat they realised he was in fact a she but they liked the name and never changed it. Jonathan played for ages with this cat until at last I said, *"I think you should put Shaun back in her cat basket, we all need to get some sleep."*

"OK," was the answer but in his enthusiasm he appeared to break the catch on the basket. I was panicking at the thought of this kitten wandering about and one of the dogs accidentally standing on her and I didn't know how they would keep her safe on the very long journey to Scotland. But I didn't need to worry because Jonathan had put his engineering brain to work and fixed the cat basket so the problem was over and we could now go to bed. About an hour later, when I was in bed, I heard noises downstairs. I'm not usually a light sleeper, but I was having difficulty that night at the thought of my eldest son going to the other end of the British Isles, which meant that I would have to get used to seeing him less frequently. I crept downstairs to investigate the noise and when I opened the kitchen door there was Jonathan sitting on the floor in the middle of the room talking away to Shaun who was in his hands.

"I'm just saying goodbye to her – I won't see her for a long time."

So we sat together for a few minutes until he finally put Shaun into the basket for the last time. It was now three thirty in the morning and the travellers would be up and about in less than three hours.

At seven o' clock we were all outside the house having tearful hugs, or at least I was. There was no room for me in the removal van. Darren, Matthew and Keith were squashed into the cab and the van itself was filled to capacity. In the back of Karl and Kath's car were two dogs and a cat, together with an assortment of boxes and bags Reluctantly I knew I had to stay at home. I made Keith promise that we could visit within a few weeks, so that I would be able to share their love of the Glen. This was agreed and so with a very sad heart I said goodbye to them all, wished them well and then, with tears in my eyes, set about cleaning up after the many people and pets that had shared the house the previous evening. The following night I drove to Leeds and met a weary band of 'Mr Shifters'. They were returning the hire van to the depot and I had been programmed to pick them up from there. It was with much excitement that I met them – I was eager to hear all the news. The move had gone well and they had seen Karl and Kath settled in their new croft.

But now it was all gone. Karl was dead.

Our first challenge was to break the news to Beccy and Jonathan who were asleep in the rear bedroom. They would probably already be wondering what all the commotion was about. Keith and I went together to knock on their bedroom door. Both of them appeared and all I could do was hug Jonathan and slowly tell him that his big brother was dead. I felt it was better for me to state the fact straight away. Keith's words to me had been *"We will never see Karl again,"* and this had sent my mind racing. As gently as I wanted to break it to Jonathan, I didn't want to confuse him. I needed to deliver it gently but straight. He was heartbroken, they both were. After minutes of hugging and holding each other we needed to make plans. Jonathan's next words were, *"How can we tell Darren? It will kill him."*

Darren and Karl were so close. Karl and Kath leaving for Scotland three years before had affected him very badly. He had lost his soul mate. Now we had to break the news that he had lost him forever. Jonathan bravely said he would break the news to him. So very soberly the four of us got into the car and drove to Darren's house in Castleford. As we all expected he was devastated and like the rest of us he was inconsolable. Through the tears, he was able to mumble a few words. *"Why has it happened to Karl? He didn't deserve to die. He was enjoying his new career and his new life and he had so much to look forward to."*

He was in a complete daze as he scooped up a few bits and pieces and climbed in to the car with the rest of us. The next point of call was Richard. We needed to get to his house before he set off for work. He was also devastated. Like Matthew, the loss of his granddad the previous year had really affected him, but he knew he had enjoyed a long life whereas Karl hadn't.

"He's too young to die," he said. *"He's my big brother and he should be here."*

Matthew was away at university and still had to be told. We had no intention of ringing him and alarming him. Jonathan, Beccy and Keith set off on a very sad journey to Stafford University to tell Matthew the tragic news. Once again Jonathan wanted to break the news to his brother. Keith and Beccy waited on one of the landings of the building as Jonathan went directly to Matthew's room. After several minutes they both appeared with tears in their eyes. Matthew collected a few belongings and they all climbed into the car for an even sadder journey home.

Darren and I were at home waiting for any news that was available. We knew very little, other that we were never going to see Karl again. Later that morning we received a call from Dennis and Maureen who said they were on their way down from their home, just over the Scottish border in Hawick, to be with us. It was a very sad day, a new experience for all of us and one we would never wish to repeat. We all cried a lot but I remember we recalled individual tales of Karl and already we were starting to re-live positive memories. But, of course, the practicalities of the situation kept coming up. What about arrangements? The undertaker, the funeral, flowers? We had no idea. Kath was his partner we would respect her wishes but we didn't yet know what they were. Her sister was communicating with us by phone but it wasn't the same as being there. It was very tough when we were over four hundred miles away. Between us, Karl's four parents, we decided that we must make the journey to Scotland the following day, even though not one of us was really fit to drive all that way, but we knew that we had to get there. Keith, as always the practical one, came up with a plan. He would get us there by hiring a minibus to drive the ten of us to Banffshire the next day. Dennis and Maureen returned home that evening and Keith went out to make all the arrangements. He then started the horrible task of breaking the news by telephone to the rest of our family and our friends. We finally got into bed in the early hours of the morning but neither of us could sleep and, of course, Keith needed his sleep that night because the plan was to drive to Banffshire and then back again to Hawick in the same day. It was a round trip of about 700 miles.

The morning came and we left early and picked Dennis and Maureen up about two hours later. It was a very sombre journey but we did talk from time to time and the conversation was always positive about Karl and his family with Kath and all their animals. I think we only stopped once to get refreshments on the endless journey. It was about three o'clock in the afternoon when we arrived at Kath's house. Her sister Shirley had moved in to support her but she also had the support of her Dad and sister Lorna who both lived nearby. Kath was in bed and the doctor had prescribed a sedative so she was too drowsy to talk to us. We talked with her father John and her sisters and it was obvious from those conversations that Kath was in a very fragile, shocked state. The biggest disappointment for me was not being able to see Karl. He had been taken to the police mortuary in Aberdeen in preparation for an autopsy. I needed to see him as I still could not believe he was dead. We discussed brief details with Shirley as she was in charge of arrangements and we were happy to fit in with whatever arrangements they felt were appropriate. This was new to us and very difficult. How were we going to get through the next week? The grief was immense. Eventually Kath felt well enough to talk to me. We were a big group, we were all family and had every right to be there, but we would overpower her if we stayed together. I went into the bedroom on my own. She was distraught. She told me that Karl was due to fly back to the rig on the Monday, so he had gone out shooting on Sunday night as a way of relaxing on his last night on shore. Midnight had come and gone and Karl had not returned. Kath had become very uneasy as he was usually in the nearby woods for about a couple of hours, and she was wondering what could have happened. When it got to 2am she became really worried and decided to ring John, her father. He would know what to do and he could be there with her in less than fifteen minutes. Poor Kath, the time between ringing her father and him arriving had seemed like an eternity. She was on her own, with all sorts of thoughts going through her mind. But John had not gone straight to her house; instead he had gone to the spot where he and Karl had spent many happy hours together shooting both rabbits and foxes. Kath heard the car pull up and her father climbed the driveway slowly approaching the house. When she saw his ashen face, she feared the worst. Karl would not be coming back. He had had a terrible fatal accident. After a few more tears she smiled and told me that on his 30th birthday only eight days before that terrible night, he had proposed to her. Despite having been engaged for some time, he had now decided that it was time to act and he had delivered the question in the traditional way, crouched down on one knee, to which she had replied, "Yes." She continued to smile and then closed her eyes as she fell asleep, exhausted. That's when I knew it was time for us to go, although I felt that I never wanted to leave this spot ever again. I wanted to stay where Karl had been happiest. While we had been in Karl's home, Darren, Richard, Jonathan, Beccy and Matthew had all been wandering freely between house and outbuildings. Feeling closer to Karl, watching the horses he loved to look after, or just wandering into Karl's workshop and feeling his presence. All his tools were neatly kept, and this was another place that he and John had spent time together, constructing fences, carrying out running repairs and building the new stable block that they had just completed. Although Karl had two fathers already who both loved him, John also seemed to treat him as the son he never had. Common sense prevailed and I knew we had to leave. Kath had her family for support and our family needed to be together to get through this very emotional period. It was mid-evening and Keith by this time was very tired but he knew he had to get us all back to Hawick. He had had a break from driving while we were at Kath's but the grief and pressure was taking its toll.

We arrived at Dennis and Maureen's cottage after midnight. Keith was the first to retire and collapsed on the bed fully clothed; that was it, he was asleep. The pressure on him that day was immense. He had to transport the whole family on a very long return journey, often driving while tears were flowing down his cheeks. He had a huge responsibility for all our lives but he completed the task with great precision and with his usual stamina and full support. I went back to the rest of the family. They were all very subdued but Richard seemed to be in an inconsolable state. He had been close to Karl whose pet name for him when he was young had been 'titch'. He talked about this and related stories from his youth and about times when he and all his brothers had been happy. Then it became obvious that he had another very worrying problem. He and Sarah were having a difficult time together and it seemed likely that they would be separating. He was very upset at the prospect and was finding it very hard to work out his future role with his daughter, Leah. Three of his four parents stayed up the rest of the night talking with Richard and trying to give him much-needed support. It was 6am when I climbed into bed beside Keith. Despite the long day, the adrenalin was keeping me going, so when Keith awoke as I slid under the covers, I was happy to talk with him. He needed to talk. He needed to be reassured that he had supported us fully the previous day. We talked about Karl who was never away from either of our minds and we talked specifically about getting home and planning for the even more grieving trip, which was to come, saying goodbye to Karl for the last time and the funeral.

During the following week we wanted to make arrangements for our return visit in order to attend Karl's funeral but because of a backlog of work at Aberdeen police mortuary, we got the same message every day for about five days. His body will be released soon. The waiting was a nightmare and we were all in limbo. Each day we were still in the same frozen state. Only the beautiful cards and letters that we were receiving daily were sustaining us through this horrendous period. Keith took over all the planning and organisation – he seemed to spend every minute on the telephone. And it was Beccy who took on the important role of making sure we had food. She and Jonathan made trips to the supermarket and made sure washing was up to date and as much as Jonathan was grieving himself he tried his best to support the family. Beccy was always at my side to keep my spirits up and to organise things. Simple, everyday tasks were at this point in time beyond me. Eventually I was told that Karl was on his way to the undertaker's in Keith. The date of the funeral was set and we could now make our arrangements. Then the following day I received a message that left me numb. I was told that I probably would not be able to see Karl because of the time lapse between his death and the autopsy I was being told that deterioration had taken place and his coffin would probably be sealed by the time we arrived. I was inconsolable. I wanted Keith to drive me to Scotland that day, there and then, as I needed to be with Karl. He had been my baby; he had been my adventurous child and most of all he had been my loving young man who had created a family with Kath for lots of the orphaned or struggling animals. Even if I could only touch his little finger then that is what I needed to do. Keith calmed me down yet again and said he would be talking to the undertaker. He promised that one way or another I would be able to say goodbye the way I needed to even if it meant setting off that moment to see him He came back from the telephone and reassured me that we were not going there and then and that I would be able to say goodbye. Although, I was very anxious, I trusted Keith. He had never told me a lie before so why should he tell me one now?

This time we travelled to Scotland in two cars and arrived at a hotel in Abelour, a small town close to Keith, the day before the funeral. Matthew had taken on the task of booking our accommodation. The owner was a very dour gentleman who showed us around and made us very welcome. He knew the purpose of our visit and indeed sympathised with us as he was still grieving the death of his wife two years before. After sorting out the sleeping arrangements, the four parents and Matthew headed off to see Kath. The rest of the group decided to stay at the hotel.

We spent a couple of hours with Kath talking over the following day. She told us about the vicar who would be leading the service. She had been afraid that, as she did not attend church regularly, it might be difficult to relay the information, which she felt would give Karl the service that she wanted him to have and he would have wanted for himself. No lamenting hymns for him or her, no long religious chants. It was to be up beat and a reflection of Karl and Kath's taste in music. She had been very pleasantly surprised when the vicar related his own love of heavy metal music and they had been able to have a laugh together at a very strained time. Kath's sister, Shirley, and the rest of her family had done a stalwart job of organising everything at their end. Everyone wanted the following day to pass as smoothly as possible for Kath. It was going to be a difficult day for all of us but would Kath get through it without breaking down? Would she collapse? She was so fragile.

We left the cottage and drove to the undertakers. This was going to be difficult. I could pretend Karl would still be coming home. I did not see him every day and therefore it was easy to pretend that he was still happy in the Highlands, his favourite spot. I needed to talk to him, I needed to kiss him, and I needed just to hold his hand.

Keith held me as we went into the undertakers. As we entered the room I saw the coffin and then I saw Karl. Wait a minute; this person has short hair! This was not my Karl! It flashed through my mind that he had told me on the phone recently that he had had his hair cut short. This had surprised me at the time, because although he had had many different hairstyles throughout his life, in the later stages it had always been long. He was wearing a grey shirt and darker grey trousers. Where were his tight drainpipe jeans and his Metallica T-shirt with the sleeves chopped off?, I wondered. All this was rushing through my brain. What did it matter what he was wearing? I touched his hair and I touched his face. Apart from a tiny scratch on his cheek and a slightly bigger purple bruise on his forehead, he was perfect. He was handsome. He was my Karl. If only he would open his eyes and talk to me. I could not let go of his hand. I could not leave him. My thoughts started to race. Our camera was in the car. I wanted to take a photograph of him. How macabre was this? I could not voice my thoughts as the others would think I was mad but I wanted a photograph of him at peace. He looked just like the gentle giant of the nickname that his teenage friends had given him. I held Karl and I kissed him and all the time I was talking to him telling him how much he was loved and how I would miss our conversations. All his life we had grown-up conversations, we had fought many battles together but we had always been united. I told him how his brothers had always looked up to him and how they were going to be lost without him at the helm. Keith and Maureen and Matthew each had their own private period with Karl and gave him their messages through masses of tears and then I gave him a final kiss on his cheek and managed to get myself out of the room. Keith held my hand and supported me to the car.

I had no idea what was happening next but Dennis drove to the glen where Karl had died; The place where he had spent happy hours on his own or with John, who had been a gamekeeper for most of his working life. Inside I was shouting 'No I can't go there. It's an evil place, I will not go'. Again this was all going on in my brain, but I was too frozen to say anything, I was in pieces. I had just done the hardest thing I had ever had to do in my life and that was to say goodbye to my eldest son. All the time in my head there were pictures of the day he was born, how happy we were and how adorable he was. The car was a 4x4 and at first it triumphed over the rough terrain but the very muddy conditions eventually proved too much for it and we climbed out of the vehicle a little sooner than intended. The five of us made the long walk over rain-soaked grass. Throughout the walk, I kept muttering to myself, *"I shouldn't be here."* Suddenly we were at the spot where Karl had lost his life and Maureen was putting flowers into my hand. She had bought some for this purpose but I had not known about them until that moment. She started throwing flowers to the ground in a random fashion and I followed suit. I remember thinking they looked pretty in the grass. Bad thoughts were being overtaken by good thoughts. I looked up and saw the area for the first time. The thick wood of trees in the distance, the mountains in the background and nearer to us a croft, which had tumbled down years before. The stones had landed randomly on the grass and this must have been where Karl and John stood for warmth and shelter on the many evenings they spent in this place. Suddenly, I felt warm and now I understood why Karl loved it here. It was picturesque; it was calm, and most of all it was a quiet haven away from the bustle of the world. Instead of raving that I did not want to be there I was now pleased I had been given this insight, however brief, into Karl's world. I could picture what happened that night from the description that I had been given. The night had been very wild. The wind was howling and it had rained most of the day. Karl had seen a fox coming into the open and he was poised to shoot. He took aim and fired and the animal was hit. He started to walk towards the fox to make sure it was dead and to put it out of its misery if it was still alive, when suddenly he slipped on the wet grass. As he slipped his shotgun went off, the bullet hit a nearby rock, ricocheted off the rock and embedded itself in his chest. By the time John arrived he was too late to help. The police dealt with things very sympathetically and told John there had been several accidents that night because of the weather condition, but none as tragic as this. They also said that the chances of the gun going off in that way and causing death were a million to one. John was devastated, not least because he had introduced him to shooting. Karl had taken to his new hobby with an immense amount of enthusiasm. While still living in Yorkshire he had enrolled at a shooting club but out here in the highlands it was different. John had given him his first shotgun and Karl had been extremely careful in building a locked gun cupboard in which to keep it and this had been inspected and passed by the local police. I could never equate the two people – Karl the animal lover and Karl who went shooting. It was all to do with beliefs and the community in which he lived. They believed foxes and rabbits were vermin and that they needed to be kept to a certain level. My love for Karl allowed me to respect his beliefs and I never said to myself he should not have been there, or that it was wrong to follow this sport. My heart told me that he was enjoying his hobby and that he could easily have been killed on his way to work in a car accident, or in the helicopter that took him to the rigs. We headed back to the hotel to meet up with the rest of the family. We had a sad day coming up tomorrow, but tonight we all needed to be together and to try to relax.

When the following morning arrived, it was a very sunny, calm day. There was no wind at all. We all ate breakfast together as we knew this would be a long day – we were driving back to Hawick that evening after the service was over. No-one had much of an appetite but we had no idea when we would next eat so we made the best of it. The owner of the hotel had left us a key as he would be out for most of the day and we were to lock up after ourselves when we left for the crematorium. He had allowed us to wander around in his own private area; he really did understand what we were going through.

It was 1.30pm on Thursday 2nd November 2000 when we left the hotel. We had to reach the crematorium for a two o'clock service. We drove into the centre of Keith where the funeral cars were waiting for us, three black beautifully polished funeral cars, large Range Rovers which were probably essential for the terrain in this part of the country. Kath arrived and was escorted into the first car supported by her good friend and neighbour. Our family was split between the two remaining cars. We started on a slow sombre journey towards the coast. I can remember thinking at this time that if the funeral had been two weeks earlier we would have had great difficulty in getting there as a nationwide petrol strike had just finished. I tried to think about anything other than the journey we were taking. At 1.55pm we arrived at the crematorium at Buckie in Morayshire. We all got out of the cars and were escorted to the front of the building. I was carefully watching all my boys and felt that Darren needed support to get into the building so I grabbed hold of his arm and linked him into the service. We sat in the allocated pews and all I could see was Karl's coffin in front of us. This would be the last time we would ever be in his presence. I wanted this moment to last forever, just frozen here with all my family. It was too painful to move beyond this. The music started up and the vicar climbed into the pulpit. What he had to say was just perfect. He had obviously listened intently to Kath and had picked up on their devotion. He had got the measure of Karl perfectly. He brought in stories of their animals with several humorous examples of his kindness. The service ended with the song 'Because You Loved Me' by Celine Dion as apparently this had been their favourite shared song. There were two other pieces of music. One was a heavy metal tune and the other was a song from the film *The Lost Boys*. The time came to leave the crematorium. After a very shaky start we filed out from the front of the building and we and the other immediate family lined up against the wall outside, after which everyone filed past to pay his or her condolences. Where had all these people come from? As we were at the front and too upset to notice what was going on around I had not taken in the size of the congregation. Seats upstairs, which were occasionally used for overflow, had been packed to capacity. I just wanted to get back in the car and disappear but we seemed to be ushered into this line as if someone were actually in charge. For the next half an hour many, many people filed past us. A number of people hugged me and others were so upset that they could hardly see through their tears. For me it was a very uplifting experience with all these people here to celebrate Karl's life. Many of them said how much he was respected and liked in the community and they all said how much they would miss him. One very difficult and enlightening thing for me was when my mother pushed her way through the crowd and came to my side. She had travelled such a long way to be with us and I just kept her at the side of me as I tried my best to communicate with everyone who filed past with their condolences. At many intervals my mother would say in her loud voice, *"Do I know them?"* as if she were 'enjoying' a party and not a funeral. The most telling scene that all was not well with my mother's mind was when she spotted Maureen, Karl's second Mum. She gave her a big beaming smile and said, *"Fancy seeing you here, it's a while since I last saw you."*

Eventually we all met in the centre of Keith at a hotel, which had been booked for refreshments. It was the first time we were able to greet my parents, my brother, sister and niece. They'd had a gruelling journey to be with us. Judith and Helen had left London and driven to Yorkshire and collected my brother John. Together they had picked up my parents in Easington, County Durham. Then they all journeyed to the station in Newcastle and caught a train to Aberdeen where they picked up a hire car they'd previously booked, after which they still had a drive of another hour to the crematorium in Buckie. Their journey was made even more difficult by the amount of water on some of the roads brought on by the recent floods, which had affected most of the country. They had arrived at the place with only minutes to spare. Endless hours of travelling and if they been thirty minutes later, Karl's funeral would have been over; It did not bear thinking about.

Many people had driven all the way from Yorkshire, including Dennis's cousin, Karl's school friends and many of his old work friends from the Sulzer site in Leeds. It was the fact that Karl's request for a transfer to Sulzer Aberdeen had been granted, that had enabled them to move to Kath's home territory. All these people had endured very taxing journeys because of the extensive distance and the very bad weather conditions. There were also many more apologies from people who would have liked to have paid their respects but for different reasons could not join us in Scotland. Keith's boss and one of his colleagues had also taken the time to be with us. All these people just supported us through a terrible time. Several people came back to Karl and Kath's house although many others had to leave straight away because of the distance. I remember standing outside the croft talking to Stuart who was Karl's best friend on the rig. I could not help but think how enjoyable this situation would have been if we were all gathered for a party and Karl was among us. And after all, they had planned to marry soon – we could have all been here for a wedding celebration.

A group of us sat round and listened to the funny tales Stuart had to tell us of their experiences together on the rig. We felt quite privileged that he and two more of Karl's work mates could be with us. While working on the rig, Karl had been unable to obtain leave to attend his grandfather's funeral the previous summer. They were only flown off the rig for members of the immediate family and, apparently, a grandfather is not classed as immediate family. So, officially, these young men were not entitled to come to the funeral of someone who was just a friend, but they had no difficulty in getting permission and a special flight had been arranged for them as Karl had been so well-respected by everyone on the rig.

A lot of the time I kept slipping away into the spare bedroom. Photograph albums had been laid out for visitors to look at. Here I felt at peace as I looked at photographs taken the previous winter when Karl and John were struggling to erect fence posts by breaking through ice as they divided up the fields. Kath was with them doing her bit. There were also other photographs of them together blissfully happy. Although Kath herself couldn't look at the photographs, she knew that other people would want to, so she had asked her sister to arrange the albums in the room. Murphy came to sit with me. I told him how much I would miss Karl and he put his head on my knee. If he could have spoken I am sure his words would have been similar. This was now twice I had seen him since Karl's tragic death. Here he was, a huge distinguished looking Harlequin Dane with the air of someone who has lost his way and his whole world. It had been a very long and taxing day for Kath but I guess she did not want it to end either, as she was getting comfort from the stories of people who had been close to Karl. Also she was telling us new stories of their life in the Glen. The ones I felt most sorry for were Kath's family who had taken it upon themselves to be in charge and make sure everything ran smoothly and empathetically. They did a sterling job while grieving themselves. I do not think John will ever recover from the shock of finding Karl's body.

For our family the day was not yet over as we still had 250 miles to drive back to Hawick where we spent the night with Dennis and Maureen before leaving for home the next morning. Jonathan and Beccy decided to stay on with them for a few days as they felt we had Matthew and Darren at home while Dennis and Maureen were going to be on their own.

Karl had died in a very tragic accident in Keith. He had been with his fiancé Kath for seven years, three of these living in Scotland. His four brothers, his parents and Kath will never recover from his death. It was devastating. For many long months it was just a very emotional and dark time for the whole family and, of course, we were all affected in different ways. We are reminded of him almost daily by his love of music, his love of animals and his quest for adventure and knowledge.

He was such a lovely gentle young man with so many skills and so much to offer.

After the funeral, Matthew went back to Stafford to resume his studies, but he found it very difficult to settle. We got very used to the road between Snaith and the university, as we brought him home each weekend and took him back for the following week's studies. Eventually he decided to abandon his university plans.

The next two years were taken up in launching another business, this time with support from the Prince's Trust. His proudest moment and ours came when he received a Young Entrepreneur of the Year award in a competition sponsored by Shell Livewire. His business involved hot foil printing on to business cards and other stationery. A very cumbersome printing machine now had pride of place in his bedroom and Keith had adapted an old cupboard for it to stand on. It was an extremely heavy piece of equipment, so heavy in fact that it took three of them some considerable time to move it from the car, through the ground floor of the house, up the stairs, and across the landing to his bedroom. He started the business with great enthusiasm but found that he had difficulty finding an acceptable audience for the cards and did struggle somewhat on the attention to detail required with this type of work. He supplemented his income with a variety of part-time jobs and short-term contracts. He continued to try to find a reason for his confused thoughts. The diagnosis of Asperger syndrome had been a major step forward at the time but no-one was able to help him to make sense of it. He would regularly have short periods of confusion that made it impossible for him to concentrate on anything. All he could do was to take refuge in his bed for a couple of hours until it had passed. He visited many different professionals, both on his own and with either or both of us in support but nobody seemed able to pinpoint the problem and Matthew just got more and more frustrated. It was easy to see why he had so much trouble in concentrating on his business and why attention to detail suffered.

For the next couple of months I also found it very difficult to concentrate on anything, but I did try. We resumed our trips to both the Goole and Hull support groups. It was at one of the Goole meetings that we met up with the mother of my special little friend again. He had now been diagnosed with Asperger syndrome and had a part-time assistant helping him in school. This was music to my ears. He would now go through school with support instead of being classed as disruptive. Someone would listen to him. There was some justice in the world and I felt that my faith had been rewarded. His mum had joined the group to gain as much knowledge as she could. Now a single parent family, she was working hard to support him as well as keeping the rest of the family moving forward. I soon realised, however, that I could not continue to attend the groups. I often got emotional at these meetings. After all, children's lives were being discussed. Children who were not getting the support they needed and some of them were not anywhere near to being diagnosed at that point. I just felt I was unable to grieve and give my full support. Keith and Matthew continued for a few more months but Keith realised that he was getting too committed. Although he was still on leave from work following Karl's death, he knew he was taking too much on. He was travelling down the same path that he had done with the church council and the magazine, and so they both decided to pull out.

As far as I was concerned, Christmas 2000 was not going to happen. I did not intend to buy any presents other than those for Leah, our granddaughter. We would not be sending any Christmas cards, after all what did we have to celebrate? Our loss was still immense. I had not been able to answer the telephone since Karl's death. Jonathan had given us his answer phone that he brought with him when he had moved back into the family home so this meant that we wouldn't miss any calls. None of us had the stamina for Christmas. As it approached, I was getting more frustrated and upset. All my boys were hurting; they were missing their brother. Darren and Karl had been more like twins than just brothers. They were born a year and a half apart but they had always been unusually close. I doubted that he would ever really recover from the loss. And Jonathan had become a different person. He had split up from Beccy and was now spending more and more time in the pub. Also that summer my cousin Sue lost her five-year battle with cancer. Ironically she was Karl's godmother. She had been there at all the main events in his life, taking her duties as a godparent very seriously. He had been away on the Alba rig when Sue had passed away and when I gave him the news on his return to the mainland, I remember him saying to me how hard he had found the task of writing a condolence card to her husband and children. He said how unfair it was that she would not see her children grow up. One thing that she had been to us all was an inspiration. She fought the illness every step of the way, always taking positive steps to keep fit to give her the best chance possible.

Within months of each other, two fantastic individuals had been snatched away from our family.

That vision of a bright future that we had seen in the Northumberland sky, way back in January, was now well and truly tarnished. After a positive start, the year 2000 had delivered a number of heart-wrenching blows and what we didn't yet know was that the year had one more cruel episode up its sleeve.

Chapter 14

GRIEVING

It was December 9th and Keith went downstairs just after dawn and saw the light flashing on the telephone answering machine. He played the message and was devastated. Jonathan was in Pontefract hospital. He had been in a car accident and could we get there as quickly as possible. How long had the message been there? Why hadn't we heard it ring? Keith was asking himself these questions when he climbed the stairs. He entered the bedroom, gently woke me and said the terrifying words.

"Pat you need to be strong. I know you can do it."

He told me what he had heard and this time I asked no questions. I followed Keith like a sheep. We found some clothes and I was soon dressed. He had already woken Darren and Matthew who were obviously deeply distressed when he told them what was happening.

Darren, in particular, was confused as he had been with Jonathan during the previous evening. There had been a party at the pub to celebrate the fact that Jonathan and his friend Mark had left their jobs at British Aerospace ready for their joint trip to Australia. Darren and Jonathan had been walking home together when Jonathan teamed up with a friend, leaving Darren to walk home on his own.

I remember it being a silent drive to the hospital. No one wanted to voice the fact that it was a serious message and maybe the hospital staff wanted to get us inside the hospital before they told us some bad news. I was just numb; surely lightning could not strike twice? We had lost one beloved son; we could not lose another. We arrived at the hospital and were shown into a waiting room. It was like watching a movie or a television programme like *Casualty*. If it was bad news they did not take the relatives directly to the patient, they always ushered them into a tiny family room where they could talk in whispers.

Now we were experiencing this it seemed unreal. Suddenly through the fear, words started to get through to me. Jonathan had been involved in a serious car accident. He is in a coma. We are monitoring him very carefully. There was my glimmer of hope; he was alive so I could click into action now and will him to get better. Many other jumbled thoughts went through my mind but I smiled at Keith. There was a chance and we had something to hang on to.

Some time later Jonathan came out of the coma and after a little while we were able to talk to him. He had broken ribs and a broken collarbone, his face was full of bruises and one eye was almost closed, but he was talking, he did have some strength. He was over the worst and now he just had to take time to heal. Naturally he was very quiet probably due to the pain but also due to the shock and the fact that he could not remember what had happened. So many questions were going round in our heads, but he wasn't able to answer any of them. We all sat at his bedside showing our support and took it in turns to talk to him. Once they realised that their brother was not in serious danger anymore Darren and Matthew decided to return home and, leaving Keith at the hospital, I drove them back. I dropped them at home, turned straight round and drove slowly and carefully back to the hospital, all the time praying Jonathan had not had a relapse. As I returned to his room a policeman was sitting at his bedside. They were talking about the accident of which Jonathan had no recollection. It was a complete blank. Apparently he had been driving his friend's car when they smashed into a fence and rolled over and over into a field. Fortunately they had seatbelts on which had saved their lives. Jonathan had been breathalysed and told that he was well over the limit and would hear from the police in due course. His friend had disappeared from the scene of the accident and had telephoned the hospital later that day to ask staff about Jonathan's state of health. We talked to Jonathan for the rest of the day and made sure we were as supportive as we could be. We knew that depression was setting in with him. We had always felt that his excessive drinking would lead to trouble but, of course, we had no way of knowing what form it would take. It was almost teatime when a male nurse came to us and said that Jonathan had been talking with him and he had expressed a wish to get help for his drinking problems. The nurse said he had had some experience in this field and after listening to him he had deduced that he was what was called a problematic drinker. He could keep to moderation generally but problems would compound and he would drink excessively and this was just as serious as being an alcoholic. He needed help and support. When we next sat with him, Jonathan told us of his plan to get help for his drink problem. He had finally admitted to himself that it had gone beyond control. That evening Matthew came to the hospital and took Keith and me on one side and showed us some photographs. After he had gone home he had visited the scene of the accident and he was chilled to the bone, so much so that he had gone home to get a camera. There was the car in the middle of the field. It was a saloon car but it had no roof on and was battered beyond recognition. It had taken the rescue team and paramedics an hour and a half to cut Jonathan out of the car. It had been a miracle that he had survived. Matthew had been so horrified that he felt Jonathan needed to see what had happened. He needed to be shocked in to realisation of the scale of the devastation at the scene of the accident. It might seem cruel, but he felt that Jonathan had no recollection of the accident and needed to know how close he had come to death, in the hope that he would never drink and drive again. Matthew told me later that Jonathan had looked at the photos carefully and although he had made no comment, he could see that he was very upset.

During the afternoon we asked Jonathan if he wanted us to let Beccy know and without hesitation he said he did. I am sure he must have been in turmoil. After almost eight years, he had told Beccy, the person who he loved most in the world, that their relationship was over. She had moved out of Reeth House and was trying to rebuild her life. After Karl's death Jonathan went into a deep depression and said he could not cope with any responsibility. He was confused and needed to be free. Now here he was letting her know he had had an accident and bringing her back into his life. I rang her from the hospital and as we expected, she was very upset. She was completely on her own as her parents were away. I felt that I couldn't give her this terrible news and then just leave her there on her own, so I suggested that I could pick her up and she could stay with us. Jonathan was in hospital and therefore they need not come in contact but at least she would have people around her. Beccy decided she would stay with us. At this point I did not know if she would want to visit him or if he would want to see her, but we were taking it an hour at a time. I left Keith at the hospital and drove to Beccy's house. She was obviously upset and trying to be strong. She asked if she could visit the hospital and so we pulled in and I rang Keith and explained the situation. Keith rang back minutes later and said that Jonathan seemed relieved and was eager to see Beccy. So we went straight to the hospital and left them alone for some time.

Jonathan did not want to stay in hospital but he had no choice as he was still suffering from shock and the doctors would not discharge him. When he did eventually come home he took several weeks to recover, and in fact, despite much physiotherapy and the daily exercises he still does today, he has never regained full use of his arm and his collarbone is much lower at one side than the other. In spite of the accident and probably because of it, he was still determined to go to Australia and this was the incentive that kept him going. He moved forward as positively as he could. He had done something foolish and he would own up to it and take the punishment. During this time Beccy stayed at his side. Although they were no longer going out to Australia together, they both planned to go independently and probably see each other when they were out there. Their relationship was now very different, but the closeness was still there.

Now I knew that Jonathan was on the road to recovery I found that other thoughts were churning round in my head. I felt for Kath all by herself with this big void of Christmas looming. She had her father, she had her sister in the same town, but she no longer had Karl. How was she going to get through?; that was my overriding worry. I had to see her. I had to go to her. We talked on the telephone almost daily. Once I picked up her message on the answer phone, I would ring her and we would talk for hours. We cried together and we laughed together. We usually started out feeling very sad but before we ended our calls, we usually managed to get to a more positive tone and always laughed at stories of Karl or Kath's antics with their many animals. Although I wanted to be there for Jonathan, as he was facing a serious drink driving case, I just knew I had to go to Scotland. The court date had been set for 21st December but I knew that Keith would be there to support him, so I felt he didn't need me. On the evening before the court day, when everyone was busy, I secretly packed a few items into a bag and took it out to the boot of my car. No-one noticed. I went to bed that evening determined to sleep well. I had to, as I had a very long journey to tackle the next day and it was too far to drive for someone who was half asleep. I had been unable to sleep in the previous weeks but that night I did sleep soundly. Next morning we were all making our own preparations for the day. I started to prepare vegetables for our evening meal but I was the only one who knew I would not be eating it. I gave Jonathan a big hug as he left for the court with his Dad. I told him we were there for him but he knew that without being told. It was a very worrying time for him – very stressful. But he never voiced complaint or showed signs of stress and he took everything in his stride and dealt with things as they came along. As soon as I heard the car drive off, I took a note from my handbag. It was the note I had prepared the night before, explaining that I felt driven to be with Kath before Christmas dawned and outlining why I had not told anyone. I knew Keith would not have stopped me, but he would have insisted on driving me there and as someone had to be with Jonathan, he would have tried to persuade me to postpone the trip. But timing was critical as it would be Christmas in three days. My mind was in turmoil but I was positive that this was the right action. I set off armed with my map book. Under normal circumstances I would not have needed a map book. Keith would have written a list of key road numbers and landmarks for me. He would have supplied some extra instructions for the town centres that I was unable to avoid. He always sees places from above, in his mind, just the way a map is drawn, and Matthew has the same skill. How I got there I will never know. Sometimes I was crying, at other times I was singing, but throughout the journey I was thinking about Jonathan and wondering how he was being treated. What would happen when he went to court? What would be his punishment? A driving ban and a heavy fine were my thoughts. I hoped that it would be no more severe than that.

To do this 450-mile journey I should ideally have set off at dawn. As I had to work around the plans dictated by the family, it was actually

10am when I left home, much later than I would have liked. By four o'clock in the afternoon I had got as far as Perth and apart from stopping for petrol I had driven continuously and felt that now I could ring home and find out the verdict. I was very nervous about ringing but I knew I had to do it soon or the family and particularly Keith would be wondering why I was not in the house, especially as I had hardly strayed out of the house since Karl's death. I had left Keith the note, but it was under my pillow so that none of the boys would find it. I rang home and Keith answered.

"What's happened?" I asked. Keith explained that the hearing had been postponed because they needed more information about Jonathan and that a new date had been set for the last week of January. After he heard my sigh of relief, he asked me calmly, "And where are you?"

My answer was "Perth," which prompted his next question:

"As in Scotland?"

"Yes," I answered.

He asked no more questions but quietly said, "What do you want me to do?"

I explained about the note and told him that as well as explaining my actions it also contained a shopping list for food for Christmas.

Our shopping pattern had been erratic since Karl's death. In fact everything had been erratic. I remember the first time we went shopping afterwards, only four days into our bereavement, but we'd had no choice. There were six of us living together at that time – Keith, Darren, Jonathan, Beccy, Matthew and myself – and as we had to eat, someone had to go out and buy food. We arrived at Safeway without a list, with no incentive and no energy. Tears were streaming down my face as I looked at piles of fruit, trying to work out if we needed any, but nothing was registering. I had looked to Keith for support but he was in a trance and unable to help. I told him it felt like an unreal state and why did we have to be there. I felt as if everyone in that supermarket knew how vulnerable we were and how much we were feeling our loss, but in reality, of course, nobody knew and we spoke to no one. We held hands for most of the time and went home with a totally unrelated basket full of items. They may not have made proper meals but they were at least food, and they would avoid us starving. For several weeks after this difficult shopping trip, Beccy and Jonathan took charge of the replenishment of supplies.

So from Keith there were no reproaches. He was totally behind me. He knew why I had to do it. He just asked how he could help, told me to drive safely and to ring when I could. He would see me when I returned home. Once I had spoken to him, I began to fall apart. There was still a long drive ahead. I did not want to arrive in the early hours or I would have to sleep in the car until daylight. I did not want to do this, as I knew I would be too nervous of the dark to fall asleep. Even so I had put a spare quilt in my little KA just in case I was caught out. It was eight o'clock in the evening as I was approaching Aberdeen, with another hour to go across to the town of Keith.

At many times during my journey I had had the radio on, and the theme running throughout the day was about Madonna. She was due to marry Guy Ritchie that weekend at Skibo Castle and guests were coming to the area from far and wide. I felt it was like a race to see who got to that part of Scotland first; Madonna or me. At least it was something else to concentrate on during a very difficult journey.

It was well after nine o'clock and try as I did I could not find the road out to Karl and Kath's croft. I had only been there a few times as they had moved to their dream home only the Christmas before. Keith had always driven on our previous visits and now I realised I'd not taken enough notice of the roads. I had my mobile phone and now was the time to use it to ring Kath. I had not made contact earlier because I had not wanted her to know I was coming and have hours of waiting. I tried to ring but found that the phone was dead. I then realised after ringing Keith from Perth that I must have left it switched on and the battery was now flat and my credit had run out. Oh, I wished I had paid more attention when Keith had showed me how to use the phone correctly. Maybe I would have to park up and try to sleep in the car after all.

Then I remembered Kath's dad. He was a lovely man who I knew would be only too pleased to help me if he only knew I was there. But how could I find him? I drove up and down looking for a police station but ten minutes later I had still not found it. It was not a huge town surely they must have one. When I found my bearings again and covered a larger area I eventually stumbled across it. I very timidly went into the police station and was questioned by a desk sergeant. He was very kind when he heard I had made such a long journey and knew the person I was looking for straight away. Firstly he had to check why I was making contact before he could put me in touch. I must have seemed a strange sight arriving late at night with an address but little knowledge of the area. When I explained my links to John it triggered off a memory for him straight away. He remembered being involved at the time of Karl's death and he offered his condolences and stated that it had been such a shock to the people in that small community. He made me a hot drink and contacted one of the people out on the beat to come into the station and direct me. A young WPC arrived who knew John very well as he was a well-respected member of the local community. Unfortunately when we arrived at his house it was in darkness. That was a setback but I did not panic because I thought that even if he was not there, I would be safe with the police and I would have somewhere to sleep even if it was in a prison cell. The police lady knocked on the door, but there was no answer. She knocked again as she said it was unlikely that he was anywhere but at home at this time of night. Eventually a bedroom light went on and John put his head out of the window. She assured him very quickly that there was not a problem and explained about me. She was conscious of the fact that John was not a young man and had received the biggest shock of all time a few weeks previously when he had had to identify Karl's body. John came down, took me in and said how pleased he was to see me, even at that time of night. He said he was very worried about Kath. She would not eat and was hardly communicating with him or with her sisters. She was becoming even more reclusive. He immediately rang her to say that we were on our way. He got out of his car and told me to follow him. In doing so I realised that I would never have found this lonely road on my own. We drove to the gate of the smallholding where John pulled in and said he would go straight back home now, but would be up to see me in the morning. It was dark and eerie as I got out of the car to open the heavy gate. I drove in to the driveway and left the engine running as I went back to fasten it again. I could hear Murphy barking as I drove the rest of the way up to the house. Kath let me in and we hugged. I was shocked, as she looked so ill. She'd never had much flesh on her, but today she was even thinner and had huge circles under her eyes. She looked like a frightened animal that feared its death. I was so relieved I had made the journey – something had driven me to come and now I knew it had been the right decision.

I was shattered having driven all day and was ready for sleep but Kath had obviously been alone for too long and needed to talk, so talk we did. We had a laugh, we cried a lot and we laughed again. She told me so many tales about herself and Karl. She always put herself down as a not very organised person, when in effect she ran that place with perfect precision. Three horses, two dogs, a cat, two snakes, two pet rats, a squirrel, a rabbit, a peacock and a pet crow had to be cared for every day. Karl had rescued the wounded crow by climbing a telegraph pole, carrying Kath's shopping bag on his shoulder to put it in. He had shinned back down with the crow in the bag and almost had a very nasty accident. Grommet, as they christened him, recovered well – so well in fact that despite their attempts to set him back into the wild, he would not leave. So now he was a member of the family living in his own cage that Karl built specially for him. When Karl was home they shared all the chores and this gave Kath a break from the daily heavy work involved in keeping the horses. When Karl was off shore, Kath went about all these jobs by herself, and now, that was all that was keeping her going. She admitted to me that if she hadn't had to get up to feed the animals she would have just stayed in bed. She had no reason to live, she felt, but she could not let this large family starve to death. When I looked at my watch I could not believe my eyes. It was 6.30am and we were still talking. We had talked all through the night and the kettle had been constantly on the boil. Kath realised she was out of cigarettes and I got back into my car and went to her local early morning shop. I should have been fast asleep by now and yet I felt OK and the cold air felt good. This was the right place to be. I needed to be with Kath and I needed to be near Karl. Since his death other events had happened which had needed dealing with and it felt as though I'd not had enough time to mourn Karl's death. Now, at last, here I was in their special part of the world. How wonderful it would have been if this had just been a normal visit to see them both. It wasn't, of course, and the shock of never seeing him again hit me as I drove back to their croft.

Karl had built stables with John's help and he had built fences with John's help. So much of Kath, Karl and John were woven into this place. As with all farms or smallholdings there is always a job to do; you never get a day off. It was very hard work but they both loved the life. Long term they hoped to have enough money so that they could work together with the horses and run a family business at the croft. Kath was a first-class trainer of horses and was well known for her skill in preparing them for shows and pageants. It was in this, along with other areas that they were hoping to develop their living. But for the time being Karl had to continue working in the oil business. He was, of course, still employed by the same company that he had joined in Leeds at the age of sixteen. He'd had a regular pattern of working which meant he was away on the oilrig for three weeks and then worked on shore for three weeks at the plant.

The following morning John visited, as promised, and then I went shopping in Keith to buy some food supplies to leave for Kath as she had, since the funeral, existed on next to nothing. She was so depressed that shopping trips were limited to the local village and I think her dad was bringing all the animal food in for her. Her friends and neighbours had been extremely supportive but at the end of the day she was on her own, in a very lonely spot, with a big responsibility for the animals. Later in the day, Lorna, Kath's sister, came to visit. We always got on well as we were near in age. Kath was the youngest daughter with quite an age gap between her two sisters and herself. Lorna had only been gone a short time when some of Kath's friends called in for a brief visit. As we waved them goodbye, it was early evening and we realised we had not eaten all day. I had in fact not eaten for two days – I hadn't stopped to eat on the journey to Scotland and, of course, I'd also missed a night's sleep. Once we had some food inside us, the two of us settled down to watch *The Lost Boys*. It was a film Karl and Kath had enjoyed and watched together several times. She had to explain some of the film to me as I did not find it straightforward but the film was not the important thing. Being together and talking about their life was the important thing. It was the early hours of the morning when eventually I just had to go to bed. I could no longer keep my eyes open; I'd now been up for forty-eight hours without even a nap. But before retiring, I had to look in the spare room. Kath had decorated this room and put all Karl's treasures in there, his books, his trophies, his favourite pictures and his ornaments. All the presents they'd given to each other over their years together were lovingly displayed. The only things not on show were photographs of him. These were all face down and photo albums were tightly shut. Whereas I took great comfort from looking at his photographs, Kath found them too upsetting.

Soon after Karl's death I had spent weeks with Keith's help going through photo albums and having pictures copied. I had over seventy-five photos copied, some of Karl alone but the bulk of them with his brothers and other family members. I have always loved photographs and have been a keen photographer all my life and thank goodness I was. Here were pictures that certainly told a story with lots and lots of happy memories. My friend Joyce, who had known Karl when they were both teenagers, later guided me in putting together a montage of these memories. As we decided on where and how to position the pictures, she asked me questions about some of the events depicted. It was all a great help towards healing.

Although there were no photos of Karl in the house, there were lots of photographs of animals, particular of Rum, Kath's greyhound, who had died earlier in the year at the grand age of thirteen. I spent a long time in this room before going next door and finally falling asleep in Kath's bed. Since Karl's death she had taken to sleeping in the lounge with Murphy and Storm either side of her. Storm was a lively whippet that they had brought to the family as a companion for Murphy after Rum's death.

She did not want to use the bed. She knew that the room would have to be decorated and things moved round before she would feel comfortable about sleeping in there again and Lorna had said that she would help her whenever she felt ready.

The next morning Kath brought me a drink. She had slept little and had already been out to feed the horses. We talked more about their plans for the renovation of the croft both inside and outside, as it was, after all, only twelve months since they had moved into their new house. Their first house together in Scotland had been just a stepping stone. They always knew that they would move again once they found a place with potential and here in The Glen of New Mill they had found just that. They had already developed a pond that they had made into a social area where they loved to sit quietly relaxing on long summer evenings. With regard to the horses, they had turned one of the fields into a separate paddock for the new foal, which was to be born the following May. This was to be Karl's horse. He helped to choose the sire and was there at conception, but sadly he would not see Katana being born.

I could see a little animation creeping back into Kath's expression. She was no longer the frozen, frail person I had found the day before. But how long she would remain like this I just didn't know. I had to go home soon, but I would be back.

Half of me wanted to stay put, to be with Kath to share our tales and our love for Karl, but I knew I was needed back in Yorkshire. So after saying very tough, sad goodbyes I got into the car. Kath was pleased that I'd visited, that was obvious, and we promised to keep in touch by phone. John and Lorna came to see me off but they were also going to spend the afternoon with Kath so the house did not feel immediately empty again.

When I arrived home late that night Keith was alone in the house. He made me a drink and a snack. We were both so pleased to see each other and to be able to hold each other. He was also very proud of me for making this long journey all on my own. I am sure it was Karl who guided me all the way. I never opened my map book on that Christmas visit. I just drove endlessly. I was on a mission. We relaxed together for a while and then Keith went up to bed and I rang Kath to say I was home. It turned out to be a longer call than I had expected. We just kept on talking and it was another two hours later that I followed Keith up to bed. This was to be a regular pattern for some considerable time. From now on Kath often rang me during the late evening, as this was the loneliest time for her. She would be so down we would talk and talk and I could never finish the call until I thought she was on an even keel again.

The following day, everyone was pleased to see me home and they had all worked to get ready for Christmas; the Christmas that was not going to happen. Keith had bought in the food we needed. But with no tree, no cards and no decorations, the house did not look festive. Festivities were not on our minds but Keith's mum did join us for Christmas dinner and we did play a couple of board games afterwards. Normally at Christmas time my mum and dad would have stayed with us but they had moved to Easington in County Durham during the same week that Karl had died and for this year at least they would stay in their new home. Keith was an absolute rock throughout this time. He was there to mop my tears. He was there to hold my hand. The one thing he never did was tell me how I should be behaving. It was a totally new and devastating experience for all of us and he had no answers. He just allowed me to grieve and he was always there for our boys and for me.

Keith was fortunate enough to be given extended leave from his company, which we all needed, and we were very grateful to his directors for allowing this. He devoted his time to grieving and supporting. We even discussed him stopping work altogether which would mean a new start, the end of the long hours and the long drives in ever-increasing traffic jams. But after a few weeks it became obvious to both of us that this was not the time for him to give up work. Yes, we could have more time together and our sons and families would see him more often, but bouncing around his head were lots of plans. He still had many areas he wanted to improve in his work, people to help who he felt may be just abandoned if he left at this point and there was also, of course, a financial consideration. It may not have been the right time for him to stop but what we did agree was that come what may, he would retire at the age of sixty at the very latest.

So he went back to work in January 2001 and set himself a three-year plan to achieve a number of changes in people development that he felt were crucial for the future of the company. This was the major advance in his thinking that had developed since his realisation about himself. He still enjoyed training but he had taken his role further to embrace the development of people. He felt that there was a better way to manage people and to motivate people than the methods that were prevalent in the company at that time.

He wanted to change the whole culture, the whole approach.

"Let's focus on people's strengths," he would say, *"rather than dwell on their weaknesses."*

It was 21st January 2001 when Keith drove Jonathan to the courtroom in Selby. His solicitor, Shaun, was pleased that they had postponed his court appearance in order to get character references and other documents. The courts had been coming down heavily on drink driving offenders in the run up to Christmas and prison sentences were being awarded quite liberally. Because of this, Shaun felt he needed as much ammunition as possible. It was about lunchtime when I received a phone call from him.

"I'm sorry, Mrs Greenwood. I have some bad news for you. Jonathan is going to prison."

Oh no! I thought. I can't believe it.

"Despite the mitigating circumstances of his brother's death, the judge feels he should set an example to all who drink and drive and feels that this is the best way to do it."

By now I was physically shaking.

"I'm very sorry. I was hoping this could have been avoided. Please do not hesitate to ring if you need anything."

I was stunned. Where is Jonathan being taken? When can we see him? Can we take him some clothes as he is dressed in his suit and has nothing comfortable to wear? These were the questions I fired at Shaun. What silly thoughts, but I was trying to be practical. I needed to act practically. It was a terrible shock but at least he was alive. He could have been killed in the accident. Now we just had to help him through this terrible time. Shaun said that he was hoping Jonathan would be sent to the Wolds Medium Security Prison, as the experience would be much less frightening than if he were to be sent to Hull prison, which is a high security unit. This would depend on space available and we would not know for another hour or so where he had been sent. I rang Beccy who was waiting for news. She was shocked to say the least but asked me to let her know when we had more news.

But the main question that was running through my head was: where is Keith?

He was supposed to be with Jonathan in court. I rang his car phone. He answered immediately as he was still waiting in the car outside the court for news. Jonathan, who told us afterwards that he suspected that prison was the most likely outcome, had wanted to go in on his own. So Keith was unaware what had happened. Nobody knew he was there and so no-one had told him. Jonathan was unable to tell him as he was led away into a van waiting at the back of the courtroom. After my call, he came home at once. We were frantic for news. We were in limbo – how were we to find out? I decided the only way forward was to ring Wolds Prison in the hope that we might get some information. I rang and was transferred to the department dealing with arrivals. No-one had arrived by that name, but then that didn't mean anything. It was too early yet to assume he would not be going there. The gentleman was very kind as it was obvious to him this was a first experience for us and I was very upset and confused. He promised to ring me back that evening and state whether Jonathan had been transferred there or not. In less than an hour we received a call to say that he had arrived and that he would be kept in a holding cell all night and directed to another cell the following morning. He told me that he had been given a sentence of twenty-eight days. I could just imagine Jonathan all on his own and probably terrified about the next few weeks. I asked the gentleman about visiting and he said that we would be able to visit the following week but that I would need to ring for an appointment and to arrange for a pass. We were allowed to take him one pair of trousers, one T-shirt, one sweatshirt, three pairs of socks and three pairs of underpants but no footwear as this was provided. He was allowed £20 in cash to buy sweets, cigarettes and for phone calls. He was allowed two magazines and one book. Before the visit I prepared all these items and as Jonathan had always been good at art and I knew he would often draw in his spare time I also got out a sketchpad and some drawing pencils to take along.

The appointment day arrived. We collected Beccy from the nursery where she worked and drove towards the Wolds Prison. With pretty countryside at either side of us, you would have thought we were on a casual day out, but this came to an abrupt end as we arrived at the car park. We went through the entrance door into a large room where we had to queue for our individual passes. After collecting them we had to walk through a scanner just like the ones at the airport. The next process was to be checked by sniffer dogs. This was all new to us and rather daunting but I can remember forcing myself to remain positive. It was a horrible place but our task was to cheer up Jonathan and not give him any glimmer of upset. They carefully checked the bag that I had brought. Everything was recorded but the sketchpad and pencils were not allowed and we had to leave them at the desk, to be collected on the way out. All other items were taken from us put into a standard issue bag with a number written on them. Not a name, just a number. Eventually we were shown to a room, a very bright airy room with light flowing through large panes of glass in the roof. There was a snack bar in one corner and several tables and chairs were placed around the room. At some of the tables were groups of people talking. We were told which table to sit at and then immediately a metal gate opened and in walked Jonathan. Foolishly I had expected him to be still in the suit that he gone to court in, but he was dressed in a blue jogging suit and white pumps. He sat down at the table. He looked tired and very gaunt but he smiled a huge smile for all of us and then another special one just for Beccy. At first, it felt like hospital visiting where conversation is often limited. The patient is not very communicative and very inactive and you feel you shouldn't rant on too much about the outside world. But it wasn't like that at all and conversation came easily. Jonathan had not lost any of his sense of humour. We chatted for a while and then I whispered to Keith that we should go and get some drinks. We placed our order at the refreshment bar and I suggested that when our drinks arrived we should stay there so that Jonathan and Beccy could have some time on their own. The guards must have been used to this ploy and one of them came over and asked us to take our drinks back to the table. Thinking quickly I said we were waiting for a toasted sandwich. And as he walked away, I ordered the sandwich. This gave us an extra five minutes, not very long but it was all the time we could manage to create so they could be alone.

After a few days, Jonathan's sentence was reduced by half, to fourteen days, and as he was only allowed one visiting pass per week we left it to Beccy to apply the following week. He was due to come home on February 5th, the day after his birthday. We had posted his birthday cards to the prison and it was obvious how low he was feeling, as he told us of his surprise when the prison officer handed the cards to him. He had no idea what the date was and had forgotten his birthday, so at least for a few minutes he was able to feel that there were lots of people who were missing him and who were counting the days until he would be home again. At last, the day of his release came and Matthew and I were up at dawn and excited that Jonathan was coming home. Matthew wanted to go by himself to collect him from the prison and so he set off early in order to be there by nine o'clock. Once Jonathan was home the three of us spent most of the day in the lounge chatting about the last few weeks and about the future.

Jonathan had only been home for a couple of weeks when he asked Matthew to take him to Leeds to book his ticket to Australia. When they returned, it was obvious that he was very pleased, as he had managed to get a ticket for only £119. Because of his stint in prison he had been unable to use the original ticket and had lost the value of it. So this reduced fare deal had helped to make up for some of the loss. This seemed like great news to me, but then he broke the news about the reason for the cheap flight. He had to fly in just six days' time. So we immediately swung into action with shopping and packing planning. Beccy came with us to Manchester Airport to say goodbye to him. It had been obvious to us that she had been pleased that he had recovered from the accident and pleased that the two-week prison sentence was behind him. And now it was easy to see that she was emotionally unhappy to see him fly out of her life. She did, of course, have her own ticket for a flight later that spring when she was planning to meet up with him, but it must have seemed very strange and upsetting to her when she had to wish him *bon voyage*.

The following morning Keith and Matthew left early for work. Keith's company had employed Matthew for a temporary project, and Keith was taking him to the location. As they drove through the neighbouring villages the sound of sirens was overwhelming. Police, ambulances and fire engines were everywhere. Because it was extremely icy, they thought that there had probably been a major accident on the M62 motorway. There had indeed been a major accident but it wasn't on the M62. It was the morning of the Selby rail crash when a Range Rover left the motorway, careered down the embankment and landed on the main east coast railway line. Minutes later an express train ploughed into the vehicle and fourteen people were dead. This had been the second tragedy to hit our local area in the past few months. Persistent rain throughout the year had increased the height of the water table. Water levels on the rivers were rising at an alarming rate and large acres of farmland resembled the Florida everglades. The school next to us became the centre of operations with a constant stream of fire appliances and army vehicles arriving on a daily basis. Sandbag mountains were being erected everywhere. Following advice from 'flood line' we had moved all our important possessions upstairs, as a precaution. In November the land drains that had been feeding the excess water into the river, finally gave up and there was nothing to stop the advancing tide. Our neighbouring village of Gowdall, trapped between this deluge from the fields on one side and the overflowing

River Aire on the other, took the full force and was quickly submerged. Many houses were damaged and several had to be completely rebuilt after the event. Snaith was more fortunate. Being on higher ground and a greater distance from the river, the water only reached the edge of the town, although a number of properties did experience extensive flood damage, particularly one of the petrol stations, which was completely covered by the muddy waters.

Before Christmas, Keith's boss Dick had contacted me to say he wanted me to know that at the forthcoming sales award ceremony to be held in February, Keith was going to be presented with a lifetime achievement award. I was not to tell Keith – I was sworn to secrecy. In giving this news to me, Dick hoped that it would give me something positive to look forward to after our recent tragedies.

Keith and I stayed at the Hilton Hotel Park Lane. We dressed for the evening and met with our party in the bar of the hotel. I was the only non-member of staff. I was trying my best to be positive as this was to be Keith's night, but he didn't know it yet. This was his fourth attendance at this event. Since its inception in 1998, he had recommended people for awards and this year was no exception, with two people in the frame. It was because of the company's success at the 2000 event, with three winners, that Keith and I had been included on the trip to South Africa and Keith thought that I had been invited on this particular evening as a special treat.

I was really looking forward to seeing his face when his name was read out. I knew he would be so proud. On the other hand I was feeling the strain of being in a big group and trying to stay positive. This seemed strange, as I was the one who always enjoyed social outings but now with so many people talking at the same time, I was finding it difficult to keep a thread going. The evening started and the meal was fantastic. A couple of times I was overpowered by grief and memories and I made a quick exit to the ladies' hoping no-one had noticed. But of course Keith had. He came to find me and he squeezed my hand and told me I was doing so well. After the meal the awards ceremony started. Thirty-four categories were announced and the winners cheered and applauded. Keith was very disappointed when his two finalists did not strike gold. And then the presenter announced the final award; The Lifetime Achievement award. He talked about a man from Yorkshire who started his career in selling at the age of twenty. He went on to give some of the highlights of his career but although Keith was listening intently, he still did not realise he was talking about him. In fact he quickly whispered to me that although there were career similarities, he had started his selling career at the age of eighteen. He had only just finished telling me this when a look of shock and surprise came over him and for a few seconds he was stunned. The presenter had stopped talking about this person and had announced the name: Keith Greenwood. By the time he rose to his feet and went up on to the stage to collect his award he had a big beaming smile on his face. The whole place cheered and as he returned to our table everyone shook his hand, congratulated him and wanted to look at his award. Kim, the managing director, had ordered champagne at the beginning of the evening; it was under our table packed with ice away from Keith's view. The champagne was opened and it was Keith's time. It was a very special moment for him. In business he had had tough times and good times but his hard work and continued stamina had been recognised and appreciated. Then Dick passed a package to me and inside was a teddy bear with a message around its neck. The message read 'please take me to your home' from everyone at Henkel. I was so touched I could hardly stop the tears from flowing but I did my best and thanked Dick for the lovely gesture. I suspected that Jenny, his wife, had arranged this – it had her touch to it. Everyone around the table had made me feel very welcome and I had talked with each of them in turn. Eventually the time came to depart and the taxis arrived. We were dropped at our hotel and went straight to our room. I could hold in the tension no longer. I just sobbed and sobbed and Keith did the same. He said as much as he had enjoyed the evening and had greatly appreciated the award, it all felt a bit hollow now we were back in our own world. Under normal circumstances we would have gone home the following day and told our sons of Keith's award and telephoned Karl or sent him an email if he was away on the rig. We just hugged and eventually fell asleep. Next day on our journey home Keith received more than a dozen phone calls of congratulation as news of his award spread slowly through the company. I was so proud of this man. He had been so thrilled to receive his award but was also very sensitive to the fact that we had only just started to work through our grief. It really was very early days, and we still had such a long way to go.

Chapter 15

BREAKDOWN

Kath had not slept easily for months before Katana's birth. The last full week before the foal was due she had cuddled up on the sofa each night and set her alarm at hourly intervals. If the mare delivered the foal and needed assistance, morning may be too late and so every hour she went out into the pitch-black night to the stables to see that all was well. On the very night that Katana came into the world, or at least in the early hours of the morning, there were several large flashes of lightning in the sky. Kath was struggling to help this little foal into the world but instead of being frightened by the lightning, she felt calmed. She believed it was Karl telling her that he was watching over the two of them. This was the first positive step forward in Kath's life. It was now seven months since Karl had gone and the winter had been horrendous for her; It was not just very lonely living in the quite glen, it was also very difficult. Heavy snow had fallen twice that winter and she had been cut off from the outside world on both occasions for well over a week. When, eventually, her father was able to visit, the closest that he could get by car was a mile and a half away, and then between them Kath and John pulled a sledge to the house, loaded with much-needed food for the animals and herself. She had grown up in this isolated area and, having learnt the routines of winter survival, had stocked up beforehand, but this year had been exceptional. Many parts of Britain had recently been affected by a foot and mouth epidemic, and although it had not hit that part of Scotland, it did have an impact on Kath. The movement of cattle and other livestock was severely restricted and this had put a stop to agricultural shows throughout the country. She'd been used to travelling about to various events in order to show the horses, but this year it was not possible and so there was little to take her mind off the fact that she was now alone.

A few weeks before Karl died, he had bought a horse transporter from a local farmer who was retiring. It was in excellent condition with plenty of room for the horses and a well-furnished cab, which enabled them and Murphy and Storm to sleep together in reasonable comfort. Their little family could now move about the country to different shows in comparative luxury and it was at one of these shows in England that they were both ecstatic when Kalibur, their chestnut Arab horse, took first prize and qualified for a place at Wembley the following season.

So now it was May, and here was Kalibur's son, Katana, a wobbly bundle of legs with a beautiful chestnut coat. Not only had Kath to feed and muck out the other horses but also she had to carefully nurse this little foal. For the first few weeks of his life she needed to feed him regularly with small amounts of food and check on him at various times during the night. Family and friends came to see him and this steady stream of visitors was good for Kath – she loved to show him off. But, of course, the strain and the grief were still there.

I decided that I needed to visit Kath again, and now Katana had been born, I felt that this was the appropriate time. Keith was working in London as usual, and so he dropped me at Luton Airport on his way and I flew by easyJet to Aberdeen and then took the train through the beautiful countryside to Keith. When I arrived I could see that she was happy to see me, and buzzing with excitement about Katana, but she also looked very tired. It felt good to be back and I knew that my decision to come was the right one. During the day, while Kath was looking after the animals, I spent time working in the garden. Everything was fresh and new, and of course, Katana was part of that newness. One of my main projects was to create a remembrance garden in memory of Rum, their greyhound, who had died during the previous year. I also got time to sit by the pond reflecting and talking to Karl. It was a time of healing. In the evenings I would relax with Kath, listening to her as she poured out her grief. It was very much like our long phone conversations but this time I could offer some physical comfort. I could see she still had a long way to go. I found it a huge wrench when the time came for me to come home, because I just felt at peace there and wished that I could wave a magic wand and transport all my family to the area. That way I could live out my life in the tranquillity of the Glen. Although it had been emotionally very draining trying to help Kath, it had helped me to be close to Karl and that was important.

The month of June arrived, eight months after Karl's death, and with support from Keith and the family I felt I was dealing with my grief satisfactorily. I had been trying so hard to hold everything together. Despite the devastating loss of Karl, I felt that I had to show the others that they were loved and cherished. It would have been easy just to make them all feel that he was the only one and that now they did not count. I am sure it can easily mistakenly come over this way, as no-one teaches you in advance how to grieve. But I did seem to be coping. Keith had bought a large-scale map of Australia and we had been eagerly tracking Jonathan's progress by marking his moves, which he communicated by email. By now Beccy had flown out and joined him and in addition to the emails we were also having weekly phone calls with them.

But then over the next few weeks I started to go downhill rapidly. The longer and longer phone calls from Kath were taking their toll on my mental state and the necessary paperwork that has to be dealt with at times like this was an additional worry. Each piece of correspondence always headed in the same way. It always began with the same line stating the fact that Karl was dead. Why were solicitors and such people so cruel? Why did they have to state over and over what was already too painful to acknowledge? Common sense told me this was necessary but it did not help me to move on and my world was becoming smaller and smaller. I had started driving to Castleford on my own; just to be in the area where Karl used to be. This reminiscing made me worse and yet I needed to do it, because it made me feel closer to him. I realised that I was living on automatic pilot and I was suddenly snapping at everyone. I was getting very little sleep, and when I did I was having horrible nightmares. The days were passing one by one, but I did not know what I was doing as each one ticked by. Everything was negative. I also realised that I was pushing Keith away, but I did not know why. He was obviously very frustrated as he was patiently trying to support me. He soon realised that he could no longer deal with this situation on his own. He needed outside help and so he contacted our GP who immediately put us in touch with a psychiatrist. That same evening we were on our way to an appointment in Sheffield.

I did not really want to go, but what else was I going to do? I'd not slept at all for the past three nights – I was like a zombie and a very irritable zombie at that.

Keith led me to the consulting room and once we were seated, Dr Kelly started to talk to me. He had a very soft Scottish lilt and that was all it took for me to break down in a flood of tears. I was straight back in the highlands with Karl. Why had I come here? Why did he have to be Scottish? And what could he possibly do for me? He would probably put me on pills, from which I would never be able to break the habit. That was not for me. I had to be strong and resist the pills. If I gave in then I would never get better, I would never be in control of my own life again. I just had a life-long hatred of tablets and drugs because of my mother's dependence on tranquillisers and sleeping tablets across more than forty years. Eventually I regained my composure and, although I was shaking, I listened intently to Dr Kelly's words. Gradually I started to trust this stranger who had just come into my life. What he was saying made sense. I was not looking after myself and if I did not regain my strength and confidence how would I be able to function properly? He convinced me that I needed to retreat from the world; to recharge my batteries and for the time being, to only think about myself with no outside problems. I could see Keith was in agreement. I felt that this had to be better than the way I was trying to cope at home, and yet I was very suspicious about going to a clinic, which is what he was suggesting. I was scared that once I was there, I would be there forever and even if I did come out, I would not be the same person. But I felt able to trust Dr Kelly and I trusted Keith, so I knew I had to go.

Two days later, Keith was leading me into the clinic in Harrogate. After checking in at the reception, we were directed to a small room and I was told that this was to be my room for the duration of my stay. It was simply furnished but adequate with a single bed, a wardrobe and a dressing table, plus an en-suite bathroom. I headed straight for the bed and lay down while Keith unpacked my things. Even though he was there in the room with me, I felt scared and lonely. He stayed with me long enough to ensure that I was settled and once he had gone,

I cried myself to sleep. When I woke up the next day, I felt confused and I started to cry again. A member of staff brought me a hot drink and tried to console me but I just cried and rambled. Later in the morning a consultant came to see me. He was a lovely gentle person called Dr Nehaul. When he saw how fragile and weepy I was he suggested that I should take a mild anti-depressant to calm me down so that I could start to relax. But even though I was far from rational in my thinking, I told him that I would not take any pills. The weekend arrived and Keith came to visit me on both days. I was eager for news of our sons, but as for the outside world, I did not want to know, it was too painful. We sat out in the garden and I can remember that we just held hands in silence. The following week started in much the same way. All the staff were very kind and caring but I was hardly aware of them, except during the night. Because they were worried about me, they checked on me every hour and my sleep was regularly interrupted by both the noise of the door opening and, when I opened my eyes, a shaft of light from the corridor. Timetables and meals meant nothing to me, all days were alike, and all were black. Dr Nehaul came to see me each day and patiently listened to me as I cried and rambled. He still felt that I should be taking medication, but he respected my wishes. By the time the next weekend came round, I was actually feeling a little brighter. I was so pleased to see Keith as I felt like I was now detached from my family. They were all going about their lives and I was no part of it. That, of course, was only my perception as in reality my family were very worried about me and concerned about my progress. We decided to go for a walk outside the grounds. This was allowed, but we had to ensure that a member of staff checked us out and checked us back in on our return. We walked along the main road into Harrogate. The roads were busy and the noise of the traffic was very frightening for me. But it was not just the traffic; the throngs of people busily shopping in the centre were just too much for me and we quickly headed for the tranquillity of the Valley Gardens. Once there we strolled along the pathways, which were lined with summer bedding plants, and I calmed down a little. In my head I can still visualise all the people milling round getting on with life, but it felt like I was looking down on them, as though I was not among them. Keith just held my hand and made no demands on me; he was just supporting me the best way he could. It was when we moved

Matthew at Claredale House, Bethnal Green as he starts his university life

Matthew, with three other young entrepreneurs, receiving support from The Prince's Trust

Holy Island on New Year's Day 2000

Barcelona

Monte Carlo

Pilanesberg National Park, South Africa

Our first Grandson Dylan

Alex and Dylan

**Dylan with Leah and her cousin
Georgina**

Leah with Alex

Keith at the motel in Fort Wayne Indiana in 2002 after he had crashed into it.

Keith with his mum, my cousin Joan, me and Matthew, Canada 2003

Snaith's first outdoor Halloween display at Reeth House 2003

Richard and Layla's Wedding 2004

Leah dancing the night away

A special moment

Keith with three of
our sons and
his mum

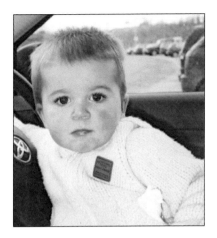

Leah   Dylan

Keith retires after 40 years in sales

Matthew launches his new business in York 2004

Kalibur – with son Katana at Karl's Croft

My dad's 70th Birthday at Reeth House

Our five sons

Exploring London

Happy Christmas

on to the steep incline that I found that I was having trouble breathing and this became more and more difficult until eventually I passed out in Keith's arms. He managed to manoeuvre me to a park bench and he sat with me and cuddled me until I came round and was able to walk again, albeit in a jelly-like fashion. It was soon obvious that I wouldn't be able to walk back to the clinic so once at the edge of the gardens Keith made me comfortable on a bench and then ran back to the clinic for the car. He told me later that he was crying as he raced towards the car. He had never seen me look as vulnerable as I did on that day. Once safely back in the clinic the nurse made an emergency call to Dr Nehaul's home and very soon he was in my room talking to both of us. He was sympathetic but firm.

"Look, you have tried it your way, but your way is not working. Isn't it worth letting me do the work by carefully planning your care and your recovery?"

I realised that he was right, of course. I reluctantly agreed to take an anti-depressant. What could I lose? I thought. After all, I was getting worse doing it my way. I was given my first dose at bedtime. At 3am I got up to go to the toilet and swiftly blacked out. When I came round, a nurse was sitting with me and stayed for the rest of the night. I knew I was not meant to take these horrible drugs. Next morning, which was a Sunday, Dr Nehaul arrived and we had a long talk. The outcome was that my tablets were changed. A slow-releasing anti-depressant called Effexor was prescribed. I was still very unsure about taking this but I did as I was told. Dr Nehaul glanced at my notepad and asked what I had been writing about. I told him that I was keeping a diary, and had been doing so from the day I had arrived. He asked me lots of questions about my family, and as Karl's loss was so powerful, he asked me to write about him. He said he would read what I had written in two weeks' time; that was my deadline. I decided to start writing straight away and although I cried a lot as I was writing, I did cover a lot of ground. The best thing to come out of it was remembering all the parties, days out, cinema trips, theatre trips, all the good times with Karl and his girlfriends. There were so many good things that remembering them all stopped everything being quite so black. When Keith visited that afternoon he listened to what had been happening and asked if he could read my story. I said yes, but only when it was finished. He tried a new strategy that day. Instead of taking me out for a walk near the clinic, he took me in the car away from traffic and the crowds and we were able to walk in the countryside. However, we soon realised it was a mistake as I started again with what seemed like a panic attack. The same thing was happening as on the previous day. I was getting more and more agitated, my limbs were heavy and my energy was draining away. There were no people there to be nervous about, so why was this happening? There was a similarity though as once again we were going up a steep gradient and it was windy and I was struggling to breathe. What was happening was common sense. I was struggling to breathe against the wind and because of the Fibromyalgia, my muscles and joints were causing serious problems. It was not a panic attack; I was simply not getting enough oxygen to my brain. It was just as difficult for me to walk downhill as it was up the gradient as I was still using a lot of muscle power, but once we levelled out and were no longer walking against the wind, we had a short rest and I began to feel a little better. It took a while for me to feel normal again but eventually we were able to walk for a little longer. As we walked, Keith kept remembering snippets from home and bringing me up to date with messages from well-wishers. I enjoyed the walk and the day in general but I was glad when we returned to the clinic, and felt even better when I reached my little room. It seems strange to think of that room now as my world, but at that time it was. I felt safe there. All I had to do each day was get up, bathe and get dressed, nothing more taxing than that. However it was not as simple as it sounds and the process took me well over an hour. When I first got out of bed my ankles would not hold me and I walked as if I was a very old person. Slowly, I began to speed up but my hips and knees were very painful. We were encouraged to take all meals in the dining room at tables of four so that we could interact with each other, but because of my mobility problems, my breakfast was brought to my room. I wasn't feeling any benefit from the tablets but I did not feel any worse and that was the important thing. Dr Nehaul had explained that it would probably take up to three weeks before I felt any benefit. My life at the clinic continued much the same over the next two weeks. Keith visited alternate evenings during the week and each day at the weekend. He was working long hours and I was making it even harder for him but he never once complained, nothing was too much trouble. He planned short outings for us on his visits and always made it a different place each time. I felt safe and under no pressure – it was just like courting all over again. During this time it had been decided that to keep things simple for me, Keith would be my only visitor and all things were channelled through him. I was unable to take a phone call at that time as I regarded phone calls as undesirable, they only brought bad news and I could not take the risk. It would actually take me nine months before I was able to answer a telephone call myself, and for a long time after that I had a fear about talking to people on the phone.

By the fourth week I was missing our sons terribly. Matthew and Darren were at home. Richard lived in Wakefield and Jonathan was still on his visit to Australia with Beccy. They all sent me messages through Keith, but it wasn't the same as seeing them or hearing their voices. Then one evening, after dinner, the door of my room opened and in walked Matthew. I was shocked and overwhelmed. I was so pleased that he was there that I hugged him continuously for several minutes. We then went for a long walk in the neighbourhood, in the dark. He looked after me and we talked endlessly. We were obviously missing each other. He had always had a good relationship with his dad and he would usually seek him out to talk about common interest subjects and business matters, but the personal bits he always saved for me. Usually when he was troubled he would be offhand with me, which prompted a discussion which would often go on for a very long time before we got to his problem. He would find it very difficult to discuss personal things and I always had to draw it out of him. On this occasion, and despite the fact he was very positive with me and not offhand, I still knew there was something he needed to talk about and eventually we got round to the problem. As would often be the case, it was reassurance he needed, not an earth-shattering solution. Although I was far from well, I was well enough to help him and alert enough to recognise that he had chosen the timing of his visit with a lot of thought. Difficult though it was, he was working very hard to manage the effects of his Asperger. His visit was a welcome tonic for me, particularly when he made me laugh by telling me about something that had happened on his journey to Harrogate. He had heard a scraping sound coming from the rear of the car and, slowing down in response, he was amazed to see one of his wheels accelerating past him. He had visions of himself driving along on three wheels, until he realised that the spare wheel holder was scraping along the ground causing the noise and it was, in fact, the spare that was racing along in front of him. As he left, he asked me not to tell Keith that he had been to see me. He hadn't spoken to his dad about coming because he wasn't sure what his reaction would be. He had arrived in Harrogate with the intention of visiting every clinic in the town and enquiring if I was a resident. Luckily, he found me at the first attempt. I agreed not to tell Keith about his visit but said that I felt he should own up when he went home. It took a further two nights before he confessed to Keith that he had been to see me but as far as Keith was concerned he was happy for Matthew to visit if I was, and he knew that his visit had cheered me up. Although Matthew had not discussed his visit with Keith beforehand, Keith was not surprised as he often turned up quite out of the blue at the most unlikely times and surprised us. The most noticeable was when we arrived at Heathrow after our trip to South Africa. Matthew had taken the last underground train, at about midnight, from Bethnal Green and slept at the airport until we arrived very early in the morning from Johannesburg. There are many other examples stretching over the years, highlighting his fierce independence, an excellent sense of direction and a marvellous feeling for theatre.

We had moved into August. It was Darren's birthday and Jonathan was home from Australia. I had now been in the clinic for over a month and knew I was moving forward as I wanted to see them and hear their news for myself. Keith booked a meal at a hotel near to the clinic and all of them came to collect me. We spent Sunday lunchtime celebrating Darren's birthday. It was a good day and one I will treasure. My time in the clinic went on and each day I felt a little more confident. Two lovely ladies, Karen and Gayle, ran daily courses, morning and afternoon covering eight different subjects: mood disorders, self-awareness, relationships, assertiveness, anger management, loss and change, feelings and emotions, behaviour types. You could choose which you wanted to attend. I went to every session and believe I took something positive from each one. It was not just about opening up and telling each other our stories, it was also about looking into the reasons why we had all got to this point, identifying our pluses and minuses and working on them. We were never forced to interact, it was our choice, and a lot of very poignant and sad stories were told in those groups. Above all, however, there was humour and I believe this was the common denominator. We were all in the clinic through different degrees of depression but eventually we all found a little humour and it was this that proved to be the healing factor. I am sure this must have been how Karen and Gayle managed to stay sane. Dealing with other people's depression, day in and day out, must take its toll. For me and for many of us they had the perfect mixture of empathy, hope and humour, all in equal amounts. Interacting with both tutors and patients was very important to me. Instead of feeling like a wet flannel, which was totally wrung out, I began to feel positive sparks. The sessions were good, very good and I mixed well both in the groups and at meal times. The rest of the time I stayed in my room and although I could not summon up enough concentration to relax enough to read, I mindlessly relaxed, watching television for short periods and, of course, writing my diary notes.

The strangest thing about this whole period was that Keith was now the carer and I was the confused person. Sometimes I was a woman and sometimes I was a child. I had always been a very decisive person and this was a totally new way of life for me – not really frightening but very strange. Keith had to make all decisions. He was leading me and this was a new situation for him as well. Once I started to challenge things again, he knew that I was on the road to recovery and he was pleased.

Every day I wrote. Sometimes it may only be lines, but some days if I were stronger it could be pages. I had started my diary on Day One but Dr Nehaul had given me a target to write even more. I had reached the target and the doctor had read my story and had asked lots and lots of questions. He said he felt he knew Karl from what I had written and would have enjoyed meeting him. As Karl's story spanned thirty years of my life, several other issues were entangled in my writing. These he discussed with me at great length and out of it several ghosts were put to bed and many issues closed instead of continually spinning around in my head. I found that writing was very therapeutic and felt as though it brought me closer to Karl. I realised that I had been pushing him away in my mind, it was less painful if I forced myself not to think about him, but writing and talking about him had helped me When Keith came to visit me, we would read my story together. We cried a lot but we laughed a lot too – it was good to remember just how many happy times we'd had together. On one particular night, after a long session with Karen and Gayle, I woke up in the early hours with a very uneasy feeling. I did not know what was happening. I knew exactly where I was. I could see out of my bedroom window and I could see that it was dark. I always left the curtains open because it helped me to connect with the world outside. Suddenly, a strong beam of light dazzled me and made me feel nervous. The light got stronger and I began to feel warm. I could see a man, a very tall person. As he came towards me, I could see that it was Karl; his gorgeous smile which always showed, his teeth, his bright blue eyes dancing, his long wavy hair. I could literally touch his hair and feel his skin. He did not speak. We just hugged and hugged; It was so immense, it was ecstasy. Then he was gone, and I felt at ease. I felt happy. I could not wait to tell Keith when he visited the next day. When I did he was very happy for me. Whatever had happened that night it stopped me pushing Karl's accident out of my thoughts and him with it. I had been unable to say goodbye to him despite the fact we went to the undertakers to see him, I needed to see him one more time and now I had. This gave me the chance to move forward from the frozen position I had found myself in before.

The following Sunday evening we decided to walk to the local church and take part in Evensong. This was our first visit to a church for purely spiritual reasons in some time. While we enjoyed taking part in the service, we felt no link to the people in the church. One gentleman nodded on our way in and from one lady in the congregation we got a smile. We felt part of God's house but not at all linked to this community. Not one person said hello; not one person came up to say welcome to us, unlike our first visit to Snaith Church when we felt welcome from the first service we attended. I thought that perhaps it was because I was not feeling well and I had misjudged our lack of welcome, but Keith said he felt exactly the same. That was our first and last visit to this particular church. It didn't really answer the question that we had been asking ourselves for some time. Did we want the church back in our lives? I certainly knew that it would be a long time before I could go back into Snaith Church because of all the memories it contained about Karl, but maybe another local church would be the answer, just not yet!

My time in the clinic lasted for seven weeks. I made many friendships and I am pleased I had this experience. It put me together again as a much stronger and more confident person. Before I went in, I had just wanted to sit and vegetate but now my brain told me to use all the experiences and to move forward. I will always be grateful to all the people in and out of the clinic for supporting me, not least Keith's boss Dick and Allyson from the human resources team who facilitated my speedy entry into the clinic through their firm's private health insurance scheme. And probably my most enduring memory is the fact that I was taught never to use the word FINE in response to the question, *"How are you feeling?"* because it means you're Fucked Up, Insecure, Neurotic, Emotional.

Keith and I both knew it was not Karl's death alone that caused the breakdown. Certainly, that was the worst thing that had ever happened to me, indeed to any of us. But it was also supporting his brothers who were all totally devastated particularly Jonathan with his accident and subsequent imprisonment. Matthew, of course, not only had the grief of losing Karl; he had the added problem of trying to make sense of his world.

On top of this was the feeling that although I loved my husband, I was never totally happy or relaxed, as so many elements of our life did not add up and so many areas were so very difficult every day of our lives.

All of these were contributing factors to my breakdown but it was the strain of giving constant telephone support to Kath at whatever time of day or night. This was the final straw that drained me and pushed me into depression.

Throughout this period Keith was fantastic. He had watched me change from a person in charge and keeping all the balls bouncing and shielding him from his everyday ghosts, to a mental wreck. He took charge of me. He delegated tasks at home and devoted his time between work and me. This was a new situation and now I was on equal terms with his job. This sounds bitter, as I have always known that he loves me but showing it was different. He always knew I would be there for him, so it was easy for him to let his work take over and to put me into the background, knowing that I would still be there at the end of it. It was invariably the boys and me together at home and

Keith always away. He struggled to get things perfect in his job, and did not have continuous energy to perfect both marriage and work. I often tried to reassure him that good was sufficient; he did not have to be perfect. This drive is in almost all Asperger people, as so many times in their lives they are accused of not trying hard enough, particularly when they seem to have the intelligence and yet get very simple things wrong. It compounds over their lives until they have no choice but to give all their energy to nearly every project they attempt. I believe this is why relationships can go wrong even when they seem so strong. It takes an impossible amount of energy to keep all the balls in the air and when they find someone who does understand them, they start to relax. They wrongly feel that they don't have to work as hard as they do in other facets of their life where people are judging them. So the partner sees them as having dual standards, which puts a huge strain on the relationship.

But when I needed him the most, he was there for me. It is thanks to Keith that I recovered and that I am here today; my eternal gratitude also to Dr Kelly for observing me and finding the best place possible for me to recover. Once I was in the clinic, the same thanks go to Dr Nehaul, who had patience, empathy and a good sense of humour to look after me, and bring me back from the brink. In addition to these people, our four sons were so supportive that I could not help but get better. I now have a much healthier perspective on life. It was only a matter of weeks before Keith's role as my carer disappeared altogether but instead of the roles reversing I was now strong enough to stand up for what I needed, so we could work together in our relationship with a much greater understanding of the power and the problems of Asperger syndrome.

Chapter 16

PICKING UP THE PIECES

In January 2002 Matthew celebrated his 21st birthday. As with all our children, he had received a small amount of money from an insurance policy for this landmark birthday. His brothers had used theirs in different ways but they had all put the money towards something special. For Karl it was a motorbike, for Darren a computer, Richard put his towards a car, and Jonathan went on a ski trip. Matthew was unsure what our reaction would be when he told us that he wanted to use his money to buy a ticket and visit New York. We were actually thrilled with his decision, as it was another experience for him and, although we were apprehensive, because he would be going alone, we knew it would not be a problem – he was self-motivated and would be busy every minute of the trip. He asked me to go with him to the travel agents and we went on our way to a yoga session in York. The young assistant was eager to get the best deal for him and as it was only four months after the 9/11 terrorist strike, air tickets had dropped in price. He was able to secure a return flight for £109, which was an excellent start. The rocky part was yet to come. Unfortunately he had not checked his passport beforehand and it was on the night before his trip that he realised that although it was a ten-year passport, because of his age, the photo should have been renewed after five years. He then spent many hours on the phone in the early morning in a desperate attempt to save his trip of a lifetime. A few hours later Keith ferried him back and forth between the passport office in London and Heathrow Airport.

Finally he boarded a plane just a few hours after his scheduled flight had departed.

He thoroughly enjoyed his ten days in the Big Apple and even took a day trip to Washington DC. He just packed as much as he could into his limited time. On a low budget he could not afford luxury accommodation every night, so he combined one night at The Hilton with several nights at an assortment of budget hotels across Manhattan. One three-night stay was an eye opening cheap hotel at the Harlem side of Central Park. All too soon his time came to an end and he rang me from the hotel on the night he was due to fly back home. *"See you tomorrow mum, love you,"* were his last words. Tomorrow he would be home and we would enjoy all his news but tomorrow did not quite happen like that.

The next phone call I received was from an upbeat American voice asking me if I would accept a reverse call charge from Matthew. I looked at the clock. He should have been on the flight by now I thought. I accepted the call and Matthew came on the phone and calmly told me that he wasn't on the flight because he did not have his ticket. Somewhere during his visit he'd lost it. The airport staff said he needed details of his booking and if I faxed the details to them at JFK Airport then they would try to get him on the next flight. Quickly and calmly I mounted the stairs to find his flight details. They were all there, neatly filed in his bedroom. Keith immediately faxed this information to the number Matthew had given. We waited over an hour and then received another call to say that nothing had been received at his end, were we sure that we had sent it correctly? Our next instruction was to fax the details direct to the Virgin flight desk. A very long two hours later we got another call from Matthew stating that he was still unable to fly. Virgin would not accept this information as proof. He was told that they needed the official breakdown of tax and other details from the ticket itself and the only way we could get that was from the travel agent in York, who wouldn't be open for business until 9am the next day. I was now getting very anxious but amazingly, I didn't panic. He now had no cash left – after all this was the last day of his holiday and he should have been on his way home by now – and there was also a problem with his credit card. It was now almost midnight and Matthew was exhausted. Yes, he could sleep on an airport bench, but that left him vulnerable and at the mercy of anyone around. We told him to sit by the phone and we would get some money to him one way or another. This was easier said than done and it took several hours and numerous phone calls until, at last, we were able to transfer some money via Western Union. We rang him for the last time at 2am, six hours after he should have been on the flight. He now had some money with which to grab a bite to eat and find a place to get some sleep.

The following morning at 9am I rang the travel agent and managed to speak to the young lady who had been so helpful in securing a good deal for Matthew. She could remember him clearly.

"Has he had a good holiday?" she said.

"Yes, very good, however he's still in New York and can't get home."

"Why ever not?" was her startled reply.

I explained as briefly as I could and asked for her help in faxing the needed information to the Virgin desk in New York.

"Of course I will. There's just one snag. Our fax machine is not working so it will take a little longer than normal. Once I have pulled out the information, I will have to go outside to send the details to him."

Two hours later Matthew rang to say that Virgin had still not received the information and I told him that the young lady from the travel agent had rung me to confirm that the fax had gone. He calmly thanked me and said he would go back to the Virgin desk again. Poor Matthew, would he ever get home. Should he cut his losses and just buy another ticket? No, he never wasted unnecessary money. In his eyes there was still a way to use his return ticket even though it was lost and even though it was a day later. The checking-in desk had all his details; he had his passport; why would they not let him on an available flight? But of course, it was only four months since the horror of 9/11 and they never wanted that to happen ever again so they were being extra cautious. Matthew had seen first-hand the devastation it had caused by visiting Ground Zero and talking to New Yorkers, and he agreed that it was only right to check everything thoroughly. He rang me back with a new fax number. This, apparently, was a direct line to the Virgin office at the airport whereas the original number was at their office in New York. I rang the travel agent again and apologised for the hassle, but could she possibly send the information again to this new number. She was still very eager to help and said this had not happened before. They'd had occasional cases of people losing their tickets but they had usually been able to come back on the original flight or certainly soon after. From her point of view she was sorry she could not do more for us.

"Leave it with me!" she said, using a very efficient tone and two hours later Matthew rang to say he would be on the flight that evening at 8pm – the same slot as the one he should have been on the previous evening. For this, he was only going to be charged £50 for transferring his ticket to the new flight. Keith was by now working at the office in London and was planning to have an early night after our lost night's sleep from the previous evening. He would be able to collect Matthew from Heathrow as he was working in the south. When no further phone calls arrived from Matthew I decided I could go to bed and try to get some sleep. Next morning I received the much appreciated phone call from Keith and then Matthew. Matthew was on British soil and was in fact halfway up the motorway with his dad. They were happily chatting about his adventures. When he arrived home we hugged and I did not want to let him out of my sight. For him, it had all been part of the adventure and the only thing he regretted was the extra expense, the inconvenience was no problem. In Matthew's mind you just work through a problem, there is no point in panicking. We totally agreed with him but it was an entirely different feeling when our son was three thousand miles from home with no ticket and no money to get home. A few days later, and after a discussion with me about what had happened, Matthew went into York and took a small gift to the young lady who had worked so hard on his behalf to secure him a flight home. What he also told me in that conversation was that he had known that he had lost his ticket way before he arrived at the airport on his return journey. In fact he knew when he arrived at the airport on the way in. He could remember putting it in the brochure pocket in front of his seat on the outgoing flight. But he had just arrived in New York when he realised and that was not the time to worry about such small details. In Matthew's eyes New York was waiting to be explored and anything else could wait to be sorted. There were places to go and people to see. In his mind, he didn't need to worry anyway because the airline had a booking for him and technically he didn't need a ticket. But of course, he was thinking about budget airlines such as easyJet and he hadn't realised the effect that 9/11 would have had on procedures.

At the end of the month he had another birthday celebration trip and this one was a complete surprise to him. We had organised a weekend trip to Dublin for him and his three brothers. They drove to Holyhead and took the ferry. Our original plan had been for them to fly but Jonathan vetoed that because his trip to Australia had made him very nervous about flying. The weekend went well and was a good opportunity for them to get closer to each other. Like most siblings, as time progresses, it is easy for closeness to slacken when jobs and partners come along. Darren took charge of all the documents and made sure everyone was up in time for the return ferry. It was a new experience for all the brothers, especially as none of them had been to Dublin before. Matthew probably did the most sightseeing as he does not drink at all and gets up early to pack as much into his trips as possible. Darren, Richard and Jonathan went at a more leisurely pace but took in some of the sights and the culture of the city before they would all meet up to eat and spend the evenings together.

Keith had now drifted back into his old pattern and was staying away again although not quite as frequently as before. Once I was home from the clinic and without my job to challenge me, I was finding it difficult to find a new balance. I went out for walks which helped my joints, but in between I read a lot and paced myself with the housework. Keith and I talked about this and I said that as our sons were all grown up why didn't I go with him on his work trips sometimes and then we could stay away together. I had made the occasional trip with him in the first half of 2001, but now we were talking about something more regular.

It was on one of the earlier occasional trips, about two months before my breakdown, that I had done something that was totally out of character for me. Keith was attending a two-day conference near Bristol and we stayed in a Travelodge in the city centre. Unknown to Keith, I was on a mission. Something I had been considering for several months. Firstly I looked for a nail salon. My fingernails were not too bad but this was my first step. I relaxed and chatted to the young beautician. She had lovely smooth skin, glossy hair and beautiful nails which were quite short as she used her hands all day long in her professional work. Once my nails were finished and the polish was dry, I asked her one final question.

"Can you recommend a tattoo salon?"

"*Yes,*" she replied positively, "*I can.*"

And after writing down the details for me, she proceeded to open her overalls, pull up her T-shirt and show me a butterfly tattooed across her midriff.

"*It's the only place I would recommend. I know of others but I have no first-hand knowledge of their hygiene standards,*" she said, with a persuasive smile.

I thanked her for the job she had done and also for this piece of information. The first part of my mission was complete. Now I was on my journey. I had to get a bus out of the city for my destination. Once I got off the bus the salon was just across the street. Now I started to get nervous. What would they ask me? What would I say? I knew I was going to have a tattoo, but I wasn't sure how to go about it. I opened the door and went inside. A young man who had tattoos covering both arms greeted me. He said that I would need to wait for about an hour. The salon did not make appointments as it was difficult to time this kind of work and they preferred not to work to the clock and create unnecessary pressure. I decided to stay but an hour was a long time in this situation and I had nothing to read. I had nothing to take my mind off the process I was about to experience, either, but I need not have worried. I was looked after and the time passed actually passed quite quickly. I was asked what I wanted.

"*Four letters,*" I replied. "*K- A- R- L. No artwork, just his name.*"

I had thought long and hard about a picture. There were so many things I could have had to remind me of Karl: skull and crossbones, an animal, a bird, a motorbike. The list was long. In the end, though, I decided that I wanted just his name. The next question was where. Kath had already helped me with this decision. On my Christmas visit when I had mentioned to her what I wanted to do she was very surprised. She probably thought I was the last person to do something like this. Karl had had his first tattoo done when he was about eighteen and had several more over a period of years. Kath also had several but none of them were obvious. That sounds strange considering she has a splendid tattoo of the head of an Arabian horse on her calf. However because she always wore long skirts, jeans or jodhpurs it was several months before we saw the tattoo and even then it was only because she was explaining it to us and revealed it. When I told her that I wanted to do this but it was just between Karl and me and not the rest of the world, she understood. If I had it on my arm it would show in summertime. We had talked about midriff and thigh but then she said, *"Why not on your ankle?"* This was a good idea as I usually wore long skirts or trousers and so nobody would see it unless I wanted them to.

The artist asked which ankle and I said I did not know. We made a decision together and he made a start. I was watching a young man in another corner of the room. He was having a large drawing on his upper arm. He looked very ill at ease. I was glad mine was only four letters. His would take forever. It was explained to me that the picture he was having was a tribal drawing. The young man was not making any noise or wincing so it must not be too painful. The artist placed my ankle in a position, which was both comfortable for him to work and for me to be able to sit for a period of time. I heard the buzz of the tool and then I felt severe discomfort as the needle touched my skin. The movement seemed to last forever and then the needle was taken away again. It went in several more times before the letter K was formed. I cannot explain what I experienced; it was not pain as I knew it but I found it very uncomfortable. I gritted my teeth and started thinking about Karl. That was the secret. I thought about the time when he had his first motorbike and how he promised me that one day he would take me for a ride after he passed his test. He later replaced the bike with one with a bigger engine, but I never got my ride. In the wintertime he always used his car and then in the summer he was always busy enjoying the open roads and the fresh air on two wheels. His burning ambition was to visit the USA and tour it on a motorbike. Sadly he would never achieve this now, but he had achieved so many other things. I was pondering on this when suddenly the young man said, *"There, you can look now."* So there it was completed. I was very relieved and I wondered how people coped with long sittings. I loved the finished product. The young man said he was sorry if it had been uncomfortable but it was a very bony part of the body to work on. I walked out of the salon with a big smile on my face. I had achieved my goal. Now I could not wait to show Keith. I took the bus back to Bristol and I walked back to our hotel. It was not long before Keith arrived and when he did I was sitting on the bed with my leg covered by my joggers. I pulled the material back and showed him my ankle. He was very surprised. He smiled and hugged me. Then he said,

"How does it feel?"

"It feels perfect," I said, and followed the words immediately with a big grin.

"I'm proud of you," he said, with a beaming smile.

Keith had been surprised at my revelation but not shocked. I had mentioned the subject to him months earlier when I was still very nervous about having it done. He understood why I felt it was a special bond with Karl and he gave his approval. His words at the time were, *"I think you should go ahead."* He had then smiled and continued with, *"as long as you don't want me to have one as well."*

I travelled with Keith for about two years virtually every time that he had to stay away on business. After his business was done we had time together for a relaxing evening. Keith could spend a full day at the office and be back at the hotel in just over half an hour. We did not need to think about cooking and we could have long walks on summer evenings and visit new places. Some days I would explore new towns or cities on my own while Keith was working. It could often be very frustrating as I was at the mercy of my energy levels and some days I spent time reading in libraries and parks. Other days I would explore museums, cathedrals and shops. I decided that I would hunt for treasure in charity shops. I could write a book about the different styles of the shops, the staff and the characters that visit. This gave me an automatic quest in a town. I could visit or not visit depending on what else I was committed to. I learned a lot about different back stamps on china and silver markings and had several genuine finds. It all added to the excitement. Some days when I was tired I would stay in the hotel room and read. Often I would type if Keith was able to leave the laptop. I had no timetable to follow so I could pick up the typing and stop as soon as I felt any strain on my hands. We visited some lovely hotels and also some mediocre ones. One of my favourite trips was when we stayed in Newmarket. The hotel was near the racecourse and close to the many different stables. Early in the morning I used to watch the teams of jockeys riding out over the downs in their splendid colours doing their daily warm-ups. It really was a fantastic sight. Some mornings I would merely watch from the window but I got more excitement being out among them on the frosty mornings, watching the icy breath of both jockey and horse. I did miss sharing something like this with Keith but after all he did have to work to earn a living. And he did work very hard. Despite the fact that I travelled with him he still put in long hours, prepared documents in our hotel rooms and could still get up ridiculously early to prepare for training courses he was delivering that day. It was while we were staying in the Newmarket hotel that Keith decided to re-decorate the room. It was early evening and we decided to open a bottle of wine. Keith has never found this an easy task and we only had a basic corkscrew opener with us. After several attempts and half a cork later Keith was much relieved to find that the rest of the cork was leaving the bottle and he was achieving his task. However, he was shocked when he realised that the wine was in fact splashing out of the bottle and landing on the newly decorated wall. He looked down in horror and saw that some had also splashed into his suitcase and stained his shirt for the following day. It was red wine and I quickly went in to action removing the stain with lots of cold water and lots of scrubbing with a nailbrush, and then I tried the same method on the wall. As I rubbed gently with cold water it was obvious I was rubbing the surface off the new wallpaper. I tried other methods but nothing would hide the fact that Keith had just designed a mural on this wall – and not one that was required. We settled down for the night, convincing ourselves that it would look better in the morning, but it didn't. He toyed with the idea of talking to the decorators who were still on site working on another part of the hotel, but decided against this. It was our last night in the hotel but Keith still had a full day's training to deliver in one of their meeting rooms. The cleaners were bound to discover his handiwork and then the management would confront him. But no-one did ask to see him, and so he made the decision to quietly leave at the end of the course. Needless to say, he never went back to that hotel.

While Keith was training in Perth, I visited Caithness Glass Factory and as I am a member of the Caithness Collecting Society I had a personal tour of the factory. I was shown how a paperweight is made, starting with the gathering of molten glass from the immense heat of the furnace, right through to dusting and packaging ready for despatch to the shops. I met individual designers and enjoyed looking at all the glassware in the museum. It was a very pleasant day, which was then rounded off by a tour around the beautiful countryside as we searched for somewhere to eat in the evening. These were pleasurable experiences for me but it was often quite a gruelling schedule as we travelled long distances in the evening. It was not uncommon for Keith to do a full day's training in Manchester and then drive all the way to Bristol so that he was in the right place for the following day's training. So we would often not arrive at the hotel until 9pm after which we had to find a suitable place for a meal. With my restricted diet, this was often quite a challenge. Despite the closer understanding that had developed between us, there was still the wall that came down whenever he was in work mode, and he would push his work time to the limit.

Christmas 2002 passed by quietly as we waited for the birth of our grandson. And some more good news came to us in the form of an engagement as Richard proposed to Layla. Between Christmas and New Year, Keith and Matthew and I went up to Scotland to see Kath and to spend some time in Edinburgh. Kath was well, but she was still finding life lonely and very hard work. However, she'd had several achievements at the horse shows that season. Sid, a new horse that she'd acquired was already showing great potential and she talked about how Karl would have loved this particular horse's personality. And Katana was now eighteen months old and looking every inch a champion of the future. Murphy had been quite ill but was now recovering and it was quite obvious that both he and Storm were still missing Karl. They had always been very playful but now they were noticeably docile. We took Kath out for lunch in the town and then headed south again. It was good for me to see Karl's place again, particularly as I was now much stronger and Kath no longer needed my support.

In the first week of January 2003 Keith rang me from London to tell me the good news from the company's annual sales conference being held at the London Planetarium. Richard had been presented with a trophy for achieving Sales Merchandiser of the Year 2002. He told Keith after the presentation that he had remembered his words one year earlier as they watched someone else win the award. "*Next year, Richard, that could be you.*" He had decided to go all out to achieve it.

Richard like Keith has a strong work ethic. However unlike his dad he has a better balance; he works hard but he also plays hard. When Richard was ten years old, Keith had taken him to Old Trafford along with Jonathan. In hindsight it seemed that he had been born with Manchester United stamped on his bottom. Already a fan, this match sealed his lifelong devotion to the team. He was a staunch supporter and he and Jonathan had this hobby in common – they would spend hours 'talking football'. Throughout their early teenage years, Keith would often be in charge of the company's hospitality box at Watford football ground. This involved ensuring that the customers had a good time and that everyone followed the rules. Keith would often take the two of them to Watford with him for the day. One particular year we all went for a weekend to watch some five-a-side games that were being held as part of a fun day. Five of us squeezed into a Travelodge family room on the Saturday night and then went to the ground on the Sunday. The skipper of the company team was panicking. People hadn't turned up and he was short of players. Although he was only fifteen, Richard was tested and drafted into the team.

After leaving school he had played football every week for his local team. He was very skilful and the talent spotters did notice him. I clearly remember when we took him to Huddersfield for a trial for their team. We were all excited but it was a bitterly cold day and there was frost on the pitch at the start of the game. Keith and the boys reported that he played extremely well. I had retired to the car at half time as I could not stop my teeth chattering and was feeling quite ill. I have always suffered from cold, probably because I have poor circulation. Richard gave a very good account of himself on the pitch and the football coach acknowledged this, but it was not quite enough to land him a contract. While at school he had achieved good results in his GCSEs and so he went on to Sixth Form College. After a disappointing first year, he switched colleges and decided to follow a sports management course. He continued to enjoy and play football throughout this time. At college he worked hard and was a very committed student when doing his placements. He was recognised as having a high work ethic and showed signs of good leadership qualities. He qualified at nineteen and then was out looking for work. He found work easily but not in his field of study. To earn money he took several driving jobs, working long hours and travelling all over the country. This developed his driving skills, his map reading skills and his stamina. He was always popular with both girls and boys but preferred close friendships to casual flings. He had several girlfriends over a number of years but eventually became engaged to Sarah. The following year they moved in together and along came our granddaughter Leah. It soon became obvious that Richard worshipped his little daughter. Feeding, changing nappies, anything she needed – nothing was too much trouble. They were struggling to the pay bills and so eventually Sarah went back to work. They shared the childcare between them until a child-minder was found. Later it was decided that Leah would go to nursery. She really enjoyed it and it was good that sometimes we had the chance to pick her up from the nursery on a Friday when she was coming to stay with us and we were able to meet her little friends. Eventually Richard got a job as a transport manager with a small company, and again he worked hard and was promised promotion. Unfortunately this kept slipping out of his grasp. On one of their visits to Reeth House, Richard said that he had been offered a job at the London branch of the company and that both he and Sarah were very excited at the possibility of moving to London. They were looking forward to starting a new life there, but weeks went by and then months and the London work was not mentioned again. We began to realise that despite Richard's commitment and hard work his boss appeared to be dangling carrots but never came through with the rewards. It was obvious that Richard was beginning to get very frustrated about his job and so when a vacancy came up with Keith's company in Yorkshire, he asked Richard if he would be interested in being interviewed for the position. He jumped at the chance, had two successful interviews and started his new role with Henkel in December 2001, a week before Christmas.

January 2003 turned out to be a good month for us. As well as Richard's good news, we were delighted when our first grandson was born on the 21st of the month. Dylan Michael Townend was born soon after midnight weighing in at 9lb 12oz. He was given Beccy's father's name, Michael. But Jonathan also wanted him to have another name in memory of Karl. Townend was one of Karl's other Christian names, which he had been given in memory of his grand father. Jonathan had spoken to us earlier in the day to say that Beccy had gone in to hospital and he was staying with her. It was a long labour and Beccy was exhausted when their little bundle of treasure finally entered the world. When Jonathan rang us soon after the birth, it was obvious he was delighted to now be part of a family of three. He was very proud of Beccy, too; she had struggled through a very tough day and they were both thrilled with their beautiful baby boy who they had nicknamed 'Elvis' throughout the pregnancy. We could not wait to hear Leah's reaction to the news of her new cousin. She had been waiting patiently for so long. Firstly for Christmas then for her Birthday on 31st December but once that was over she was having a hard time waiting for the birth despite counting the days. Her granddad Keith had told her that she would have to go to bed and then get up on twenty mornings before 'our baby' would be born. Leah always referred to the impending arrival as 'our baby'. Matthew and I visited Beccy and Jonathan at the hospital on the following day and Matthew was the first to hold Dylan. He said he was amazed how tiny he was and began to examine his fingers and toes – it was as though he was investigating a miracle. And then it was my turn to hold him. I looked down at his tiny face and despite being very bruised there was no mistaking who his daddy was. He was just like a miniature Jonathan, the same nose, the same chin, exactly the same profile.

I assured Beccy that before long he would resemble both of them but she too said she could see a perfect likeness to Jonathan. Over the next few days all his grandparents and his uncles and aunts visited him they were all very proud of this new member of the family and could not wait to spend time with the three of them in their own home. When it was time for Leah to see him she immediately wanted to hold him. Beccy showed her how to sit and support him and once shown she did not want to leave him. It was great to see them together and to see the happiness on everybody's face, especially Jonathan's.

Jonathan was a very happy child and I am sure he must have had a smile on his face even when he was still in my womb. In his childhood he always expressed what we used to refer to as his cheeky grin. Karl and Darren had been eager to welcome him into the world and having two older brothers probably made him quite content with his lot. He was full of energy and was the first child to climb out of our cot, the first child to climb on the table and the first to accidentally move my uncle's JCB a few feet across the barn, an action which required quick thinking, and even quicker action by Keith to avoid a serious accident. When it was time to visit playgroup he became extremely unhappy so we postponed this for a while ready to retry a few months later. In the meantime we moved to Snaith where the school joining age was lower than that in Bradford so he never did go to playgroup again. In fact, we arrived in Snaith on a Saturday and he started school the following Monday. Going into school was always a problem for Jonathan, as he did not like to be jostled in the crowd. As the bell rang and all the children were hurrying towards the school door, he would always walk back towards me and give me a last-minute kiss thus ensuring he could walk down the path on his own after the crowd had gone in. Sometimes other mums would remark on this or just smile as it was part of his daily routine. Once inside school, he enjoyed learning and he also enjoyed the company. He started to develop a small group of friends and throughout his school life was always a popular class member. However, he never went to school birthday parties at junior school whereas lots of the other children seemed to be involved in these. I found out the reason one day at the school gates one Monday morning when the mum of his best friend came up to me and said,

"Did you enjoy your weekend away?"

"We've not been anywhere," I replied.

"Oh I'm sorry, I thought you must have been away with Jonathan not attending James's birthday party."

I apologised and said I had not seen the invitation. It turned out that Jonathan had had the invitation for two weeks but kept it hidden in his tray at school. We never pressed him to attend children's parties but we did encourage him to bring children home for meals and to play. This he often did but occasionally, when he felt he had had enough, he would come to me and say, "Will you send them home now Mum? Tell him it's bedtime or something."

He obviously wanted time alone, but found it difficult to tell them himself, so I carried out his request and supported him. Even when he was older he often found it hard to say no to friends. He enjoyed reading and drawing and was always telling jokes and dressing up and acting, and we felt sure that one day he would end up on the stage. He joined the cub scouts and was a member for a few years, attending the annual cub camp, which we visited during the weekend to enjoy songs around the campfire. Despite his natural shyness he was always the first to join in the acts when the annual gang show took place. He enjoyed acting in sketches or reciting prose. He was never a child who became bored easily and soon became engrossed in whatever he was doing and was always ready to visit new places and try new experiences. My former husband Dennis had helped Karl and Darren to buy motocross bikes, a hobby they were developing together. At the same time, Richard and Jonathan, who were always very close, had a track bike, which they used to share. They each got helmets and protective gear as Christmas presents but in the event they were often quite nervous and both decided they were happier with a football at this time in their development. Even as a young child, Jonathan seemed to understand the minds of all his brothers. He was the one I can thank for my sanity. So many times when Matthew was having tantrums and I was dealing with the situation by myself, Jonathan would often say to me, *"Don't shout Mum, calm down."*

He was always right – shouting never solved the situation; in fact it aggravated it – but often I was so frustrated that I could not always see this for myself. By the age of ten, Jonathan had changed from a noisy whirlwind into a gentle person with a calm nature and his calming influence always helped the situation. Like Karl, he was always a deep thinker and an observer. He was happiest sitting in a group observing the interaction. When he moved up to the secondary school he found the general pressure to study and exams in particular very hard, as he had, by then, developed quite a full social life and he got up to lots of mischief as most young boys do. But he was very creative and loved English language, literature and drama, and in his spare time we would often find him sitting on his bed either sketching or writing stories, when his imagination would carry him to great heights. His love for sport continued and he was picked to represent the school at county level athletic tournaments and won several titles. He was also a dedicated member of the school football team. Whenever I was able, I would go and watch him play, sometimes enjoying the match sitting on the grass with other parents and cheering and occasionally standing on the sidelines if the weather was inclement. I remember one day in particular when Jonathan was enjoying a match and suddenly the hailstones started to bombard us. The footballers huddled together for a few minutes until the worst passed and then they began to play again. At the first opportunity Jonathan came close to the touch- line where I was standing and whispered across to me, *"Mum, do you think you could run me a hot bath?"*

I was relieved to be given permission to get out of the cold. We only lived next door and I followed Jonathan's instructions to the letter. As soon as he walked through the door there was a hot drink waiting for him to take to the bathroom. I used to wish Keith would go to some of the matches but I knew that, even when he was at home and not working for the company, he would find it very difficult standing with a group of parents for an hour and a half. When he was in year nine, Jonathan asked us if he could go on the annual ski trip. We agreed and he thoroughly enjoyed it. He had two further ski trips before leaving school plus two more after he left. He encouraged Matthew to go with him on the school ski trip as soon as Matthew was in year seven and this was good for Matthew's development. It also enabled him to keep an eye on Matthew and protect him from some of the school bullies. We often had problems with Jonathan not coming in on time on school nights. He was never desperately late, but he always liked to push the boundaries. Saturday evenings were more relaxed: as long as he was in at a reasonable time we were happy. One particular Saturday night we were getting quite concerned at his lateness when we received a phone call from him asking if we could pick him up. Instead of him being in Snaith where we thought he was, he was in the nearby village of Pollington. He had been mediating between one of his friends and his friend's fifteen-year-old girlfriend. The girl was very unhappy at home and had decided to run away with her boyfriend and was not going home that night. The boyfriend was obviously not happy about this situation and Jonathan had tried his best to persuade her to ring her mother. He knew by this time we would be concerned about what had happened to him but he did not feel he could go home and go to bed and leave the situation as it was. He was concerned that her parents would be worrying about her and asked me to ring her mum and tell her where she was. We went to the scene to collect him and the girl's mum came to collect her and was so pleased to have found her daughter that there were no recriminations. They just hugged and went home together. We praised Jonathan for his responsible act. He did however say it was always much easier to sort out somebody else's problems rather than his own. Over the years, there were many other situations where he became an 'agony aunt' to his friends. In his last year at school Jonathan decided he did not want to go to Sixth Form College. He wanted a job, he wanted to work and so he left school at the end of the summer term but was unable to get work straight away. When term time restarted we stated that as he did not have a job he ought to at least be following some further education and so, reluctantly, he signed on at the college in Pontefract. Officially he continued until the end of the Christmas term but we had been having regular phone calls from the college telling us that he was not attending lectures, so after much discussion we felt it was pointless forcing him to stay at college as he was not committed and was having to be deceitful. He tried again to get some work and this time he was successful and, although he knew it was not what he wanted to do long term, he was much happier. He applied for several jobs including finding out information about joining the navy and then in the following summer he was successful in securing himself an apprenticeship at British Aerospace based at Brough. He was highly delighted, particularly as only twelve people had been accepted from three hundred applications.

And so his apprenticeship began and just as at school he was popular with his peers and soon made a small but close group of friends. They would often arrange social outings near payday each month. It was on one of these evenings that he had met Beccy. She had gone along as a friend of one of the female apprentices. Up until this point Jonathan had had several long-term relationships with girls and we were aware of most of them. Now Beccy had come into his life, but it would be a few more years before we were introduced to her.

As they lived forty miles apart, he only saw her at the weekend or the occasional night through the week. He still had male friends at home and spent some evenings during the week with them in the local pub. But his relationship with Beccy developed and he was accepted into her family. He built up a healthy relationship with her two brothers and her parents, and he joined group visits to their family in Holland. When Jonathan and Beccy had returned from Australia, they had clearly rekindled their friendship, but they were certainly not an item. On their return, they lived together in Snaith for the first week and then Beccy returned to her family home and then in to a house which she rented with a friend. However, for a couple that were not going out together they saw each other on a very regular basis. As well as being lovers they had also been best friends and Beccy had been there to support him through his grief after Karl's death, his accident and the subsequent brief spell in prison. Their liaisons grew more frequent until eventually, once again, they set up a home together, this time in the village of Hessle, just outside the city of Hull.

Keith's company, Henkel, recognised long service with them by awarding the employees with a cash figure, which increased as each five-year milestone came around. In celebration of 35 years with the company, Keith received the allocated amount, which we put towards a new fireplace in our lounge. But in addition he was awarded the cost of a weekend away for the two of us, anywhere in the UK. He decided to combine the weekend with a training assignment that he had accepted. It was spring 2003 and we flew from Liverpool John Lennon airport to Belfast. After picking up a hire car at the airport we headed up to the north east coast of Ireland, to the seaside town of Portrush. We stayed in a hotel near the seafront for three nights. Keith ran a two-day training course in the hotel and then had a day's work around other parts of Northern Ireland. It was a very peaceful break for me while he was training, and then on an evening, we would take a drive along the coast visiting the local beauty spots including the very impressive Giant's Causeway. On the third day I went with him as he visited a number of towns, names that I could remember from the news bulletins over the years, Omagh, Londonderry, Coleraine.

On the Friday night, and with Keith's three days of official business behind us, we began our weekend. We were booked in to the Hilton Hotel in central Belfast. It was my first visit to this part of the country but Keith had been before, in the late 70s when murders and bombings and street violence were a daily occurrence. We spoke to several people who said that the visit of President Bill Clinton in 1998 had made such a difference to the atmosphere and was a turning point for the city. And while we were there, they were expecting a visit from President George W. Bush who was coming over for talks with the British and Irish prime ministers at Hillsborough Castle.

We were shown to our room and given a key to the executive suite. After booking an evening meal in the dining room, we went to explore the executive suite. There were about six couples already seated at individual tables all enjoying drinks and canapés. We joined in conversation with another couple but Keith spent most of the time looking out of the windows at the splendid views over the city. This was his way of gaining space from this group of strangers with whom he was reluctant to get involved. This was a typical reaction from him. If I hadn't been there, I am sure he would have chatted away, but subconsciously he saw them as an intrusion into our private time together. The time came to go to the dining room and enjoy our dinner. We ordered wine and our meal was served. We chatted about what we had seen earlier in the week and expressed pleasure in how lucky we were to be able to share these experiences together. I watched the couple at the next table. A tall distinguished man in his forties with a tall, equally good-looking teenager, probably about sixteen, was my guess. I overheard snippets of conversation. The father was giving the son the choice of places to visit the following day. Why was there no female? Was the mum dead or were they divorced? Did son live with mum and was this quality time for father and son? Now suddenly I was able to feel myself analysing all this. Stop it! It's nothing to do with you, I was saying to myself. I cannot stop my natural curiosity but I can now stop myself from using unnecessary mental energy sorting out things that do not concern me. Being in the clinic and understanding myself taught me this. Now I could prioritise. I no longer needed to waste valuable energy this way.

There was an air of optimism about the centre of the city as we walked around on the following day and yet on the outskirts it was easy to see that the divisions between the two communities were still there, just under the surface. We took a bus tour that meandered around the contrasting areas. You didn't need to be a rocket scientist to establish whether you were in a loyalist or a republican stronghold. The flags, the murals and the general graffiti told their own story and the heavily fortified police stations were for me the most poignant reminder of a divided society. On Sunday morning we visited Milltown Cemetery. It was so sad to walk between the hundreds and hundreds of graves and read the inscriptions for many young lives lost over thirty years of violence. The cemetery was a hive of activity with little clusters of people busily placing fresh flowers and generally tidying the graves. It was obvious that it wasn't just a fleeting visit. In every case it was as though they were here for the day. I could imagine them having a picnic here later, with their departed loved ones. A black taxicab arrived with another family, obviously the driver's family. The Irish tricolour flew from the cab's aerial. They didn't stay very long. Flowers were placed beside a large memorial stone and within minutes they were gone. We went to the stone; a list of thirteen names stood out in gold lettering and underneath were the words, 'Murdered by the British Army'.

At work, Keith was getting more and more involved with the development of people and had become very much a consultant to his sales director in these matters. A profit warning from the company's head office in Germany had meant that they had to look for savings. His training budget became an early casualty and had to be frozen for the year. As part of the discussions about the future, Keith suggested that his own early retirement would help the situation as they could get away without replacing him if the workload was delegated to the line managers. This strategy had, in fact, been part of Keith's three-year plan anyway. After some discussion a date of 1st April 2004 was provisionally agreed.

It was now almost three years since Karl's death and I felt that I had finally picked up the pieces of my life. Things were by no means perfect, but then in life they never are, but I did feel on top of the current situation and more importantly I felt confident that I would be able to deal with the many challenges that undoubtedly lay ahead.

Chapter 17

A NEW BEGINNING

It was a cold day in the February of 2003 when Matthew took the call. He had been successful.

It was back in November that he had attended a weeklong interview process with Coca-Cola. He had shared with us, at the time, the experiences that were evolving during the sessions and he was quite confident in his performance. With two stints of self-employment behind him, he felt that now was the time to get some experience by working with one of the top brands in the world and they didn't come much bigger than Coca-Cola. And now they were saying yes! We'll give you a chance – your induction starts next week. He was ecstatic. The last six months had been somewhat frustrating for him as he went from job to job and he had done some pretty meaningless tasks. The worst must have been the few days he spent extracting discarded plastic mouldings from brick rubble. Apparently his employers had been informed that they must remove these from the site before it could be re-developed.

And so off he went into the sunset with a very smart uniform and a Coca-Cola van to develop the sales of their products through small independent retail shops. Each day he came home and related his experiences. But as the time went along it became clear he was struggling. He didn't seem to be getting help from his manager. He kept making mistakes, as everyone does in a new job, but he got the feeling that, rather than wanting him to succeed, his manager was quite happy to see him fail. That was probably not the whole truth but it was

Matthew's perception and because of this, his motivation dropped and his performance reflected this. It was a downward spiral. So it was not such a surprise when, in May, I received a phone call from Keith on his way home from London. Matthew had contacted him for a chat and they had met in a hotel halfway up the A1. Matthew had met his manager and a person from human resources. His three months probation had come to an end and they were unable to confirm his continuing employment with Coca-Cola. The following day he had to return the van and all the equipment. I followed in our car in order to bring him home and I could see that disappointment and confusion were written all over his face. Although the relationship with his manager had been a strain throughout this period, he started to have self-doubts about his abilities. Perhaps he was not cut out to be in business. One of the criticisms from his manager had been that he didn't communicate well with the customers. Keith volunteered to help him by finding out what the customers actually thought about him. He put on the Coca-Cola jacket that Matthew had retained and, pretending to be a customer service manager, asked a cross section of them how Coca-Cola were doing as a supplier and, as part of the conversation, he cleverly asked about Matthew's communication with them. After the exercise was completed, Keith was convinced that Matthew didn't have a problem in this area. It actually reinforced what he already knew, because he had acted as a trainer for him for a couple of days when he was selling the business cards and had been very pleased with his basic approach to the generation of sales. More importantly Matthew was pleased with the results of Keith's investigation and it restored a degree of confidence in his mind. So, in essence, it came down to lack of concentration and he knew that this was, as always, being fuelled by his obsessive thoughts.

Fortunately he didn't have long to brood about the past. Keith was recruiting for a project team and he needed someone to help out in Scotland for a three-month period. Matthew was happy to accept this short-term opportunity and the manager of the team was happy to take Matthew on as he had worked for him before and he knew that he was competent. He enjoyed the travelling up and down to Scotland. The work was not taxing and he had the opportunity to visit a variety of places in his spare time, but he did find it very lonely and this was highlighted on one particular evening when he turned up at home unexpectedly. After finishing that day's work, he had driven down from Scotland and the following morning he had to drive all the way back again. He had, in fact, checked in to a hotel for the night but after a short time, he had checked out again and was heading south. We were very surprised to see him as he walked in at about midnight and, without talking to us, headed for his bedroom and stayed there until we retired for the night. We knew instinctively that something was wrong and we also knew that it was better to leave him alone and that he would come to us when he was ready to talk. As we were getting ready in our room he came in and sat on the bed. His trusty quilt was with him. He sat with us, our six-foot-three-inches tall, twenty-two-year old, looking unhappy and bemused as he sniffed the corner of his quilt. When he was a baby and sleeping in his cot he was in the habit of sniffing the corner of his quilt. He never chewed it but he used to rub it with his finger as he sniffed it. It was probably the soap powder he could smell as I washed it regularly. One day I was tidying his cot and I noticed that the corner was threadbare and a hole had formed. I could not afford to buy another quilt cover so I studied the quilt and decided it was big enough for me to cut a border off and sew it up and make it look new again. So out came my machine and I made the required alteration that I felt looked very professional. Evening came and it was time to put Matthew to bed. He sat there and grabbed his quilt to his face as always. Then he turned the quilt and turned it again and again. He went round all four corners and could not settle because he could not find his trusty corner. I was appalled at what had I done; I had destroyed his comfort zone. I had not thought this through at all and not realised that this corner and the ritual surrounding it were so important to him. Now it clicked that it was not the quilt he was attached to, but one particular corner and that's why I only had to repair one of them. What a cruel mum I was. Here was my little boy looking for his comforter and it would never appear again. Eventually he did get to sleep but had a very disturbed night. The next four evenings were very similar but by the time the fifth night came along Matthew had created his own customised corner and was happy again. I swore I would never touch his quilt again except to wash it. As he grew bigger and went into a bed he did the same thing with the larger quilt; he always had one favourite corner. Keith and I used to joke with him and say that in the future when he had a long time girlfriend, he would be able to share his 'cudder' with her. This was the family pet name for his customised quilt. Once when my mum was staying I overheard her joking with Matthew.

"I don't know Matthew; will you still be sniffing that quilt when you are twenty-one?"

She didn't realise at the time how accurate her prediction was.

None of my boys ever had a dummy as I always felt that they demeaned children and whenever they were upset, I found myself able to calm them without the use of dummies. I did wonder, however, if I had allowed Matthew a dummy maybe this would have been better and he would have moved on from it by now, but then again, maybe he would still have been sucking the dummy at twenty-two, which would look a trifle more eccentric than his cudder.

So what was the problem tonight and why did he look so unhappy? He was lonely; he wanted a friend, someone to talk to, and someone to confide in. Most of all he wanted a girlfriend. He had had a number of brief relationships with girls but they had all faded. At one time he had fears that he would never be able to approach girls. He found it as difficult as Keith had done in his youth, but he had overcome that hurdle, and now his problem wasn't starting a liaison with a girl, it was in sustaining it. I listened to him and I cuddled him. Somehow our statements that it would all come right in the end seemed rather hollow and empty. He also told us about an incident at another of the hotels that he had stayed in while in Scotland. The manager brought it to his attention that someone had complained about some very loud noises that appeared to have been emanating from Matthew's bedroom. He had talked his way out of the situation by apologising, and saying that he had, unfortunately, had the television volume turned up at a particularly high level. In reality he was the one making the noise. Loud internal screaming sounds made through clenched teeth, very similar to Tourettes and accompanied by an aggressive slow clapping of the hands. These were sounds with which we were familiar, as he would often make them in the house, usually in jest, but we appreciated that they were allowing him to release some of the tension that was building up inside him.

The month of August arrived and I received yet another of those heart-stopping phone calls from Keith as he drove up the motorway.

After a brief greeting he sighed and said four very poignant words. *"We have a problem."*

Keith had organised a two-day meeting for the team at a hotel in the Midlands, and this included activity in the form of paintballing. Although Matthew had enjoyed the event, he had also found it very difficult and had told Keith that he didn't feel able to finish the contract. This gave Keith two problems; Firstly, how to achieve completion without Matthew's help and secondly, and more importantly, how to explain Matthew's reason for pulling out to the team's manager. But even more important was the fact that Keith could see that Matthew was struggling to make sense of his life, and he knew that he had to do something more to help him. The following day Matthew stayed at home and Keith went to the office in London to see Dick, his sales director. Dick was, of course, fully aware of Matthew's difficulties, as Keith had confided in him six years earlier about the diagnosis when he had requested a change in his responsibilities. Keith said that he needed to bring his early retirement forward by three months to the end of the year, as he had to help Matthew with his future. Dick was very sympathetic and agreed to discuss it with Keith as soon as it was practical, but for now, he suggested he took a few days' holiday.

By the time he came home that night, Keith had sorted things out in his mind.

He had already contacted the team manager and told him that Matthew needed to terminate the contract immediately, because an opportunity had presented itself to him and he had to take advantage of it quickly. He had also worked out a strategy to complete the work that Matthew was unable to do. He told Matthew that he intended to take early retirement and then asked him what he thought about the two of them working together so that he could help him to develop a new business. Matthew's reaction was very positive. He had been very disappointed and upset about the previous day, but the fact that there was a way forward gave him hope. I too was keen to help in this new venture. I wanted to be part of the new beginning. The very next day we headed for York. We were looking for inspiration and felt that we might find it there, as it was a city that Matthew had grown very fond of over the past two years. We walked and we talked and we tossed ideas about. At the end of the day we had a list of elements that we felt had to be embraced by the business:

Hotels and restaurants
Leisure and tourism
Business people
Food,
Children
Guided walks

Five of these elements were ones that had kept popping in and out of Matthew's thoughts throughout his life. His early career aspirations had been set on becoming firstly a hotel manager and then ultimately owning his own hotel. When he was at school and looking for work experience he was determined to gain this by working at a high-class hotel. He had bypassed the normal school procedures and written directly to the hotel that he had selected, which at that time was the only five-star hotel in the north of England. After an interview, his application was accepted and he thoroughly enjoyed learning about what makes a good hotel tick, as he moved between departments. We had bought him a black suit for the period and he wore it at the interview, but also on each and every day that he was employed. Both Keith and I felt very proud when we saw him in that suit; he looked very professional and it was obvious that he felt very proud to be wearing it. When he was asked to work in the leisure club area, he was told that he could wear casual clothes, but he refused. He felt that he had to wear the suit, even though he had to do jobs like cleaning the toilets. It was very reminiscent of his refusal to go to school in casual clothes on non-uniform day – it just wasn't the right thing to do. After one day in the leisure club he asked to see the duty manager and requested a transfer back into conference and banqueting where he felt he would learn more about the business. The duty manager fully understood his reasoning and his request was granted. He found the whole experience of the work at the hotel of great benefit to him and the only negative comment came from his school's career officer, who had been critical of Matthew's enterprise from the start. He took a very dim view of pupils deciding to decline his range of work experience options in favour of something completely different, and his criticism increased when the head teacher called at the hotel to assess Matthew's progress only to find that he was not there because his shift had been changed to fit in with his request to transfer between departments. The sixth element, guided walks, came from Keith. He had said for some time that, on retirement, he would quite like to be a tour guide. When we had been in San Francisco we had joined a guided tour of Chinatown and he had been stimulated and moved by the enthusiasm of the guide and had talked for days afterwards about how he would love to do something like that.

The next time Keith had a meeting with his sales director, they came to a definite agreement. Dick had tried to persuade Keith to stay another year until the end of 2004, as there were a number of issues that needed sorting out. After a lot of discussion Keith did agree to this additional year, but only because it was on the basis of a three-day week and as it transpired this was actually an ideal solution for us, as it meant that we could get used to a reduced income as a prelude to full retirement. And, of course, it meant that he would have time available to help Matthew set up the new business.

In September Matthew came on holiday with us and we also took Edith, my mother-in-law and Matthew's nan, who had yearned to visit Canada for some time. She had enjoyed many holidays with Keith's dad and, since his death, had taken to travelling to many varied destinations, mainly in Europe, but had also ventured on a trip to Egypt. She was great company on this trip and despite her age of seventy-eight, she often put us to shame with her stamina. The day we arrived we all had jet lag, but after checking in at our hotel at midnight, she was eager to put on her swimming costume and join Matthew and Keith in the hotel swimming pool. She was ready for any experience that the trip handed out. Our days often started at seven o' clock in the morning and occasionally we were still out after midnight but Nan was still there, taking in the atmosphere. Our journey, which started in Detroit, took us through Ontario and Quebec and the American state of Maine with a conclusion in Boston, Massachusetts. We covered some two thousand miles, which were driven mainly by Matthew. The holiday really began with a few days' stay at my cousin's house near Toronto. My special time was when Joan my cousin and her husband Barry took us to the Lake of Bays and to the cottage of their daughter and family. To me this was just out of this world. We arrived on a hot lunchtime and were shown around the cabin where the blinds were drawn to keep the cottage cool. We went outside and I gasped at the view, a large tranquil lake, surrounded by forest-covered hills with very few signs of habitation. It was beautiful. Within minutes, Matthew was back at the car getting his swimming shorts and was changed and running down onto the boardwalk. He jumped in and was happily swimming about like a puppy that had hit the water for the very first time. My cousin had prepared a huge picnic lunch for all of us and we sat at the table under the shade of the cottage enjoying both the food and the breathtaking views. Just below us was the jetty where their son-in-law moored his boat. I could not help thinking what wonderful experiences their two children would enjoy while growing up here. They went to the cottage most weekends in the long summers and had also been known to struggle into the area in deep snow which was a totally different experience and one that seems quite natural for Canadians who make as much of outdoor life in the winter as they do in the summer.

Just one year earlier Keith and I had stayed at my cousin's house as part of our first full holiday together without children. Keith was never really what you would call a holiday person and regarded holidays as something you might do if you had any money left, which, of course, we never did have. If I had realised this fact sooner in our relationship then I would have taken charge, made plans, and made sure we had those missing holidays, but I didn't, at least not until more recent times. On that 2002 trip, Keith had driven from Boston to Chicago without any major mishaps, well, except for trashing a motel, that is. He had sent me in to the reception area of a motel in Fort Wayne, Indiana to enquire about accommodation. When I arrived a man was already speaking to the receptionist so I waited patiently. After a few minutes, the relative calm of the evening was shattered by what sounded like a major road traffic accident on the highway. We all ran to the doorway and I was astounded to see our hire car firmly embedded in the front of the building. Keith had been waiting for me with the engine running and had not engaged the hand brake. He had accidentally slipped the automatic gearshift into the drive position, enabling the car to lurch forward into one of the bedrooms, which had unfortunately been occupied at the time by the motel manageress who was sleeping between shifts. Keith was very apologetic about the incident but, nevertheless, still insisted that we could only stay at her motel if we were able to borrow a hairdryer from her. As well as staying with my cousin, we also spent a night at the house of a friend who had lived near us in Bradford but had emigrated to Illinois back in the 70s. We concluded our trip with a week in Janesville exactly thirteen years after I had flown out there on my own. It was a fabulous holiday and we were both totally relaxed and aside from the warmth of our hosts, the highlight of the trip was the stunning autumn colours throughout New England. We did still get some challenges from Matthew, however, even though we were so far apart, but they were not too challenging. He had sent us off with a list of books that we had to buy and a project to investigate the state of the market for home fruit bottling kits. However, he did provide us with a very pleasant surprise when the hotel receptionist at our hotel in Boston brought us a fax. It was a message from Matthew: 'Happy Special Anniversary'. It was twenty-two years since our marriage but that trip was an early celebration of our silver anniversary.

One year later, we were here again in Canada and after our peaceful day at the lakeside cottage, we headed in a north-easterly direction towards Quebec. It was in the city of Montreal that we saw the first signs that things were, once again, getting too much for Matthew. One evening, he went out on his own, after the 'oldies' had gone to bed. The following morning he was very quiet and not very communicative. Keith and I both sensed immediately that something was wrong. After breakfast, we decided on our plans for the day. Keith and Matthew were going on a walking tour, and Nan and I were going to walk around the shops. Then we would all meet up in the afternoon and go to another tourist attraction together. When Nan and I arrived at the agreed meeting point, there was Keith, but no Matthew. He told us that Matthew had decided to go off somewhere else and would see us later, but I could tell from Keith's expression that it was more than that. He told me later that, on the guided walk, Matthew had said very little, and appeared completely withdrawn. Keith's mum was unaware that he had been different that morning, as she was totally immersed in the experience of being in Canada. But then, nobody other than Keith and I knew about the torture that Matthew went through on a constant basis, and, of course, we didn't really know what it was like inside his mind.

When he did come to us with his thoughts, we could only listen and try to console him, and because we didn't understand, it became very heated as he got frustrated and accused both of us – but me in particular – of not listening.

The three of us moved on to an exhibition of sculptures made entirely from trees and plants which was housed next to a redundant power station. Then, we joined the underground system and headed back to our hotel. As we approached the hotel, my heart skipped a beat. There was Matthew waiting for us. He was sitting on the steps at the entrance to the building. He looked scruffy and tired and very sad and lonely. He just looked like one more homeless person, like the ones you see in shop doorways in every city in the world. All that was missing was a blanket and a collecting cup. As soon as he saw us he stood up and tried to appear normal, probably for Nan's sake, but once inside, when it was just the three of us, he broke down in tears. He had taken a walk on his own the previous night and this had allowed his thoughts to wander and anxiety about his future to take hold. In all this confusion he had tried to move the car, shortly before we saw him on the hotel steps and, in the process, damaged it. Keith went with him to check it out and to re-assure him that it wasn't a big deal and that it could be fixed. After we talked, he seemed more relaxed and the four of us went out for a meal.

Our next port of call was Quebec City where we stayed for two nights. This turned out to be a nightmare for him. It wasn't anything to do with Quebec itself – it could have been anywhere. After a head-splitting day for him, when it was obvious that he was having difficulties, he asked us to go out with him for a drink, just the three of us. We tried our best to say the right words, but it all went wrong and he left the table and stormed off into the night. Keith and I were mortified and didn't know how to resolve things. And then he came back, and after more talking, we made our way back to the hotel. It was a slow journey, as we kept stopping for more discussion.

I was very concerned, because he gave the appearance of being suicidal.

"What is the point of it all? Nobody understands me, nobody likes me."

He was heartbroken. Eventually we got back to the hotel and we went to his room to carry on the discussion. He lay on his bed and I cuddled him until he asked me to go and leave him on his own. The following day his severe depression had lifted, but, of course, we were no longer fooled into kidding ourselves that it had gone forever. We knew it was still there; he had just managed to work hard and mask it, just as he did on most days. Oh, how I wished I could help him!

The final night of the holiday was spent in Boston; Matthew had a surprise for us and had booked tickets for a comedy club. Unfortunately Nan was not used to the modern style comedy and the regular four-letter words offended her ears. She could see that we were enjoying the humour, if not the bad language, and she just waited patiently until it was over and then said, *"Well, I'm afraid I didn't enjoy that at all."*

On the previous evening we had taken her to a branch of Hooters, a restaurant chain that only employs waitresses who are blessed with large breasts. She had chuckled constantly at the way they all cavorted between the tables, and said that she would easily fit in there as she thought that she had a bigger pair than many of the staff.

We now look back on that holiday with a great deal of pleasure fuelled by the memories of some spectacular places, but it did, of course, create a very mixed bag of emotions with some of the most challenging difficulties for Matthew. That said, it did not stop us achieving one of our key goals which was to gather lots of information about the tourist trade in general and guided walks and tours in particular. And once back home the research continued as over the following months a variety of trade shows, guided walks and tourist attractions were visited in order to get more information and ideas. Matthew would regularly hitch a lift to London with Keith in order to visit a trade show. His decision to go was often last minute and sometimes he would tag along when I had already agreed to be with Keith and so, on numerous occasions, we were three in a room that had only been officially booked for one. This clandestine arrangement became quite hilarious whenever we stayed in a hotel at the same time as a group of company people were staying. Many is the time that Keith would be standing in the corridor of the hotel as a look-out to ensure that Matthew and I were not spotted as we sneaked out of the hotel the following morning. During one of Keith's sales conferences, we stayed with him at a luxury hotel at the side of the Thames in Chelsea. Matthew and I decided to leave the hotel by the rear entrance and walk along the river side to a nearby restaurant, thereby avoiding company delegates who we were sure would leave by a coach at the front entrance. When Keith returned to the hotel later in the night, it amused us to learn that the group had, in fact, also walked to the river bank where they had boarded a ship for their evening meal and entertainment.

One particular weekend, Matthew decided to visit a trade show in London that would be open on the Saturday. His plan was to go down with Keith on the Friday, keep busy during the day while he was at the office, and then the two of them would visit the show on the Saturday. This sounded a good arrangement so I decided to go along as well. On Saturday morning we pulled up outside Olympia Exhibition Centre and wondered where the usual crowds were hiding as it was unusually deserted. Keith and Matthew walked the perimeter of the building looking for a way in and somebody to talk to. Eventually Matthew found some contractors, but they knew nothing about the show that we were looking for. Not disheartened, he suggested we go to Earls Court as we must have the wrong exhibition centre. After a short drive and a quick discussion with the car park attendant, he realised that he had been right in the first place. We had gone to the correct exhibition centre. The show was definitely on at Olympia but unfortunately not this week. We were one week too early. He had read about the show some time ago in a magazine on the shelf in a bookstore, but hadn't written it down – he was relying on his memory and what he thought he had seen. As an alternative we drove to Hampstead, an area of London that Matthew has always liked very much, and for which he has high aspirations. I was interested in looking at the home of the singer, Boy George, located near the Heath. Keith and I were both astounded when Matthew just walked across the road towards the house without checking the traffic conditions. He saw the house on the other side of the road and he just went. Like so many occasions before, he just seemed to be in a world of his own and totally unaware of what other people were doing or of any danger around him.

On our first visit to the USA and Canada, Keith and I had both been impressed with the way virtually every house had been decorated for Halloween. Everything from very simple trimmings on some properties to others with fantastic garden displays featuring both humorous and scary characters, which had obviously taken a lot of time and effort to construct. Because our next visit fell in September, the house displays were not there, but the materials were in the shops in abundance. Keith decided that this year he would create a display. He would be the first house in Snaith to have a Halloween scene in the garden. Once we were in to October, he set about assembling the various bits and pieces that he had bought, some in America and some from shops in England, whose ranges had greatly increased from the year before. And he sent Matthew and I in search of a bundle of straw, which we purchased from a nearby farm. Throughout the construction period and during the whole of the month he was like a little boy who had built his first model. He would constantly seek my approval and would display a cheeky grin and dance with joy when I gave it. The straw was the centrepiece and this was surrounded by pumpkins of various sizes and above the straw bale, he created a display of witches and ghosts and skulls, all of which were illuminated at night by the coach lights on the garage that he covered with orange-coloured scary faces. Several children came 'trick or treating' on Halloween night and both they and their parents confirmed their appreciation of the display. We rounded off the period with a family Halloween party that gave us a chance to experiment with some festive treats from a recipe book that we'd purchased on our holiday.

Now the holiday was behind us, I was feeling more positive about things and I was determined to get myself off the anti-depressants that had been prescribed while I was in the clinic. I had not wanted to start them in the first place, but once I was on them I found no side effects, except maybe my imagination was not as sharp as it had been previously – something I felt was actually not a bad thing. I now felt calm inside and no longer irritable as I had been through the dark period.

My first attempt to stop taking the tablets had been some twelve months earlier, after our first holiday to Canada. I had seen Dr Kelly and we had agreed that it was now time to cut back and eventually stop taking the antidepressants all together. I had followed the guidelines and on a smaller dose I had seemed to be doing well, but once I had stopped altogether, I was a complete nervous wreck. I was without support and I was back to my previous state of anxiousness. What was aggravating this was the immense pain in my joints. It felt as though knives were being turned in each of the small joints throughout both my hands, and my neck struggled to hold the weight of my head, making it very difficult to turn to either side. I was unable to drive because of the very restricted movement I had in my neck. The pain at the bottom of my spine was excruciating and both my hips and knees were restricting my movements as well as causing pain. Basically I was a mess and I couldn't understand what had happened to me. I was also in tears all the time and I did not know why. There were no real reasons for it, other than I just did not feel well. So Keith had taken me to visit Dr Kelly, who felt that in hindsight it had probably been too soon for me to manage without the anti-depressants and also, as it was the build up to Christmas, this was adding unnecessary pressure. It was probably just the wrong time of the year to have tried to make the transition. He was also very aware that I was struggling to find some outside support for my mother who was by now suffering from short-term memory loss and he was helping me in this endeavour as well. He reassured me that a setback like this often happens, but it did not mean that I would be on the tablets for life. But for the time being, I had no choice. I had to go back on the tablets. Within days of resuming them, I was my old self again.

So now, twelve months later, despite it being that same time of the year, I decided to have another attempt at withdrawal. Unknown to Dr Kelly or even to Keith I had slowly started weaning myself off the antidepressants. To say I had no more success than the previous time would be wrong. I didn't have the anxiety attacks and I didn't really feel unwell but the end result was just the same. All I could feel was constant pain from my joints and muscles. My movements were very restricted. I could not grip the handle on Dylan's pushchair and there was no way I could hold him. I could not drive as the pain in my hands was excruciating. All in all I was a mess once again but despite all this I could reason, my head was no longer a problem. After several discussions with our GP, I decided to take the tablets again. The alternative was regular doses of strong painkillers but I had tried this before and it gave me side effects of severe stomach problems. I decided that going back on the anti-depressants was the best way to go forward. This decision was vindicated by the fact that research had shown that low doses of anti-depressants had been helpful to patients suffering from Fibromyalgia. Once back on the tablets, although I was not completely free of pain from day to day, I was able to put it in the background and get on with my life, If I was more relaxed and not tense all the time, then it followed that there would be less strain on my joints. I had now accepted that there were some things I could not do such as peeling vegetables or scrubbing awkward stains on clothing and I often found simple things like washing my hair very difficult. So, I learnt to pace myself and be sensible, and to seek more help from Keith. It made perfect sense but I could not always see this previously.

For most of the previous six years, Darren had made his home with us in Snaith. He had made many friends in the area and they complemented his friends in Castleford. In the autumn of 2003 he decided to get on the property ladder and purchased a cottage in the town and then spent several months renovating it. Although Darren has an intellectual brain he has always had a fascination for how things work. This was certainly put to the test when he was required to learn a few new skills. The cottage had to be re-wired and partially re-plastered and a new chimney had to be constructed. With the help of friends and family he had to decorate and re-fit throughout. He installed a new shower cabinet, built fitted wardrobes in the bedroom, made a bookcase and a computer cabinet in the lounge, laid a slate floor in the entrance porch and sanded and varnished the wooden floors throughout the cottage. What had once been the outside door, but was now an inner door due to the addition of a porch, contained a beautiful old panel of stained glass, which had a couple of pieces missing. He tracked down a specialist who took the panel away and remade it using all the original materials and restored it to its 1920s elegance. It looked stunning as you entered the cottage. Finally, furnishings were added and this was done with the same taste and thought that had gone in to the redesign of the property.

For a number of years he had had a daily journey of thirty miles to Leeds to the offices of Yorkshire Electricity where he worked. He was originally employed in a temporary position, but then took up a permanent role and seven years later was still employed by the same company, albeit now under different ownership. Sometimes he had a lift, sometimes he travelled by train and bus, but mostly he arrived there under his own steam although he did have some horrendous journeys. This was due to a number of less-than-reliable second-hand cars, one of which blew up on him.

And then, at the beginning of 2001, he was extremely happy to hear that the job he had been interviewed for before Christmas was his. He had been promoted – his studying and hard work had paid off. As well as a more challenging job and an increase in salary, the added bonus for him was that he would now have a company car. His own car had been constantly failing and it had let him down on several occasions when it would not start in the morning. He had been buying the vehicle on a leasing agreement and now he did not need it, it would have to be returned to the dealership. By the time the dealer came to collect it, both he and Keith had struggled to get it in an acceptable state in order to avoid a financial penalty. In fact, on the day of collection, Keith had managed to get it started early in the morning and kept it running for a while to warm it through. In the event the collection driver didn't attempt to start it, he just hooked it on to a breakdown truck and drove it away. When Darren returned from work that evening, he gave a broad smile of relief when he saw the empty space on the drive.

Since his diagnosis seven years earlier, Matthew had been to see three different therapists to help him cope with his communication difficulties, obsessive behaviour and short periods of depression. Many of his obsessive rituals revolved around water, washing his hands, bathing, watering the garden and washing the car. He eventually came to realise that these compulsions were, in fact, a form of release for his over-active mind which wasn't allowing him to relax naturally. This was a clear example of how Matthew and Keith behaved differently. Keith didn't suffer from the obsessive thoughts and actions which were plaguing Matthew at this time and yet Matthew didn't share Keith's fear of social occasions and, in fact, embraced and enjoyed them.

His communication difficulties were centred more on the family than the outside world and I believe this was a subconscious reaction to my decision, without his knowledge, to inform the family about his diagnosis.

Way back in the period just before Christmas 2000, Matthew, Keith and I had accepted an invitation to attend a meeting, the subject being 'Dealing with an Asperger partner'. It was held in a Victorian building with high ceilings in the centre of Manchester. There were four professionals leading the discussion, two men and two women. The delegates, however, were all women except for Keith and Matthew.

The delegates were all having great difficulty coping with their aspergic partners and were looking for help. I found it quite interesting that I was able to contribute and offer a lot of tips to the gathering and Keith and Matthew being there, and able to confirm and indeed illustrate my points added to the validity. Following that meeting, I started to get telephone calls. The professionals had put my name on a list of people who were prepared to offer help. Over the following three years I had long chats with several frustrated women even though I was far from strong myself and it was probably towards the end of 2003 that I felt I was the most productive with the advice that I was giving and it obviously helped them as I am still in contact with a number of ladies today, the frustration has eased slightly and they have moved into a different more positive stage of their life. The main difficulty that most of them had is that their partners did not accept that they had Asperger syndrome – in fact some of them didn't know the condition existed. And very much like an alcoholic, firstly they have to accept it, secondly they have to want to change their behaviour and finally they have to accept help. It can be a long, hard slog and for some people they feel it is a battle not worth fighting.

By the time the tulips and daffodils had opened up to signify that spring 2004 was in the air, Keith had started his three-day week. Generally he would work on Monday, Tuesday and Wednesday and would then use the other two weekdays for research for Matthew's new business. We had a daily delivery of The York Evening Press from which he would cut out relevant information and these cuttings would be stored alongside the numerous guide books, magazines, leaflets and general notes that we had collected since the idea had first been formulated the previous August. Despite the fact that this was to be his final year at work, and the fact that he was only working part time, in no way did he take it easy, or appear any less committed. Not that I expected it. It was just not in his nature. He worked in line with the demands of the job and sometimes he would switch his days to the end of the week in order to accommodate an important meeting; some weeks he would work for four days, and in one particular week he actually worked for all five days. But his commitment to Matthew's venture was just as real, and all the extra days were clawed back and used efficiently for the research project. I was often confused when he was locked in the study, not knowing who he was working for on that particular day, because to him, there was no difference – both needed total concentration and commitment and a full day's work. It was going to be a busy year for both of them, pulling everything together, but they knew it would be well worth it, and they were eagerly looking forward to their new beginning.

Chapter 18

PAIN AND GAIN

The best days of the week for me at this time were often the ones I spent with Dylan. When he was only a few months old, Beccy was planning to return to work as a nursery nurse. My heart went out to her; she loved motherhood and she had brought all her skills to bear, fully immersing herself in her new role as a mother, but financial pressures meant that, although reluctant to return to work, she had no choice. I thought long and hard before I volunteered my services as a baby-minder for two days each week. I was determined to help them as much as I could, but felt I could not commit more time as it was unrealistic for my state of health and I did not want to be unreliable which would then mean that Beccy, in turn, would be unreliable in her job. Keith was fully behind my decision but suggested that the two days should not be consecutive, because it would probably be too tiring for me. I soon developed a regular pattern, up at 5.30, in the car and on my way to Hessle by 6.30, arriving about 7.15 so that Beccy could be at work by 7.30 or 8.00 depending on her shift. Initially she would cycle home at lunchtime to be with Dylan but as she only had a half-hour break, it was really too much for her. She had a group of energetic four-year-old children in her care and needed that half hour to relax between morning and afternoon sessions. And, of course, she needed to eat something as well, so after a couple of weeks, she realised that it would be far better to save her energy for the nursery. Sometimes Dylan was awake and fed by the time I arrived, but often he would still be in his cot. Whenever possible, weather permitting, I would take him out in his pushchair, even if it was only for a short period, as I felt the fresh air was good for him and it was certainly good for me. I don't think a day went by that he didn't get a compliment as passers-by would often say what a lovely little boy he was, what beautiful eyes he had and how happy he looked with his big smile.

During the warmer weather we would go for long walks together, or rather I went for long walks, while he rode in the pushchair. Not far from their home was a large park and this included a well-stocked bird garden. Ducks, hens, canaries, cockatoos, all the usual birds were there, but there were lots of lovely variegated or vividly coloured ones too. Dylan seemed to have a natural affinity with birds and was happy to spend hours in this park. Even on the journey there and back, he would be constantly on the look-out for pigeons on chimney pots or blackbirds on the grass verges, digging for worms. But his favourites were always the ducks, probably because he found them comical as they waddled on the ground and splashed and played in the water, and it wasn't only the park that held his attention in this respect – a little stream close to the local Sainsbury's store provided endless excitement for him. There were usually a few ducks swimming up and down this little stream, but on one particular day, to my amazement, one of them came swimming towards us with a group of eight ducklings following. It was just wonderful watching Dylan's face. His lips parted and his mouth started to move as if he needed to tell me something but as yet he had not the capacity to say complete words, however his eyes told the whole story, and they were dancing as he watched the baby ducks swimming after their mother. Every now and then a straggler would swim away from the group and she would have to leave the head of the line in order to round him up. The baby who was left leading the line would panic as it lost its mummy's secure direction, but it wasn't long before mummy returned to lead her family once again. Every time this happened Dylan would be chuckling at their antics, he was so happy and he was learning all the time. After that day, I made sure that we visited the stream at least once a week so that we could watch the ducklings grow into adults. As well as the park, we would often visit the village shops. Jonathan usually left for work before I arrived and he would occasionally leave me a note asking me to do certain tasks, nothing difficult, just things that we were able to help with as we were on our travels. I have kept one of these notes in my Memory Box, which Beccy had given to me as a gift. The note asked me to do several tasks, buy books of first and second class stamps, pay a cheque in at the bank, take a passport application to the post office to be checked, buy a newspaper – all very simple tasks – and then at the bottom of the note he had written in big letters, 'After you have done all this, if you have any time left over, you can put the kettle on and have a drink.' We also had lots of fun in the house on inclement days playing with toys, enjoying games and reading stories. I would talk to him all the time both inside and outside the house, explaining what was happening at every stage of the day, and it was this simple act, which gave me immense pleasure, not least because it created flashbacks in my mind back to the time when Karl was a young child. I would regularly give him a cuddle but apparently I was not talking to him regularly because my Gran said to me one day, *"Pat, that little boy might not be able to talk to you, but he needs to hear your voice and to hear your words for his vocabulary to develop."*

I had not thought in those terms and yet it made perfect sense, and so I had immediately put her advice in to action. And now, thirty-three years later, here I was with Dylan still remembering her advice as I sang songs and recited nursery rhymes and counted in low numbers over and over again. Whenever possible we would eat our lunch outside. I would sit on a bench, Dylan would sit in his pushchair and we would dine while watching the world go by, looking for birds and dogs and people to study. But it was while Christmas shopping together that Dylan and I discovered the delights of dining in Debenhams. As they had a microwave in their toddler area, I was able to heat his baby food and then, when he was a little older, the dinners that his mummy had carefully prepared for him. In between feeding him, I would try to pick up forkfuls of salad for myself. It could get rather complicated at times but we laughed and giggled together as we ate. He was so placid, so trusting and so eager to learn. We were in the centre of Hull the morning that the gardeners came to erect the huge Nordic spruce tree that decorated an area for the Christmas festivities. We saw the tree moved into its place and then the huge covering bag was split and taken away. They used metal ropes to get the enormous tree in place, a difficult and skilful job for the men concerned, not helped by the many passers-by who stopped and made it difficult for them to do their job safely. It was an icy cold morning and, although Dylan was dressed in a cosy jacket, hat and gloves, I did not want him to get cold, so I started to push the pram away from the area, but he objected very strongly to moving, and I was so pleased that he did. Once the tree was erected, the men assembled the lights and, before they could go, they had to test them. The delight on Dylan's face was such a picture when he watched the tree lights being switched on for the first time. He was a little disappointed however when they were switched off again, but he soon seemed to realise that the men had finished their task for the day and he was ready to move on. Several weeks later, in early January, we were passing the same spot and surprisingly the same team of men arrived, this time to take the tree down. Again we stayed a little time as the men carefully lifted the lights from the tree and put them in a huge storage box. I asked Dylan if we should move on but no, he wanted to see the action and so we stayed and watched as the team sawed through all the branches and stacked them in the trailer ready to take away. At each stage I explained to Dylan what was happening and in his own little language he acknowledged what I was telling him and made several responses. It was such fun, we were interacting without Dylan speaking complete words, but all the time I knew what he was telling me either from his expression or from the movement of his hands. His index finger on his right hand was like radar; it made constant responses to everything we encountered. As springtime came around again, we were able to start visiting the park more often. Once again it was the birds that held a great fascination for him, although he also took great delight in watching the grey squirrels that came close to us and, of course, now a year old, he also enjoyed the swings and the slide in the play area. So Mondays and Wednesdays were good days for me, and ones that I looked forward to with eager anticipation; physically, Dylan drained a lot of my energy but mentally he recharged my batteries.

In June, Keith Matthew and I had booked Keith's cousin Jo's caravan for a week. We needed a break and felt that we would benefit from this, particularly as we knew that before too long the new business would be up and running and it would not be possible to have a holiday. The caravan was luxurious and sited in a beautiful part of Wales. We were looking forward to our time away, but as it got nearer I was feeling that we would have to cancel our trip as Keith's mother was becoming very dependant on me and could not make the simplest decisions without my help. Thyroid problems had caused severe depression and confusion and I was by this time doing all her shopping. On the days she did not join us for meals I had to leave suggestions of what she should eat. A few days before we were due to leave, I talked to Keith about my concerns. He had just assumed we would go away and she would be there when we got back but I told him that I was afraid she would deteriorate and struggle or worse still end up in hospital. I told him that in my opinion we had two choices, either we cancelled the trip or she came with us. We decided on the latter but in hindsight the sensible thing would have been to cancel our holiday. It was a very difficult time for all of us and I don't think any one of us got much pleasure from it. Each day we planned a trip out but she was never sure if she wanted to go, but neither did she want to stay on her own at the caravan, and, of course, that was why we had taken her with us, as we did not want her to be on her own. Whenever we got out of the car she questioned what we were going to do and for how long and how much would it cost. Her saying that she would wait in the car for us blighted every activity, firstly, and then after one of us spent time and energy convincing her to give it a go; she spent the time being very negative, thereby spoiling it for the rest of us.

I don't think we had one day that wasn't difficult and every mealtime was a nightmare. When we went out she could not make her mind up what she wanted to eat. The process just seemed to go on forever and even after it seemed that she had finally made a choice, she would invariably confuse the waitress by changing her mind yet again. Without fail, when the various dishes arrived she would look at someone else's meal and express the wish that she had picked that one, rather the one she had chosen, and then when we were all enjoying our food she would pipe up with, "I won't be having that again," and telling us that it was too cold, or too hot, or too dry, or not enough of this, or too much of that. After a couple of days we decided it was too frustrating to eat out anymore, so we'd cook at the caravan. In this way we could, at least, take out the choice element, but it wasn't much better as there was still something wrong with the meals we prepared.

Matthew was the most frustrated of the three of us. Naturally he had come on holiday to relax but, as usual, he wanted to visit lots of new places and although he was very patient with her, it annoyed him when his nan constantly disrupted these new adventures. The hardest thing for all of us was her inability for compromise, a typical aspergic characteristic, and the best example of this was in a morning. She would lie awake for a long period before the rest of us were ready to get up, and could have easily been the first to the bathroom, but she always waited until Matthew was there, and then spent twenty minutes pacing the floor and knocking on the bathroom door shouting, *"Have you finished yet, Matthew?"*

Without fail, this happened every morning, despite us suggesting she had her breakfast first and then went to the bathroom. Keith and I knew that it was not going to be an easy week, but we had not expected to be so excited about going home and so relieved that our holiday was over.

At the end of July, wedding bells were ringing as Richard and Layla were joined together in marriage. Despite Nan's protestations that she was not well enough to go to the wedding we convinced her that she would be upset at a later stage if she had missed it. I had to sort out an outfit for her to wear and her jewellery and pack her overnight case as we were staying at the hotel where Layla and Richard were to be married. It was only three days before the wedding that I had bought my own outfit and up until one day before I was in danger of not having any suitable shoes to wear. It's not as though it had been a last-minute arrangement as Richard and Layla had been engaged and the wedding arranged for over a year. My problem was that I had to have an operation to remove my appendix. It was all part of a reversal of the Ace procedure that I had gone through five years earlier. Although my new plumbing had worked successfully for about four of those years, it had now ceased to be effective. In future I would have to rely on good old-fashioned laxatives and lots of fresh fruit and vegetables. If this didn't work, I'd just have to hope that someone, someday, would come up with a solution for my ongoing difficulty. The operation had been originally planned for April and as the wedding was to be at the end of July; in my mind I had plenty of time to recover and plenty of time to buy my outfit. However, due to a shortage of beds in the hospital, the operation was cancelled twice and was finally carried out in July, not leaving me a lot of time to recuperate. So, that is why, I, the person who packs her suitcase for her holidays two weeks before she is due to go, nearly ended up at the wedding wearing my nightie.

Throughout the day of the wedding Nan's only conversation to anyone she met was, "*I should not be here; I am not well enough am I?*"

She really was unaware that it was the bride and groom's special day and that everyone was enjoying being with them. It was sad for all of us to see how Nan had deteriorated but it must have been the hardest for Richard as he was so happy with his new bride and wanted to enjoy the day to the full, but from time to time he felt that he had to boost Nan's feelings, as he could see that we were all trying and it was proving difficult. We had all been so used to seeing her getting immense pleasure from social outings in the past. Today was a perfect example of how far she had deteriorated. Sadly, however, she did none of this quietly. She still, quite selfishly, had the need to be the centre of attention at all times, and really couldn't understand why Richard and Layla were often getting more attention than she was. It was yet another very typical aspergic action.

The bride looked radiant throughout the day. Her sister and cousin were both adult bridesmaids and another cousin was a pageboy. They all looked stunning but it was the six- year-old bridesmaid who stole the show. Leah just couldn't stop smiling. She smiled during the service and carried on smiling throughout the day as she wandered about in her beautiful dress. Darren, Jonathan and Matthew were all ushers and Richard's best friend was his best man. However he had accepted the role of best man on the proviso that he would not have to give a speech. To Richard this was not a problem as he asked his two dads, Keith and Dennis, to be deputy best men and for each of them to give a speech. It was a good family day and great to get to know Layla's parents, Phil and Michelle. Phil was so nervous about his speech and concerned that everything was going smoothly and yet at the same time he was getting so much pleasure from his family and friends and he kept coming up to me and telling me how much he did not want the day to end.

Leah was just so happy she had her dad and Layla and all the rest of her family around her. She spent much of her time on the dance floor just enjoying every minute she could. It was a super enjoyable day with brilliant sunshine as well, and we took some great photographs to add to our memories.

Keith, however, felt that his speech was not as good as he could have delivered. It was an emotional time for him because of Karl's death, less than four years earlier, and that of his dad the year before that. He was supporting Richard and supporting his mum and once the tension of his speech was over he seemed to go to bits. It was the length of time he had to be in constant communication with so many people that was his problem. So we left the hotel and went for a little walk in the surrounding area. Not the most comfortable of walks in my new shoes and suit on such a red-hot day but calming Keith down was my mission. We walked for almost an hour and he talked to me for most of that time. Then I suggested that we turn back as everyone would be wondering what had happened to us. By the time we reached the hotel again, Keith was feeling much better. I won't say relaxed, as he can never relax in a large group of people, and needs regular bouts of space, but we had achieved a breather for him and we were now onto the next lap of the day.

Despite the marvellous atmosphere at the hotel, Keith wasn't the only challenge that I faced on that day. There was still his mum, of course, but now, in addition, there was Matthew. I just wanted to say 'Beam me up Scotty' – take me away from these problems. But as we know, burying your head in the sand is no solution to any problem. During the proceedings I had watched Matthew go from quietly enjoying himself to looking confused and latterly to looking very unhappy. I was conscious that our absence might have disturbed his already shaky feelings, so as soon as we returned to the hotel, I went to look for him. When I found him, he said he was about to leave to go home. When I asked him why, he told me how lonely he was. I know this to be true as he tells me on many occasions and every time it hurts me so much. It's such a simple thing to have a friend, to have a laugh and to relax together but Matthew finds it so difficult to form relationships as he always feels an outsider. We just sat together and talked. He felt lonely, he felt that he may never have the opportunity to marry; so many things were upsetting him. I explained that out of all his brothers, he was probably the one with the most organisational skills. As soon as I had said it, I felt that, although true, it was probably not the right quality to push at this time and so I went on to reassure him that he was tall, slim, good looking and intelligent and that he had a lot to offer to other people. I went on to remind him that he was also very kind, very generous and very empathetic when the need arose. It was so heartbreaking listening to him pouring out all his fears. It must have been almost an hour and a half later when finally I felt Matthew, if not happy, was at least much calmer and I did persuade him to stay. I said that I just had to be with Nan for a while and establish if she wanted to sit through the evening party or if she would prefer to go to bed and then we could all enjoy the evening together and maybe dance as well. Nan did want to go to bed – she was tired by then and so I got her a drink and settled her into her room and then into her bed. Poor Nan, it was like putting a child to bed. Once laid down she seemed to relax and was straight off to sleep. It was so sad to see her in this state, especially when I remembered how fit and active she had been in North America less than a year before.

Now, at last, it was time to relax with Keith and Matthew and, of course, the happy couple. It would also be good to talk with Jonathan and Darren, both of whom I had seen little of during the day. Jonathan delivered my next challenge. He explained to me that his new partner would be arriving a little later in the evening, and that he wanted to introduce her to us. This news came out of the blue and took me by surprise. I had been looking forward to meeting her, ever since he had told us, but I hadn't realised it would be at Richard's wedding, but then I thought that our first meeting was probably better if it was in the relaxed atmosphere of an evening party, rather than 'under the spotlight' at our house.

It had been two weeks before the wedding that Beccy and Jonathan's long relationship had come to an end, despite their engagement back in May. Jonathan had proposed to her after she had been involved in a fun run supporting a breast cancer charity; they seemed very happy and quickly made plans to marry in September, precisely five weeks after Richard's wedding. Dresses and suits were ordered, the church was booked and a meal was arranged. We kept telling Dylan he was going to two weddings during the year, and Leah was really looking forward to him being a page boy alongside her at Richard and Layla's wedding. But because of the break-up, the little fellow missed out on both weddings.

A couple of weekends before Richard's wedding the men had been to a stag night in Manchester and the girls had a hen night in York. We were looking after Dylan and during the evening we played games with him, went for a short walk and generally had lots of fun together, as usual. The following lunchtime we took him for a visit to a local baby animal farm, and he had a great time feeding the sheep, goats and ducks.

Beccy, who had arrived back from the hen party that morning, had planned to join us on this visit, but a phone call from Jonathan, meant that she had to alter her plans.

When we returned home, neither of them was there, just a note from Jonathan asking us to take Dylan back home to Hessle. When we arrived, Beccy was waiting for us and ready to give Dylan a bath before his bedtime. Keith and I said our goodbyes and left a very happy but tired little boy. The following evening I had been watering the hanging baskets and tubs in the garden when Keith walked out of the house with a very sad expression on his face. He grabbed hold of my hand and said simply, *"I have just had some bad news. Jonathan and Beccy have split up."*

I couldn't believe it! Tears just washed down my face and it was ages before I could speak and ask Keith for the details. All I could think about was Dylan and how this development would affect him. But Keith didn't have any details, except to say that Jonathan would explain things to us as soon as he was able to, and the fact that my baby minding services wouldn't be required on the following day. It was that last piece of news that had really brought it home to me and had made me realise that my world was changing yet again. A few days later, Jonathan paid us a visit. He had come to explain about the emotional torture that he had gone through during the past few months.

The roots of his dilemma stretched way back to the late summer of 2002 when he and Beccy had returned from Australia and gone their separate ways. It was at this time that Jonathan had formed a relationship with Ruth, a former girlfriend from the days before he had met Beccy. It was only a short relationship and before too long he and Beccy were getting closer again, they moved in together, and along came Dylan. But at the start of 2004, Jonathan's past caught up with him. Ruth had approached him with the news that, in her opinion, he was the father of her seven-month-old daughter, Alex. His initial response had been to deny it, but Ruth was persistent, kept up the pressure and eventually he knew that she was right, even though he wasn't quite ready to admit it to Ruth. So this was his dilemma. Two women who had each given birth to one of his children, and he loved them both. But he had to choose one of them. Did he stay with Beccy, or did he leave and go to Ruth?

He thought he had made his decision when he had proposed to Beccy, but as the wedding date came closer and closer, he knew that it was the wrong decision, and he knew that he had to face up to his responsibilities.

On September 2nd 2004, a little over a year after the idea had first been formulated, and after months of reading and learning, Matthew and Keith first appeared on the streets of York in their brand new tour guide uniforms, ready for business. They were delighted that they had two customers on the very first public tour they had advertised. The business was under way and over the next few months they would try a variety of tactics as part of their research into the best direction to develop things for the future. It was so good to see the two of them working together and particularly special to see Matthew charged up. The previous months had not been easy for him as he hadn't had a clear role and found it difficult to fill his day. Although Keith had been very conscious of this, he felt he had to carry out the research on his own and he had to spend time getting his knowledge up to a level which would make him feel comfortable when he was taking a group of tourists around York. Now that had been achieved and he could switch his two days a week from research to the 'real thing'. Matthew now had something solid to build on in the form of a business that enabled him to use his communication skills. Like Keith, he struggled with many aspects of communication, but in a business situation, and providing he carried out the correct level of preparation and planning, he came across in a very professional and persuasive way.

Autumn arrived and it was now a full two months since our first introduction to Ruth. She was part of a very close family and this showed in her caring nature. She had been eager to become part of our family as quickly as possible. At the weekends when they were not at work, Ruth and Jonathan would pop in for short visits and bring our new granddaughter Alex to see us. She was a gorgeous blonde bundle of energy and full of questions. While very shy for the first couple of visits, she very soon learned that our toy store was in the garage and her hand would come out and she would take either Keith or me on a toy hunt. It did not take long before she was relaxing with both of us and of course Darren and Matthew, her new uncles. We now had three grandchildren, Leah, Dylan and Alex, and it meant that now Keith had yet another reason to roll about on the floor and play games. On Halloween night Alex dressed, as a ghost, and Leah, eager to play with her new cousin, became a very effective witch. Keith had once again made a pumpkin display outside the house and Matthew had dressed the dining room in ghost and pumpkin fairy lights. He had decorated the table and cooked a traditional Halloween meal for the whole family. The lights were low and small pumpkins and candles illuminated the table. The girls loved it and were so excited all evening. Leah held Alex's hand most of the evening as she felt it was her responsibility to explain to Alex all the customs that she had learnt at seven years of age. It was so much fun seeing them together and watching the pleasure they were getting from sharing a family party evening with each other. However, I also felt a little sadness because Dylan wasn't there. Since the breakdown between Jonathan and Beccy, our access to him had been curtailed, and this was, unfortunately, to continue for several months.

The year moved into December and Keith finally realised that his retirement was almost upon us. Despite the shorter working week, it had been a very busy year for him, tying up loose ends, training his successor and his biggest challenge of all, launching a health and safety guide for the field based sales team. This involved him chasing around the country to ensure that every one of the seventy-five sales and marketing people fully understood the implications of the new guide. It was the culmination of a three-year project that had involved him gaining approval and endorsement from the board of directors. His chasing around the country gave me the opportunity to sample one or two more good quality hotels before my trips came to an abrupt end. These trips had been great for our sex life and I've lost count of the number of different beds in which we made love. We found that the best time was around six o'clock in the evening when he returned either from the office or from the training course being held elsewhere in the hotel. I would be all ready for him, bathed and suitably dressed and by the time he had stripped off his suit, taken a shower and had a glass of red wine, he was relaxed and ready for a cuddle.

The final trip for me and also for Matthew was the week before Christmas. Keith had been invited out for an evening meal in Cheshire by the technical team who wanted to say goodbye to him, and the following day all three of us had been invited to a retirement lunch at Brocket Hall in Hertfordshire. So while Keith was tucking into a Chinese meal in Holmes Chapel, Matthew and I were enjoying the splendour of Cranage Hall, one of my favourite hotels, and one that I had stayed at with Keith on many previous occasions. The retirement lunch was fantastic for all of us, not least for Richard, who had also been invited. I felt so proud of Keith on that day, as each person stood up and talked about him and his contribution both to the company, but more importantly to the individual people he'd helped and encouraged over the years. I couldn't help smiling to myself and remembering all the heartache I had gone through trying to keep things together at home, while he was out there helping and encouraging these people, several of whom were complete strangers to me. But I didn't feel bitter. How could I, when I had also seen the other sides of him, his inner pain and confusion and his boyish innocence? Keith's retirement period seemed to go on forever. It had started at the beginning of December, when I had been invited to join him for a night in London, dining and enjoying a visit to the theatre with his closest colleagues. It ended two days before Christmas when, at the annual sales force party, he was given a standing ovation and received numerous gifts including a painting of the medieval walls of York and a scrapbook of letters of thanks and best wishes from dozens of members of the team.

And in between these events there was a very special evening organised by Matthew. He had wanted his dad's retirement to be shared by all his brothers so he booked a private dining room at a country hotel. This meant we were able to dine, talk and relax together without affecting other people. After a sumptuous meal we retired to a private lounge where we enjoyed coffee and other drinks and played quizzes and board games and just relaxed together. Keith was overwhelmed as he thought we would be having a quiet evening at home watching television. Matthew sprung the surprise on him as they were returning from a day in York, and when they got home Darren, Richard, Layla,

Jonathan, Ruth and myself were all there, relaxing and talking and ready to continue the retirement celebrations.

For the second time in five years Christmas just did not happen for us. My brother John brought my mum to us from her house in Easington on the day before Christmas Eve and the plan was that she would stay with us until Boxing Day and would then go to my brother's house for a few days. When she arrived, she looked very frail and was more confused and frightened than I had ever seen her before. It had only been a few days since I had been to visit her, and although my telephone conversations with her since that visit had alerted me to the fact that she had been having problems, seeing her like this was a total shock. I just couldn't understand how she could be in this state. She had very little energy and we had to help her to walk everywhere, to get on and off the sofa and to get up and down the stairs. One of us even had to lift her legs into bed for her. The following day Keith and I managed to manhandle her in and out of the bath and once I had helped her to bathe and washed and cut her hair, she looked lovely. This was my mum back again, not the bedraggled stranger who had arrived the previous evening. But she seemed very tired and what I didn't realise at the time was that all this exertion was probably draining what little energy she had, though it did seem to help her to feel more relaxed. I tried to find out from her why she was so ill, but she was just too confused to be able to explain. She spent most of the day sleeping, in between watching bouts of Christmas programmes. I have one special memory of her watching *My Fair Lady*. Keith was doing last-minute jobs around the house as it was Christmas Eve but every now and again when a well-known song appeared in the film, he would sit down and sing along with it. This in turn would prompt my mum to dig into her very limited memory bank and sing along with him. Their rendition of 'Get me to the church on time' was priceless. I do not think she really had any idea which film she was watching – she had not been able to follow a programme of any consequence for a few years – but I was in no doubt that the singing was good for her and it was during those brief moments that she seemed happy. After each song, Keith would go back to his jobs until the next outburst, and mum would nod off again and I would sit there watching her and worrying how to support her. She seemed to be getting weaker by the hour. She stayed in bed through most of Christmas Day, missing the excitement of Alex opening her presents and did not get up until teatime. Even then she only had a very light meal before we had to take her back up to bed, as she was falling asleep again. Keith and I both looked at her in the bed and then looked at each other. I knew that he was thinking exactly the same as me. If we don't get her to hospital she won't last the night. When the paramedics arrived they agreed with us and she was promptly taken to Goole hospital. Extensive tests revealed that she had suffered a major heart attack and needed cardiac care, not available at Goole, and so she would have to be transferred to Scunthorpe. I travelled with her in the ambulance and throughout the long journey, lengthened by a mechanical breakdown and icy road conditions, I was trying to work out how she could have had a heart attack without us noticing.

Once we reached Scunthorpe, she was taken straight to the cardiac department, and I joined Keith and Matthew who had made the journey by car, and had been anxiously waiting for us. It wasn't long before a doctor came to talk to us. He had carried out a number of tests and he was able to tell us that my mum hadn't had the heart attack while she had been at our house. It had actually happened a few days earlier, and it was obvious that she had not had any treatment at the time. And then he hit us with the tragic news that there was nothing they could do for her, other than to keep her comfortable. She probably had only a few hours to live. I was stunned at this news, even though common sense had told me that in the state that she was in, her quality of life was miserably poor. But I still hoped there was a chance. And so as Christmas Day moved in to Boxing Day, I began a bedside vigil as I was determined to give my mum the best support that I could in the last period of her life.

My mum's dementia had started some six years previously when she and my dad were still living in Bradford. She had started to become very aggressive towards my dad and because of this and the fact that he no longer had any family connections with Bradford, he had decided that they should return to live in their childhood village of Easington in County Durham, where his sister still lived. Mum's aggression increased and now focused not only on my dad but also on Easington itself, and once they had moved, she lost no opportunity in telling all its residents what a rubbish and hopeless place it was, thereby losing any chance

~ 315 ~

of making new friends. Because these comments were usually made very loudly in public and because of very insensitive statements made by her about people she saw out and about, my dad very rarely went out with her as he became too embarrassed. Gradually, one by one, her former skills had disappeared. She had always been an excellent cook and her fruitcakes and pies were second to none, well loved by all her family and friends. But now all that was gone – as was knitting and sewing and even reading. And, of course, along with all this, she also lost her confidence and her self-esteem. She started to neglect herself and the house, and my dad was having to do more and more to help her, to support her and in fact to protect her, even though he was himself in a fragile state of health. Once outside the home he had to walk with the aid of two metal crutches. For a long time he had kept the lid on their situation, telling no one, not even me, how bad things were getting. He tried his best to get help for her but it was all in vain. He was told that it was just a bad marriage and that they had to sort it out; nobody would take the responsibility of diagnosing dementia. So he struggled on until he could stand it no more and had to tell me what was happening. We had known about her verbal attacks on him, we had seen it for ourselves, but we didn't realise how bad it had been. Whatever he had attempted to do to help her was wrong, he could not get it right and she always found something to criticise. Keith and I knew that we had to do something to help them. We needed to visit them more often, but also we needed to help my dad in his quest to get official recognition for Mum's condition and consequently some structured help for both of them. Initially we would take them both out for the day, for a meal, to the shops, to museums, but it was obvious that she did not enjoy these visits as she always became impatient, aggressive and verbally abusive. Most of it was directed at my dad, which made him feel very uncomfortable and embarrassed. She had no awareness of the loudness of her voice or how cutting her comments were, as she accused passers-by of being too fat or wrongly dressed or simply not being a pretty person. So we very quickly realised that we had to keep them apart and usually it would be a case of Keith being with Dad, while I took Mum out. Although she was better in these situations, it was still very difficult to control her, and it was very upsetting to see her in this state. One very upsetting thing she started doing was picking up other peoples discarded cigarette ends from the floor. At first I tried to ignore this but she persisted and would often try to distract me so that she could bend down to pick them up thinking that I hadn't seen her doing it. She had cigarettes in her pocket – it was not as if she had run out – but it was just her frugal way taken to its extreme. On most visits I went with her to play Bingo. Dad had encouraged her to join the local club not long after they had moved to Easington and, despite disliking the game himself, he had joined in with her. But that was, of course, before the aggression had reached such a high level. It had taken a whole year of appointments with local specialists before Dad and I finally had a breakthrough and, although not yet acknowledging that she was suffering from dementia, she was granted a place at a day centre for two days a week to enable them to monitor her situation. This was certainly a move forward and we all felt a little easier about things. But her condition continued to deteriorate; she was eating next to nothing, paying little attention to personal hygiene, spending more on bingo than their pensions would support and was banned from Asda because she had been seen putting pick and mix sweets in her pockets. One of the clearest signs was the repetition. Every visit she would tell us the same things and go over the same ground and it was usually about my dad and how he was a 'shit house'. She was totally unaware of how hard he was working to help her. It was now easy to see that his health was suffering and I was afraid that my dad, who had always had a laid back attitude to life, was showing the signs of having a nervous breakdown. His patience had been tested to the full time and time again and it seemed inevitable that he would get worse. The final straw came for him at a review meeting at the day centre. Dad, Keith and I gave the panel of five professionals an update on her condition and how the situation at home was becoming desperate. Generally they were all quite sympathetic, though they didn't commit themselves. They then asked a nurse to bring my mum into the meeting, as it was one of her usual days at the centre. She looked confused particularly when she saw the three of us in the room, but before long she was talking to everyone in a very positive manner. The consultant asked her a few questions about how she felt, and it was like opening the door of a store cupboard that had been overfilled. She just launched into a tirade of abuse about Dad and about how he never did anything for her and never talked to her and dragging up incidents from the distant past. He couldn't take it, he just stood up and hobbled out on his crutches, and he said very little to us for the remainder of that day. On our next visit, he took me on one side and told me that he had made a decision about the future. He was planning to move into a ground floor flat for his own health and what's more he would be moving on his own. I was so upset by this and yet I knew that it was the only solution for him. In turn it would hopefully force the required help for my mother. With our help, Dad did eventually move into a bungalow of his own although, as promised, he still kept an eye on Mum. At first he would call at her house to see if she needed anything but she always hurled abuse at him, in between asking him if she could go and live with him. She could not understand that if she calmed down and met him halfway he would gladly have taken care of her, but it was the abuse twenty-four hours each day that he could no longer live with. The next few months saw Dad become a little stronger in his health, even though mum continued to pester him on the telephone and make demands on him for shopping and other errands, all of which he honoured. But Mum was very unhappy. In her muddled state she knew deep down that Dad was protecting her from the world, but now he did not live with her the abuse became stronger, as she became even more confused and lonely. I found the situation hard to deal with, but I was the best person to do it. Dad could not help her as she pushed him away with criticism, but fortunately she never abused me or my brother or my sister. From then onwards, we made sure that we visited Easington every two weeks, now, of course, with two houses to visit. But I didn't feel I could leave Mum for that length of time without contact, in fact, now that she lived on her own I felt I had to make daily telephone contact with her so that I knew how she was every single day. Each day the conversation was the same.

"*Have you had your tea? What did you have? Are you settling down to watch any television programmes?*"

She would pick up the TV Times and tell me which programmes she had circled to watch. Then I would always tell her a little of what was going on at my end but nothing taxing and nothing in detail as she could not follow for long and it would be obvious when she had lost interest as she would say, "*I'll let you go now, love,*" or she would discuss what was on the screen in front of her. I was quite happy with that, as all I was doing was giving her the daily opportunity to communicate, even if it was only by telephone.

Daylight came to Boxing Day and Keith and Matthew went home to telephone the family with the latest news, and then drove up to Easington to collect Dad, who wanted to be at her bedside. Her children and grandchildren came to see her during this critical period and even though she must have been in severe pain for most of the time, she did manage a few smiles and the occasional chuckle. She didn't say a lot to her visitors except to ask them all, in turn, if she could have a cigarette and to remind them not to forget to enter her National Lottery numbers. On some of the days Keith's mum would come to the hospital with Keith but did not grasp the seriousness of the situation despite being told by both of us on several occasions. She always managed to say the wrong thing. For example we were talking to my mum and comforting her when at one point Nan said, in a loud voice, *"I don't think she looks too bad. I am sure I am worse than she is."*

On numerous occasions she would ask if it was time to leave, as she was very hungry. It became obvious that she hadn't come to the hospital to see my mum; she had come because she wanted company and it was something to do. The days went by and when New Year's Eve arrived Keith decided to stay the night with me, as by now all the visitors had gone, and this would be my seventh night in the hospital. John and Janet had been every day. I had eventually persuaded them to go home as mum still seemed to be reasonably alert. We had all remarked on how tough mum must be, fighting on through all the pain, especially when the doctor had felt that she had only hours to live. Midnight came, Mum was asleep and I decided to try to get some sleep myself. The nurses had supplied me with a mattress that was positioned at the foot of the bed. And while I slept, Keith sat in the chair. It was almost 9.30 when I woke next morning and mum was sleeping peacefully. Keith told me that during the night, although she was sleeping, Mum had reached across to him, taken his hand and kissed it. He felt sure she was saying goodbye. Keith left for home about midday and I carried on feeding and talking to Mum. She was extremely weak. Halfway through a tub of ice cream, she stopped eating it because the effort was too much for her. Once she had regained a little energy, she opened her eyes and smiled at me. For the next couple of hours I held her hand as she drifted in and out of sleep and her breathing became more shallow and laboured. I decided to ring Keith so that he could tell the family that the end was near. I left the ward and went to the telephone area. I had said nothing more than hello to Keith when I heard a commotion in the corridor and a nurse shouting to the rest of the staff in a very loud voice, "Mrs McGee." I quickly told Keith to stay put and I would get back to him. I only had yards to walk but by the time I reached my mum's room a nurse was sitting her up and trying to get a suction tube down her throat. Two nurses took my hands and tried to lead me out of the door and comfort me but I had no intention of leaving. Whatever happened now I was staying put, and then another nurse came to me and confirmed what I already knew.

"I am sorry, but she has just slipped away."

I passed the sad news on to Keith, and he promised to contact everyone, everyone except my brother, John. I wanted to do that myself. John and I had always been close, as children and that had continued throughout our adult life. I knew that he would be upset when he was told that his mum had died and I knew that I had to be the one to tell him. I knew that, like me, it had distressed him to see her deteriorate over the previous few years and it was particularly hard to watch her suffering in the hospital on a daily basis. I went back to Mum's room and yet it was not her room any more, her presence had gone. No more wheezing, no more coughing and worst of all no more little smiles in between her sleeping and drifting. I sat and held her hand and I talked to her about happy occasions and about times when she had supported her grandsons and me. I told her that I had appreciated all the dresses she had made for me as a child and as an adult. The cardigans she had knitted for her grandchildren and the beautiful fruitcakes she had lovingly made for us at Christmas time. I think I talked non-stop for about fifteen minutes and then I kissed her and sat in silence by her side, holding her hand as the time disappeared. After several years of confusion and a long period of pain, she was now at peace.

A week later all the family were together again as we celebrated Mum's life at the crematorium. Just as he had done at his granddad's funeral six years before, Matthew read his own emotion-filled tribute to his Gran. I was very proud of my youngest son, and I know that, in her own way, so would she have been, if she could have seen him. But as I listened to him and as I watched him through my tears, I also felt very worried about him. He had certainly been more settled since the launch of the business, but in no way could you describe him as happy. The sad thing, however, was that this was only evident to Keith and me, because when he confronted the outside world, he hid, as he had always done, behind a subconscious mask of confidence and humour.

After the funeral life seemed strange for a while. I still thought about Mum every day, not least of course now there was a big hole around the time that I used to ring her. Keith's mum, who failed to recognise my sorrow, didn't help my grieving, however. She continually demanded my attention, thereby mentally draining me during this difficult period. But as we moved further in to 2005, I began to feel a little more positive about things. I had experienced a fair bit of pain in recent times, both physical and emotional and I didn't imagine for one minute that there wasn't more to come in the future. I had also made a number of gains, and one of the best was having Keith around more often. Despite his retirement, he was still incredibly busy, trying to balance his time between Matthew's business and projects in the house and time with the family. But the good thing was that, even though I always seemed to have something to do, we were able to make time for each other, time to be happy together, to laugh together and to love together and it was with these elements in mind that we decided to have a weekend away, just the two us, around 1st April to celebrate the anniversary of our magical weekend twenty-five years earlier, when we knew we had fallen in love with each other. When it came to deciding where to go, well there was only one place it could be.

It was late in the afternoon when we arrived at the hotel car park and the sun was still shining through the trees. We were both very happy and very much in love. Keith clasped my hand and gave me a gentle squeeze as we walked towards the front door. We entered the reception and a smartly dressed young lady asked if we had a booking. Keith, as usual, gave all the information that was needed. While he did so I took the opportunity to look around. Everything was just as I remembered it, the chaise longue, the chandelier, the extensive library, the roaring fire and the polished horse brasses. Surprisingly, and reassuringly, very little had changed. The place was still familiar and still felt like a haven to me. Keith came back to me, squeezed my hand once again, and we both smiled at each other – we were relaxed and we were happy. A warm feeling rippled through me and I knew that Keith was feeling the same. He picked up our small case and guided me to the lift. After all these years together we had got it down to a fine art; I no longer felt the need to bring along half the wardrobe, just in case. We emerged from the lift and Keith unlocked the bedroom door and lifted the case inside. The room was pretty and from the window I could see the hills rising steeply towards the sky. Sheep and cows were happily grazing in several of the fields around the hotel. I could see walkers wearing hiking boots and jackets and one man running with his long legged greyhound, which was gracefully retrieving a stick that had been thrown by his master. Everything was so peaceful, so perfect and my mind began to wander. I started to reflect on the past and what I had learnt about myself and Keith and Matthew and Asperger syndrome, but not for long, because at that moment Keith walked across to me and took me in his arms. He gently cuddled me and squeezed me and then he kissed me softly and lifted me very gently in his arms and carried me over to the huge double bed, which looked so inviting. He began to kiss me again and this time the kisses became more urgent than before. In that second I knew that my reflection would have to wait.

Chapter 19

REFLECTION

May Day 2005, just one month after that magical weekend in Reeth and the relative peace of our house was shattered as two mini-whirlwinds flew through the door. Our two youngest grandchildren Alex and Dylan had arrived, accompanied by Jonathan and Ruth. They were eager to show all of us what they had chosen from the toyshop that morning, but I was the only one in the house. Both children had a bubble making pack, a small tennis racquet shaped piece of metal immersed in a soap filled cylinder. They blew furiously in fierce competition to create the most bubbles. They were dancing about, they were giggling, they were happy.

As I watched the bubbles rising towards the ceiling, I remembered something that Matthew had said to me once when he was struggling to make me understand what was troubling him. He said it was like living inside a bubble in his own little world to which nobody else had access.

My thoughts were soon broken as the bubble blowing tubes were discarded and I was despatched to the garage to collect a selection of games and toys for them to enjoy. They played happily for a couple of hours and then they were gone. The house was quiet and once again I began to think. Firstly I thought about Alex and Dylan and how good it had felt to be with them. It gave me a warm feeling inside.

Then I thought again about the bubbles and about what Keith had told me after his realisation about himself back in 1997. He had told me about his childhood and how he had felt lonely, insecure and different to all the other children at school, and that many of those feelings were still there over thirty years later. He hadn't been able to tell me about those feelings earlier in our relationship because they had obviously been locked away inside his bubble. The more I thought about those conversations, the more I realised that a journey that had started with that strange behaviour from Keith way back in 1980 was at an end. I was now in harmony with the person who I truly loved – and I felt so loved in return.

There were many times in our early years when it could have been a very different story. We could have been another sad statistic; just another second marriage that didn't work out. We were both already adults with families, therefore we came to each other with a set of important responsibilities, which could never be ignored. My husband had one son, I had three sons and we worshipped them all; they were our life. I never had great career dreams at school. Yes, I wanted to work and earn my living but my main ambition in life was to be happily married and have children. One child or ten children, I had no idea of numbers; I just knew I would not be fulfilled until I was a mum. Coming from a close family as I did, people were always more important to me than possessions. When I was young I was very shy and tended to sit in the background, watching. I suppose I have always been a people-watcher. I could be in a crowd of people happily enjoying myself, but I always ended up watching, studying, and seeing a pattern. If I saw someone acting strangely, I realised it was always necessary to dig deeper to find out why, rather than labelling them odd or weird, as most people would do. I suppose I started being a people-watching Sherlock Holmes at a young age and thank goodness I did because it has helped me with relationships over the years. But I never realised it would help me to unlock the happiest relationship of my life. It was just the way I was made. Everyone has at least one 'gift' in life. Some gifts are obvious, for example the ability to sing or to dance or to play a musical instrument or to excel in a particular sport. However, other gifts are less obvious and many people do not recognise their gift. Spotting patterns in people and understanding how they tick is a gift, but it can also be a curse, as it does not mean you can solve everything, it just means you have an insight into identifying problems. Some people do not want to be helped and sometimes it is very difficult to find the key to unlock their thoughts. A person who has Asperger syndrome invariably has a difficult life. Many things go wrong for them and they often have no idea why. They continue to make the same mistakes over and over, so to help that person in the best way we must love them but be truly honest with them. Most of all we must communicate, as this is something they find difficult to take the lead in, and sometimes they find it impossible to communicate at all. If the aspergic person listens and begins to work on their communication skills, it makes relationships easier for them. It's all about giving them confidence that they will not automatically fail at relationships and they don't need to withdraw to their own narrower world where they feel it is safer than failing again and again. Most strategies are common sense. If you love the person and start to look deeper, you start to discover the underlying chaos.

From my own experiences, initially, I could not understand how the person I lived with and loved and I knew loved me, would be the most attentive person one minute and yet could totally ignore me the next. It took so long to get inside his head. Eventually I did get inside it. There were many incidents and a lot of sadness building up inside me. I often felt I could not address the things that were truly upsetting me.

The key was communication but it had to be two-way communication. I now know Keith will do anything for me – I only have to ask – but from the beginning of our relationship I wanted him to share with me, to interact and not be prompted all the time. I felt as though I was nagging him continuously. It would have been much easier to point everything out as it went wrong, but when you are looking for sharing and spontaneity this is the last thing you do. He had a good job; we were reasonably secure and all the family seemed happy, a situation for which many people would be grateful. He always gave 110% of his energy to every task he started and I could see he was regularly struggling to deal with everything. Everything, I felt, except for me.

How could I be so selfish as to think like this? He loved me, this I knew, he was a good dad to all our children but there was always one thing missing. What was it? Would I ever find it? Did it exist? Or was it me being an over-possessive woman? I felt we were so close; we could talk to each other about anything, be that funny or upsetting, and we always had a laugh together. If I were down he would sometimes see this and do his best to make me laugh. The hard part to live with was that lots of things were building up in my mind, that was putting a strain on my part of our relationship, but he was totally unaware of this. In those early years I was very happily married but I could not understand why I was not happy. He was buzzing and happy; it had to be me. Whichever way I analysed it, I was the one who was not happy, so it had to be my fault.

It's common sense that children need time and room to learn and develop, but, of course, we should continue to learn and develop throughout our life. I feel that to truly love another adult you must be truthful, loving, sharing, patient and empathetic. And most of all you need to give the other partner space to continue to learn and develop. Temper, jealousy, point scoring and especially sarcasm are all a recipe for disaster in a good, strong, loving relationship. To an aspergic person they are even more disastrous as each of the above throws that person into an alien space. In my husband's case he could not respond with any of these styles, it was not in his nature, so he became confused and withdrawn.

What first attracted me to Keith was his honesty and his simple, unworldly, non-devious niceness. There were no sexual innuendoes; there was no feeling of being mentally undressed. Many women would have found him boring, but to me it was great. As I got to know him, I saw that he could put on an act if required, but with me he never needed to. Although I saw a completely different side to him once we came together, I never felt that he had tried to deceive me. As the years rolled on, I realised that, in effect, what I saw on day one is what I got. What I learned to do, was to help him to overcome some of his hang-ups and fears and, once he accepted the need to change, I was able to help him again. I have seen him grow from a person with very low self-esteem to a man full of confidence, albeit on the outside; A person who became something of an expert in mediation. On numerous occasions he successfully brought people in conflict together in order to reach common ground and move forward. He also prided himself on creating opportunities for others to use their skills.

"*Let's not dwell on their weaknesses,*" he would say. "*Let's celebrate their strengths and give them a chance to use them.*"

Although he still finds it very difficult, he has surprised himself by planning and organising a number of family and friends' social events and whereas it used to be Pat doing 100%, Keith 0%, it's probably 70/30 now. Not the ideal 50/50 but who knows, in a year or two it might be.

Of course, Asperger syndrome is a life-long condition and despite these improvements, he does still have his quirks. Inwardly he still has difficulty in social situations but has learnt to mask this very well. He organises himself so that he reduces the risk of having to be in a 'difficult' situation. For instance, when he was working, he would make sure that he reached the office for 6.30am, which meant a very early start and a two-and-a-half hour drive down the motorway. In this way, he could ensure that he was the first to arrive and would not have to go into a room full of people who had 'already marked out their territory'. When he was training, he had no problem whatsoever with the training itself and he could stand up all day in front of a group of people and interact with them perfectly. But at the end of a course, when everyone sat down for a meal, he had to carefully choose his position to avoid causing himself too much 'social discomfort'. He needed an escape route, in case of difficulty and he would always leave the group at the earliest opportunity. Whatever the social gathering, he has to employ these tactics each and every time. He often uses visits to the toilet as a way of removing himself from a "difficult" situation, enabling him to avoid conflict and to diffuse his overloaded mind.

Keith still needs his nightly 'letting off steam' session as he climbs in to bed – his release of the tensions of the day. As he was growing up, Matthew would mimic this behaviour and developed his own routine. It was a comical scene as I reached our bedroom after cleaning my teeth. The two of them on our bed, beaming faces, shouting, screaming, clapping and reeling off a list of fictitious names and phrases that they have conjured up, or fallen in love with over the years.

Guru Sisterfield, Danny Cahoolaghan, Douglas Debavnoff, Alice. B.Topcliffe, Grebus, Horace Benfleet, Crusher Wilson, Tullis, Snodgrass the third, Studabaker Billy, Rowlimental, Gootaraisa, Rostapovitch, Devillbiss and Tin-How-Mew-Cow and, of course, Underpants on the Highway.

I join in the laughter; I can't help it, because despite being quite repetitive, it is actually very funny. Several comedians have made a good living by creating a character who displays behaviours which often mirror some of the unusual actions of an aspergic person. Jim Carrey has played these types of characters but Rowan Atkinson's Mr Bean is probably the best example. Matthew loved the Mr Bean character as a child and began mimicking him. He has a natural talent to mimic, his own, and other people's behaviour in a very humorous and non-offensive style.

Keith still needs a lot of help in spotting when one of our sons or our parents needs some help or support, but I only have to mention it and he's there like a shot. I still surprise him from time to time by predicting things in the family that are about to happen or are likely to happen. He trusts my judgement when I predict the event and he always admits he had not seen it coming. When I put the pieces of the jigsaw together for him, he always has a good laugh. We regularly joke together that between us we make one good, whole person. For example with his short-sightedness I have to read the cast and the titles for him on a television programme but he has to read the TV Times and tell me what programmes are coming on, as I cannot read a paper or book without my reading glasses, which I usually misplace. With regard to the television, virtually every programme that comes on has me studying the actors and linking them to another actor, saying that it's somebody's son or daughter or brother or sister. It's infectious and some of our sons have caught the bug. When it links back to a programme from years ago both Keith and I dig into our memory banks to recall the name of the programme and usually come up with the answer in the end. Keith will also be able to recall the theme tune and sing or hum it perfectly; he has a wonderful memory for tunes, even ones that he hasn't heard for over thirty years or more. Way back when Matthew was learning to play the piano, Keith would help him to practise and I didn't feel it would take him long to pick it up himself, but surprisingly he didn't seem that motivated, and when Matthew decided to retire from this activity, Keith also gave his fingers a rest.

Keith still has something of an obsession about tidiness. Not cleanliness, you understand; tidiness, in the sense that everything should have a home. He says that it is easy to keep a house tidy if everything has a place and I have to agree that this is true. I had first seen this, of course, with the children's toys but now it is with anything that is left round the house. He has often moved other people's things that they have left in a strategic place so that they wouldn't be forgotten, and, of course, because he has put them away, they have been forgotten. As soon as we buy a picture and return home with it, before I have even had time to get the feel of it in our surroundings, he has his hammer and picture hooks at the ready. I try to remind him that I need time to decide where it goes and that he will have to wait. He usually gives me an hour or two and then asks again. At Christmas, when either of us unwraps gifts of pictures, ornaments or small furniture it's exactly the same. Before we even sit down to Christmas dinner he will want to know where the items are to be located. I always try to remind myself that I am lucky he is interested and is enthusiastic about doing the task. My job is to channel his energy so that he puts the picture up when I have had time to assess the situation. Occasionally he will suggest a sight but usually wants me to give the instructions. The only time he did hang anything on the walls without consultation were two mirrors which he hung so high up I could only see the top of my head in both of them. I did not complain as he had used initiative and I knew he would be hurt if I pointed out the error. It was my mother-in-law who is a little shorter than I am who said one day, *"Who on earth put these mirrors up? They are far too high. I can't see a thing."*

His other obsession is lists and notes. I call it an obsession, but actually it is an organisational strength which I, and other people, have benefited from.

He creates regular 'To Do' lists and has yellow reminder stickers all over the study.

The first experience I had of his notes came within the first week that we were together. After he had gone to work one day I found a little note with a button on it. A circle had been drawn around the button and from the circle an arrow pointed down to some words at the bottom of the note. 'Please would you sew this button on my blue shirt?' I found this very endearing.

If something breaks down in the house, I have to write it on a note and leave it in the study; otherwise it will not get done. I found out from experience that just to tell him verbally was not good enough. When he first asked me to leave him notes of tasks to be done, I found it strange, as though he was just a workman that I had called in to do a job. However, I soon got used to his system and now it's just a routine. Every now and then he will transfer the information on the various notes on to a To Do list. Once on his list, however, there is no guarantee when it will get done. He has little pockets in his mind that things are slotted in to. He has now retired from full-time work but is still very busy as he is helping Matthew with his business. When he has a space he will look on his list and take the required action. So if something breaks down on say Monday, it could be the following week before 'household jobs' comes in to his action plan, so we have to do without until then, unless, of course, I or one of the boys can fix it. However, we have to be careful, because he can get quite possessive about these jobs and will see it as a criticism of his systematic approach if someone else steps in. Nowadays, however, he does see the funny side of it all, and it's not a major problem. Regular maintenance jobs do benefit from his methodical approach. He has a monthly checklist, which covers all the household appliances both inside and out including the cars. So nothing gets overlooked as he goes from one to another with his clipboard on the first day of every month. Recently he was prescribed a six-week course of antibiotics, together with another tablet, so true to form he created a pill management tick sheet which he attached to a clip board and he kept it in the study, religiously ticking the list as he took the pills.

In no way could you describe Keith as a follower of fashion. He still has the same haircut that he had in his twenties; only the colour has changed. It is good, of course, that he still has a good head of hair to be able to keep the style. With regard to his clothing, he keeps to a very safe style of dressing. He still needs the sections in his wardrobe that distinguish between work and casual, new and older. Occasionally I still see him standing looking into his wardrobe as if to say 'Please jump out at me, I am trying my best'. This often happens if he is going to a situation that is not familiar to him or to meet new people. When I see this look, I always suggest something and his face lights up and he gets on with the next task quite happily. When he used to set off for work early, and this could often mean him rising at 3.15am for a 4.00am departure, he would always prepare his clothes the night before and leave them in the study in neat sections, so that he wouldn't disturb me in the early hours. And this precision and order does have advantages because generally he sticks to certain clothing for certain jobs, thereby keeping his better clothes in good condition. For instance he has a routine when he comes home of changing into 'house clothes' as a priority. Besides the clothes in his wardrobe he has boxes marked 'decorating clothes', 'gardening clothes' and 'outside dirty jobs clothes' which he keeps either in the loft or the garage. This may sound a trifle obsessive but it is really quite practical. However, he does sometimes cross over the boundaries. When he is doing one of the tasks, let's say decorating, he suddenly realises that he needs some paint. He jumps in to the car and off he goes. Fifteen minutes later he is walking around the shop dressed in old flared trousers, a very old T-shirt and a pair of deck shoes without laces and with gaping toes. All this is topped off with a nice coating of dried white emulsion paint both on the clothing and on his hair, hands and face – not a pretty sight.

One positive step he made along the way was with regard to slippers. As a child and in the early days of our marriage he used to wear slippers. One day he made a conscious decision not be associated with them. It was just after Leah was born and he said that he didn't want her to think of him as an old granddad. He wanted her to think of him as an energetic and fun granddad.

Although quite meticulous in some aspects of his life in terms of planning and preparation, sometimes he just rushes in and gets on with the job. His enthusiasm gets the better of him and there are consequences. Like the whole contents of a five-litre tin of paint split on the hall floor, or the numerous items of furniture and fabrics ruined by testing new company products in the lounge. His insistence at using his unprotected hands to do jobs around the house, including spreading concrete, makes his skin far from smooth when it comes to stroking my body during lovemaking. Just imagine having sandpaper dragged across your breasts and legs – it's not much fun, and, of course, the stockings that he has me dressing up in are only good for one session.

I am constantly trying to get him to slow down and relax. He does everything at high speed. He never reads a novel because it is too long for him and he can only allow himself time enough to read snatches from newspapers or magazines. He does look after himself, however, and sticks to a good diet, walks regularly and has a weekly session at the swimming pool. Keith and I had enrolled Matthew as a member of the Goole swimming club when he was sixteen, while he was away on a ski trip. We felt that it would be a good place for him to combine healthy exercise with the opportunity to meet new people. On his return, and although he liked the idea, he had no intention of going on his own, so Keith said he would also join the swimming club, and they enjoyed these Sunday evening sessions together for many years. It's still a regular session for Keith and Matthew joins him whenever he is free.

In summing up how I feel I have helped Keith, I would say that he came to me as a boy and is now a man – but from time to time I happily get a glimpse of the boy still inside him. He has, of course, helped me to change. I am now much more organised and I plan things in a systematic way. He gave me confidence in myself, confidence to keep going with the typing when I never thought I would make it, confidence to take on the magazine advertising and confidence to keep going when the pressure got tough at Rawcliffe School. He was also there to support me during that horrible period at the end of 2000 and particularly during the following year when my brain went in to meltdown and I just couldn't cope.

Weird, strange, stupid, rude, selfish, odd, geeky, eccentric, obsessive are just a few of the words that I have come across over the past few years as a description of aspergic people, but the word that I have heard more times than any other is abnormal. Because of my experiences with Matthew and Keith and many other aspergians, I would like to challenge the term abnormal and pose the question. What is normal? Who decides what is normal?

Remember those bubbles? Well, just imagine that every one of us lives inside our own unique bubble. After all, every human being is unique. The majority of the bubbles only have a thin shell and it is comparatively easy for those bubbles and the people inside them to interact with each other. It's also easy for the person inside to look out through his or her own bubble to see the world outside. Although the view that each person sees will be similar to other people's, there will always be some differences.

Some bubbles, however, have a thicker shell and it's much harder to interact with the person inside. Their view of the world when they look out through their bubble has many more differences and this ultimately affects their behaviour.

I have a vision for the future and it's quite simple.

A world where we are able to respect each other's views and, more importantly, respect our differences.

After twenty-five years, I have reached the end of my journey. Keith and I continue to learn new things about each other all the time and we are optimistic that the road ahead, although challenging, will be full of rewards. So why do I feel it is the end of my journey? Because I have found what I have been looking for. I have found the thing that eluded me for so long.

I AM HAPPY. I HAVE FOUND TRUE HAPPINESS!

My personal journey has ended, but OUR happy journey continues.

The final words belong to Matthew.

I have followed my mother's progress with this book over the past few years with a cocktail of emotions; my overwhelming feeling being one of pride and admiration. It fascinates me how she is able to express her innermost thoughts and feelings on paper. It is without doubt a valuable gift. I felt from an early stage that I would like to be involved with the book and fortunately this has been made possible by the regular read-throughs and consequent editing involved in creating a book.

Before you start getting worried, let me assure you that I am not going to take up valuable ink talking about how hard my life was while I was growing up. After all, nobody wants to hear that. Besides, to me my childhood felt normal and I was happy. What I would rather talk to you about is what I have learned about myself as I moved through adolescence and into adult life.

As far back as I can possibly remember, I have always had an almost extraordinary quest for learning. As a child I would ask questions like a machine gun dispensing bullets. My parents joke that the first word I learnt to say was why, and that overwhelming curiosity is still as strong today as it ever was.

When I received my diagnosis I did not accept it at first. However, I soon realised that the reasons I felt different fitted the new label that I had acquired. I have been fortunate enough to inherit boundless optimism from my parents and I quickly used this optimism to see the positive side of my condition. I read about many famous people who were either known to have, or thought to have Asperger syndrome. I was fascinated by how they had managed to create something so positive often without any recognition that the reason they felt different was based on a medical condition. Something equally significant was happening in my life at this time. Two years earlier, I had been introduced to business studies at school and was now finding that the subject was extremely interesting and stimulating. In my spare time I had found my passion for reading again, however this time the books were biographies of famous entrepreneurs like Richard Branson and Bill Gates. This was not simply a passing phase: to date I have read over 150 biographies of entrepreneurs, business leaders and other influential people. The more I read the more I identified with these people. I admired them and looked up to them. What I realised was that these people were all 'outsiders'. By not running with the pack, it had enabled them to see the world differently and to create a different world. Where many aspergians would have been interested in the financial side of business such as stocks and share prices, I was not. I was interested in the personalities and the human interaction involved in business. I was starting to see a potential outlet in the future for the natural leadership qualities that I had displayed during childhood. I soon realised that I had an opportunity to turn my disadvantage into an advantage.

Quite simply, this was the start of a long mission to prove that Matthew Greenwood does understand people, does empathise with them and does know what drives them. I have spent years watching and studying people, listening to what they say and remembering it. I will then build up a profile of how they think, what their beliefs are, what their interests are. I also study what makes people happy and what makes them sad. Over the years I have become a chameleon, able to adapt to the environment around me and able to fit in with people of all backgrounds. This doesn't sound like the typical behaviour of somebody with a social communication condition, does it? Aspergic people aren't supposed to understand social communication and are often 'geeky'. What is even more incredible is that it never felt like hard work. I feel incredibly fortunate to have realised my strengths and weaknesses early in my life. The passion for learning about the people around me, both in my local community and in the world at large, has become part of my personal crusade to play my part as the world evolves and people start to become more aware of Autistic Spectrum Disorders and the unusual behaviour they create. What I have achieved so far is one small step for Matthew but what has been achieved since I was diagnosed is one giant leap for thousands of individuals of all ages across the world. My mother's journey has concluded, but my journey has just begun.

Matthew Greenwood

May 2005

Brotherly Love

I remember the day well. I sat alone watching television after school. The Mardi Gras float pulled up outside the house and three figures cart-wheeled on to the pavement. It was my parents and my little brother. All three, in time, came spinning down the drive, through the doorway and into the living room. My mother turned off the television and the happy trio burst into a song that broke the news that my brother has Asperger syndrome and carried on rejoicing at the fact there are many benefits to this condition.

OK, that never happened.

But neither was there a mournful, tearful scene with the news being broken to me and the rest of the family.

In truth, I don't remember ever being told, but I do know Matthew has Asperger syndrome and I've known for a long time. The knowledge came slowly over a long period as a series of doctors of one kind or another, unearthed pieces of a jigsaw. Other doctors, however, were unable to unearth anything at all and a few really struggled when they tried to attack Matthew's stone quarry mind with nothing but a JCB.

My brother doesn't have the plague. He's not ill or damaged in any way. He's my brother, an individual, just as my other three brothers are individuals and I love him just as I love them. He is family and it is easier to get on with members of your own family than it is with strangers. Matthew has put up with things about me that others wouldn't have tolerated and I have treated him the same way.

It can be easy for people that Matthew meets to be put off by his nature. He is strong-willed and confident which can easily be taken as brashness but this is simply a veneer and just below the surface there are a full range of traits and abilities. Given time, most people invariably see him as a very lovable person. However it can take a lot of time and effort, which is why people with a temperate character will usually take to him better than extroverts.

In the most non-medical, un-jargon-cluttered, paint-by-numbers english:

I like having Matthew as my brother.

Jonathan Greenwood

May 2005

Karl, Our Gentle Giant

Joseph

Alex

Anna

Jamie

Leah

Dylan

Ruth

Layla

Richard

Jonathan

Darren

Matthew

Me

Keith

My dad

Six Years Later

I am writing this in March 2011, six years after that second romantic visit to Reeth. We now have six grandchildren.

LEAH is a tall, slender, beautiful young lady of thirteen who loves to participate in energetic pursuits such as netball, gymnastics and cheerleading.

DYLAN is an eight-year-old dynamic whirlwind, very athletic, who excels at many sports, particularly rugby and football.

ALEX (seven) is very artistic and creative both with her hands and with her expressions. She also enjoys gymnastics and many other sports and is always willing to try something new.

During the last six years, Richard and Layla have brought JAMIE (four) and JOSEPH (one) into the world, two typical boys, full of mischief and very boisterous.

Then in June 2010, ANNA MAY was born, a welcome new family member for Jonathan and Ruth and a beautiful sister for Alex and Dylan.

DARREN works in the electricity industry dealing with people requiring new or increased power supply for their business or home. He is very knowledgeable about anything to do with computers and has a passion for photography. He is gradually building both his knowledge and his collection of cameras and ancillary equipment and his portfolio of photographs is increasing as he continues to receive more and more requests to shoot occasions such as weddings and christenings.

RICHARD and Layla live in Castleford, West Yorkshire. Richard currently travels the country as an account manager negotiating the sale of leading-brand stationery products to the educational industry and regularly commutes between home and the company offices in Hertfordshire and Cheshire. He still plays five-a-side football on a weekly basis and is a lifelong supporter of Manchester United. He was fortunate in being able to travel to Moscow in 2008 to see his team lift the European Cup.

JONATHAN and Ruth live in the nearby village of Gowdall. Jonathan has worked for many years as a maintenance engineer with a wide variety of employers. His current role takes him all over the country helping to keep sewage flowing. It's not a glamorous industry, but it's nevertheless essential. He likes to keep himself fit and jogs regularly, plays cricket when time allows and enjoys active sports both with friends and with his family.

MATTHEW has been running his tour company, exploringyork. com, for six years and business has increased each year with many customers providing repeat business on an annual basis. His activities have extended outside of just walking tours and he is involved with treasure hunts, team-building activities for corporate clients and has created walks for other organisations such as York Brewery and Science City. He has received accreditation for guiding in York Minster and is a holder of a York-Badge which recognises excellence in guiding in the city of York. He is also studying accounting at York College.

During the past six years he has organised and funded numerous surprise trips for us to a large variety of places. Salzburg for my 60th, Madrid and Andalusia for Keith's 60th and trips to The Bulb Fields at Keukenhof and Tallinn and Prague as a thank you to Keith for his support in the business. His attention to detail for these trips was first class, with nothing left to chance.

KEITH works for Matthew as and when he is required. He still reads the York Press every day and pulls out any snippets of information which he feels will enhance his own and Matthew's knowledge. Additional knowledge is also gained from regularly purchasing and reading books about York. He is a walk leader with the Snaith & Cowick Walking Group and is currently part of a team working towards securing grants for the expansion of walking facilities and heritage information within Snaith and neighbouring parishes. He is much more relaxed these days and the jobs on his 'To Do' list get done much quicker. However, he is not happy unless he has a 'project' and is currently planning a budget holiday for us for later this year. A four hundred-mile bus trip from home to Falmouth in Cornwall, using our National Bus Passes (free travel) and special offer Travelodges.

KEITH'S MUM passed away in 2009 after four years of very poor quality life as she lost her motivation, her self-confidence and her friendly sparkle.

MY DAD is the only remaining family member from his generation. He is a lively eighty-nine-year-old with an active mind and a good sense of humour. He moved to Snaith in 2007 following the death of his sister. He is very independent and can often be seen struggling along the high street on his crutches on his way to collect his pension or buy some lottery tickets.

AND MYSELF. Well I continue to do what I do best: watching people. I love to keep an eye on the whole family, particularly our lovely grandchildren who give me immense pleasure, but I have learned not to instantly interfere when I sense a problem. Keith has taught me to take a more cautious approach. Fibromyalgia continues to reduce the strength in my muscles and means Keith increasingly has to take over many of the household jobs, which he does willingly. He also does most of the cooking now. After fighting against it for many years, I now relax more and accept my limitations. I love reading and typing although I can only carry out the latter in short stages. When it comes to gardening, my favourite activity, I like nothing better than a whole day of planting, weeding, trimming and tidying. However, one day at a time is all I can manage and I am often in pain for a few days afterwards. Nevertheless, it's worth it. I can also say the same about the walking I do with the Snaith group, with other groups and with Keith. It is worth it, despite the pain that undoubtedly follows.

Keith and I have grown even closer since his retirement and we love nothing more than spending quality time together. But I also value my friendships; Friendships with other couples, some that we have known for many years, but particularly with four personal friends. The roots of the first of these was the counselling that I was giving to a woman frustrated by her husband's aspergic behaviour. By helping her, I was also helping myself and through the process of getting to understand each other's situation, a good friendship developed.

Two outstanding women came into my life back in the 1980's at Rawcliffe School and today, as very good friends, we are in regular contact and meet up for a good natter every couple of months. And once a fortnight I drive to Leeds to visit a very special friend. We worked together at a hairdressing salon when we were both teenagers, became very close, but then lost touch. Then quite remarkably while watching the local news on television in the year 2000 I saw her again. She was being interviewed following a robbery at her house during which her partner suffered a fatal heart attack. I tracked her down and after a gap of thirty-three years we met once again and our close friendship was back on track.

Sadly, my dad Jim McGee died whilst this book was in the final stages of production. We had been planning his ninetieth birthday party, but he died on 20th April just 73 days before the event.

He will be greatly missed by his children, his grandchilden, his great grandchildren and all his family. The love he showed us and the skills he taught us will live on.

Acknowledgements

My grateful thanks to the following people who helped me to make this book a reality.

For their help in manuscript reading, invaluable feedback and positive encouragement

Di & St John Meyers
Mary Skilton

Photographic Consultant

Darren Ingham

For their help and understanding during difficult times

John McGee
Janet Pilley
Dick Norris
Allyson Mee
Dr Andrew Brews
Dr Chris Kelly
Dr John Nehaul
Dr David J Pearson
Jo Baxter
Geoff Baxter
Graham Harrison
Steve Fowler
Dave Farrimond

And several members of the National Autistic Society